RELIGIOUS NATIONALISM

Selected Titles in ABC-CLIO's
CONTEMPORARY WORLD ISSUES
Series

For a complete list of titles in this series, please visit **www.abc-clio.com**.

Books in the Contemporary World Issues series address vital issues in today's society, such as genetic engineering, pollution, and biodiversity. Written by professional writers, scholars, and nonacademic experts, these books are authoritative, clearly written, up-to-date, and objective. They provide a good starting point for research by high school and college students, scholars, and general readers as well as by legislators, businesspeople, activists, and others.

Each book, carefully organized and easy to use, contains an overview of the subject, a detailed chronology, biographical sketches, facts and data and/or documents and other primary-source material, a directory of organizations and agencies, annotated lists of print and nonprint resources, and an index.

Readers of books in the Contemporary World Issues series will find the information they need to have a better understanding of the social, political, environmental, and economic issues facing the world today.

RELIGIOUS NATIONALISM

A Reference Handbook

Atalia Omer and Jason A. Springs

**CONTEMPORARY
WORLD ISSUES**

 ABC-CLIO

Santa Barbara, California • Denver, Colorado • Oxford, England

Copyright 2013 by ABC-CLIO, LLC

Library of Congress Cataloging-in-Publication Data

Omer, Atalia.
   Religious nationalism : a reference handbook / Atalia Omer and Jason A. Springs.
      pages cm.
   Includes bibliographical references and index.
   ISBN 978–1–59884–439–9 (cloth : alk. paper) — ISBN 978–1–59884–440–5 (ebook)
   1. Nationalism—Religious aspects. 2. Religions. 3. Religion and politics. 4. Religion and state. I. Springs, Jason A. II. Title.
BL65.N3O44   2013
320.54—dc23   2012039404

ISBN: 978–1–59884–439–9
EISBN: 978–1–59884–440–5

17 16 15 14 13   1 2 3 4 5

This book is also available on the World Wide Web as an eBook.
Visit www.abc-clio.com for details.

ABC-CLIO, LLC
130 Cremona Drive, P.O. Box 1911
Santa Barbara, California 93116-1911

This book is printed on acid-free paper ∞

Manufactured in the United States of America

For three teachers and mentors:
David Little, Ronald Thiemann, and Jeffrey Stout
Who, in their own relentless grapplings with religion, ethics,
and politics,
taught us everything we know.

Contents

ix

Preface

This book investigates the concept of religious nationalism. It provides an account of how different forms of religious nationalism emerge and evolve, and overviews the debates about whether nationalism is an essentially modern development, or dates back much further than the onset of the modern era. From India to Israel/Palestine, from Northern Ireland to Sri Lanka, to Serbia and Egypt, this book unpacks and examines a range of examples of the ways in which religious and national identities interweave, sometimes fuse together, and interact in many of the most persistent—and in some cases explosive—political, ethnic, and cultural conflicts in the 20th and 21st centuries. No less importantly, we investigate how nationalism and religion can, and often do, blend and lace with exclusivism and chauvinism even the most seemingly stable and self-avowedly just and inclusive of liberal-democratic societies, such as the United States and France. Finally, we explore possibilities for thinking differently—perhaps constructively—about the ways that national and religious forms of identification have, and do, intersect, reinforce, and/or conflict with one another.

Motivating Questions

A central aim of this book is to challenge the common understanding that *religious* nationalism is a uniquely volatile and antimodern form of nationalism because it is religious in one sense or another. A second aim, which parallels the first, is to challenge the common presupposition that secular (nonreligious) varieties of nationalism are intrinsically more stable, rational, and benign than what typically gets categorized under the banner of religious nationalism.

To unpack the case studies and debates we investigate here, we take up four lines of questions in the following chapters.

First, is religion uniquely prone to cause violence? Why, and to what degree, have so many people in the modern era come to understand "good" varieties of religion as those that remain essentially personal and contained within the private sphere, while "dangerous" religions are those that assert themselves in public and political life, and thus are likely to interact in volatile ways with national identities and causes?

A second line of questioning asks: What are the links between (1) organized religious traditions and institutions; (2) the various potentially harmful *and* potentially beneficial ways that religiously motivated actors and ideas might be present in public, political life; and (3) manifestations and assertions of national identity? In what ways do national identities selectively retrieve and make use of practices and understandings drawn from organized or historical religious traditions (rituals, symbols, myths, sacred spaces and times, etc.) to imagine, justify, and perpetuate themselves? Are such links always and necessarily destructive and exclusionary? Is it possible to critically assess negative versions of such interconnections and to reconceive and deploy them constructively? What might constructive examples look like?

Closely related to this, we ask, third: How does the complex and often conflicted inter-relation of religion and nationalism challenge the idea that "the religious" and "the secular" are clearly distinct and easily separable ways of being in the world? In what ways does the airtight opposition of religious versus secular limit and obscure different avenues for critically understanding and perhaps constructively engaging nationalism more generally, and religious nationalism in particular?

Fourth and finally, we pursue a line of questions that ask: Is nationalism itself a form of religion? How do nationalisms provide forms of collective identity, generate solidarity, and articulate values and moral ideals? Does nationalism operate like a religion for societies and national contexts that deliberately, and in some cases even aggressively, identify themselves as nonreligious? How, and to what degree, does religious nationalism exert itself less conspicuously, but therefore all the more insidiously, in contexts where formal religious and state institutions are structurally kept apart?

Chapter 1 approaches the lines of investigation that appear under points one, two, and three above. Here we identify one widely influential understanding of religion versus secularity, and argue that this understanding is far too limited and one dimensional to adequately deal with the complex challenges presented by religious nationalism. We then examine several cases of religious nationalism in detail to demonstrate why and how analytical conceptions of both religion and nationalism must be nuanced and expanded in order to grasp the multilayered, continually shifting, and thus synergistic interface between religion, nationality, and ethnicity. Over the course of Chapter 1, we move back and forth between the cases of Northern Ireland, Israel/Palestine, and the former Yugoslavia (i.e., Serbia, Bosnia and Herzegovina, and Kosovo). The second half of Chapter 1 recounts the history and debates over the emergence of nationalisms in both modern and premodern variations. Here we overview cases of religious nationalism in India, Sri Lanka, France, Egypt, and Spain.

Chapter 2 offers sustained focus upon the questions that appear under point four discussed earlier, before returning to consider the remaining questions under point three. Here we draw sociological discussions of "civil religion" into conversation with debates about religious nationalism. How do these developments—both emerging from processes by which groups generate collective identity and sustain solidarity—fit together? What, if anything, makes them different? We explore a range of possibilities for conceptualizing the ways they relate with specific attention to the workings of civil religion in the United States. We then return to our discussion of why it is not only untenable, but analytically counterproductive, to draw an easy and iron-clad conceptual partition between religious and secular domains, and further, civic and religious forms of nationalism.

Chapter 3 concludes our arguments in the book with extensive overview and assessment of religious nationalism in Israel and the United States. By applying the conceptual tools, insights, and arguments from the previous chapters, we demonstrate that in both cases, forms of religious nationalism exert themselves in chauvinistic and discriminatory ways. However, in both cases, those very traditions and resources that fuel and facilitate religious nationalism also provide means by which exclusivist tendencies can be challenged. Our analyses of both of these cases offer cautionary reminders that liberal democracies are not immune from chauvinistic tendencies to which nationalism in all of its varieties is prone. Chapters 2 and 3 adapt a few paragraphs from Jason A. Springs, "Civil Religion," in Richard D. Hecht and Vincent f. Biondo III (eds.), *Religion and Culture: Contemporary Practices and Perspectives* (Minneapolis, MN: Fortress Press, 2012).

Finally, Chapters 4 through 8 provide readers with a set of reference tools (chronology, biographical sketches, data and documents, a directory of organizations, further resources, and a glossary) which aim to facilitate further reading and research, and orient our audience to the many broader debates surrounding religious nationalism.

1

What Is "Religious" about "Religious Nationalism"?

Defining Nationalism

In the modern era, nationalism refers to a group identity defined in terms of political, ethnic, or cultural identities, associations, and attachments. Based on this understanding, nationalism is identified by common features that a group of people recognize as holding them together as a nation ("a people"). For example, such attachments may relate to the operations of a particular state or government (e.g., French or U.S. nationalism), participation in the life of civil society (e.g., civic nationalism), or an identifiable ethnic, cultural, or racial community (e.g., black nationalism in the United States).

Misconceptions about Religious Nationalism

Many people assume that nationalism is basically a nonreligious, or secular, phenomenon and that religious nationalism alters or perverts that phenomenon by adding a religious component. On this account, religion is usually viewed as a matter of personal belief and practice, and thus something that should be contained within the private sphere. Furthermore, proponents of this perspective believe that religion and nationalism should not be mixed because doing so leads to dangerous, fanatical, and uniquely explosive results. In other words, religion infuses nationalism with an "otherworldly" significance, which is considered superstitious,

1

based on mere belief, not subject to reasoned debate. As such, it is prone to authoritarianism, prejudice toward people who belong to other religions (or no religion at all), and violence.

This understanding of religious nationalism has been pervasive throughout the modern era and into the present. However, this view makes a mistake of oversimplification. Namely, it associates nationalism with modernity and progress, and religion with premodernity and ignorance. To call nationalism "modern" suggests that it reflects the important progress by which human societies emerged from the dark ages of premodern and early-modern eras. On this account, modern societies progressed from ignorance to enlightenment through the discoveries of the natural sciences, the development of political and social sciences, and the emergence of the nation-state. This viewpoint holds that modern societies are better than their premodern precursors because they have separated the public sphere (places where members of society engage in issues of mutual interest, such as government, laws, and rights) from the private sphere (places where people can exercise individual authority based on personal beliefs and opinion, such as the home or family). Religious belief, practice, and institutions are associated with the private sphere in modern societies. They should be separated from the public spheres of government and the state. Consequently, this perspective regards religious nationalism as an antimodern and outdated form of social and political engagement because it mixes religion with politics. Moreover, this modernist approach assumes that religious nationalism is likely to result in fanatical, arbitrary prejudices instead of logical political debate and procedures.

We highlight the assumptions in this understanding of religious nationalism because such oversimplifications make it impossible to address the intricate ways that religion and nationalism relate to one another in even the most modern of societies. Such oversimplifications also obscure the complex purposes that each can serve. They prevent us from accurately identifying the weaknesses and dangers of religious nationalism. Most importantly, these assumptions prevent us from understanding the potential strengths of certain manifestations of religious nationalism. In short, when religion is viewed as essentially negative in modern contexts, it becomes difficult to think constructively about how religion might make positive contributions to contemporary politics, overcome political and social conflicts, cultivate self-critical and self-correcting forms of solidarity, pursue more just laws and political institutions, and build sustainable conditions of peace. To approach this topic from a more constructive angle, we introduce the concept of religious nationalism by first exploring how it has been examined in an area of study that focuses on the role of religion in conflict.

Challenging the Religion versus Secularism Model

We use the term "secularism" to refer to the thesis that as trends of modernization increase, the influence of religion in public, political life gradually disappears. The phrase "trends of modernization" refers to ideas, practices, and institutions typically understood as characteristic of the modern era; these include the human ability to measure and control the workings of nature through the natural sciences, evidence-based forms of reasoning, industrialization, bureaucratization, social forms that place a high premium upon the freedom of individual choice, and political forms based upon the separation of religion and state (Douglas, 1988, 467–474). In many cases, because thinkers who hold to this secularism thesis view religion as not requiring empirical facts or verifiable evidence, they claim that it is outdated and irrational. Some claim that its public relevance is rendered implausible by the increasing diversity in public spheres. Some aggressively secularist positions even regard religion as the opposite of progress and modernity. Generally, secularism holds that nationalism and religion should be separate because it assumes that religious nationalism will be inevitably pathological and uniquely volatile.

Juergensmeyer: Supporting the Religious versus Secular Model

In *The New Cold War? Religious Nationalism Confronts the Secular State* (1994), sociologist Mark Juergensmeyer presents one of the most influential accounts of religious nationalism in recent decades, but he also falls into several misconceptions of the strict religious versus secular model. According to Juergensmeyer, religion and secular nationalism stand in direct opposition to one another. As he puts it, they embody "competing ideologies of order" (Juergensmeyer, 1994, 26–44). On this account, the secular state

believes that religions that assert themselves publicly and politically will inevitably lead to exclusiveness and divisiveness. As a
result, religion must be relegated to the private sphere and kept
out of political life. To illustrate this point, Juergensmeyer points
to Western colonialists who established secular political systems
and systematically marginalized religion in the Middle East, South
Asia, Central Asia, and Eastern Europe. However, Juergensmeyer
argues, religious forms of nationalism have become increasingly
popular around the globe because they have the capacity to facilitate a synthesis of ultimate meaning and political power that
bridges the supposed abyss between religion and nationalism.
Religion provides substantial meaning, a sense of collective identity, and ultimate value that humans naturally need and that secular social and political orders (and thus, secular forms of
nationalism) are not able to provide fully. And yet, in portraying
religious and secular political states in a basically oppositional relationship with one another, Juergensmeyer's account relies on the
secularism thesis described earlier in this section.

Hibbard: Challenging the Religious versus Secular Divide

In contrast to Jurgensmeyer, political scientist Scott Hibbard
offers a more complex picture of how and why religion remains
relevant to modern politics. Instead of supporting the religious
versus secular model of nationalism, Hibbard argues that secular
state actors and political elites fuel exclusivist and divisive religious politics, even though they often intend to do the opposite.
Secular elites try to push religious voices into the private sphere
and keep them contained on the margins of political society.
However, the more that religious people are told that they should
just keep their religious views to themselves, the more many of
those people feel compelled to assert their religious beliefs in
forceful and even confrontational, political ways. The result tends
to be the opposite of what the political elites and other secular
state actors intend. And yet Hibbard's account does not portray
the relationship between the secular state and religious actors as
simply oppositional. In fact, the two have often interacted in symbiotic ways (i.e., in a parasitical relationship where one uses resources provided by the other, or in a relationship of mutualism
where each benefits through instrumental interaction with the
other). For instance, in some cases, political elites increasingly
needed, and sought, support and legitimation from religious

figures. As a result, they often publicly engaged religious leaders and institutions to selectively co-opt religion for their political purposes. "It was mainstream political elites, in short, who helped to normalize illiberal [exclusivist] religious ideologies and brought these ideas into the political mainstream," Hibbard argues (2010, 5).

This example of the complex inter-relationships of public religion and secular politics demonstrates that it is important to challenge the secularism thesis that informs many common assumptions that politics and religion inhabit separate spheres in the modern era. Typically, the secularism thesis overlooks the fact that religion can play multiple roles—many of which may be constructive—in public, political life, and especially in increasingly diverse, pluralist, modern contexts. Hibbard subsequently argues that "religion remains relevant to modern politics because of its close association with communal identities and moral legitimacy." The authority of religious *institutions* may be less centralized in modern social life when compared with some previous eras. But this fact does not make that authority insignificant or negligible. In fact, Hibbard concludes, "religion remains enormously influential in the construction and mobilization of collective identities. This is especially relevant for modern nationalisms and other forms of political communalism." This happens, in part, because religion "becomes deeply intertwined with patriotism and is invoked to demonstrate cultural authenticity" (Hibbard, 2010, 6).

Nations may be perceived as natural entities that have remained unchanged since ancient times, but in reality they are products of history. The strength of national identities is grounded in a subjective belief in the features of identity that bind them together. The bases of group identity are often experienced by members as obvious, and as the essence of the individual and the community. Though nationalisms are products of history, they are also real. Consequently, to understand nationalism (religious and otherwise), it is necessary to explore how power interests and symbolic resources (including stories that recount the group's origins and its persistence through history, symbol systems, ritual practices, and communal fault lines) as well as their historical circumstances and developments (e.g., the history of colonialism) affect how national identities are constructed and reproduced to appear as "natural" and "given" realities.

Religious Aspects of Religious Nationalism?

A man in Northern Ireland was stopped in the headlights of a police car while walking home one night. Demanding that he identify himself, the officer called out to him:
   "Protestant or Catholic?"
   "Atheist!" the man replied.
   The officer paused and called to the man again, "Protestant atheist or Catholic atheist?"

What is religious about religious nationalism? One might identify a clear example of religious nationalism in the Islamic militant group Hamas's aims to establish an Islamist, Palestinian nation-state. The Palestinian Hamas movement emerged from the Egyptian group the Muslim Brotherhood at the outbreak of the first Palestinian uprising (the first intifada, 1987–1993) against the Israeli occupation. Hamas's primary objective is nationalist in that the movement aspires for political self-determination on the entirety of the land of Palestine. But intertwined with this objective has also been a strong program for the Islamicization of Palestinian society (guiding the society by the teachings of the religious tradition) and the reclaiming of broader trans-national Islamic unity and territorial integrity. In other words, Hamas interprets the liberation of Palestine as a religious duty. Hamas activists understand this to require jihad (meaning literally "to struggle" and denoting primarily a spiritual struggle) against Israel (or as Hamas calls it, "the Zionist entity"), the West more broadly, and the evils and decadence of secularism. We can begin to detect how political and religious objectives are conflated and interwoven. In each of these ways, a movement of national independence and self-determination is motivated by, and aims to achieve, objectives that are taken from its understanding of the Muslim religious tradition.

Similarly, one finds religious nationalism apparent in a messianic Jewish settler's commitment to maintain her home in a wealthy, gated enclave that is situated in the middle of impoverished Palestinian villages in the West Bank. Internationally recognized as Palestinian areas, the West Bank and Gaza Strip have been referred to by Israelis as Occupied Territories since Israel seized control of them during the Six Days War (1967). The settler believes that the prophesies of Hebrew Scriptures will be fulfilled, and the arrival of the messianic end times will occur, if this land (known in the Bible as Judea and Samaria) is filled with Jewish inhabitants and the Jewish state (Israel) grows.

In these two examples, the religious dimensions of the nationalist enterprise appear to be straightforward. In other cases, however, it may be more difficult to uncover the religious aspects of religious nationalism because religion may function in more complex, or more subtle, ways. For example, should we classify the eruption of sectarian violence in Northern Ireland (Protestant versus Catholic), Iraq (Sunni versus Shi'ite), and Lebanon (Muslim versus Christian) as "religious" in any sense of the word?

Case Study: Northern Ireland and the Troubles

In Northern Ireland, the Protestant Christian majority (known as Unionists) sought to keep the region unified with the United Kingdom. The Roman Catholic minority (known as Nationalists) sought to reunite with the Republic of Ireland. In this conflict between Protestant Unionists and Catholic Nationalists, religion functioned as a marker of national identity for each group. And yet it was not only a hallmark of national identity. Religion also greatly influenced socioeconomic status and cultural forms of identification. To understand the different ways it did so, we must examine the case of Northern Ireland in greater depth.

Known as the Troubles, the conflict between Protestants and Catholics in Northern Ireland could never be characterized as exclusively religious. It was also political and socioeconomic. And yet group identities were formed with reference to religious creeds and institutional affiliations. Those identities continued to be embodied in rituals and invested with significance through symbolic practices. One analyst of Northern Ireland, Claire Mitchell, points out "that religion does not just mark out commu-nal boundary ... but ... gives structures, practices, values and meanings to the boundary" (Mitchell, 2006, 1–2). One cannot simply point to theological differences between Protestants and Catholics (e.g., their differing creeds, doctrines and beliefs about God, and ways of worshipping and other religious practices) as the cause of the conflict. At the same time, however, it would be equally incorrect to claim that because the conflict between Catholics and Protestants did not focus upon theological differ-ences, it was therefore "not really about religion." It would be inadequate to characterize the conflict as religious "only in name," that is, because some of the markers by which the groups distinguished themselves from each other refer to religious traditions (i.e., Protestant versus Catholic).

Mitchell demonstrates the importance of understanding how religious ideas, symbols, rituals, institutions, and individuals (religious leaders and lay people) actively shape and give meanings to communal identities in ways that help create, prolong, and aggravate political and social divisions, and fuel conflict. In other words, communal identities do not occur merely when political elites manipulate popular religious sentiments, or religious institutions and leaders. Rather, the religious identifications of Protestant and Catholic in Northern Ireland became interwoven with highly complex power relationships. Religious identity markers formed boundaries of inclusion and exclusion that permeated socioeconomic and political arenas.

The Troubles in Northern Ireland lasted from the 1960s through the late 1990s. And yet, like many other nationalist conflicts, its roots can be traced back to British colonialism in the 17th and 18th centuries. After conquering the territory, Britain sought to incorporate Northern Ireland by settling English and Scottish people in regions formerly populated by native Irish and English Catholics. The English separated Northern Ireland from the Irish Free State (later named the Republic of Ireland) in 1920, partly as a reaction to the growing unrest that resulted from the emergence of Irish nationalism. Irish nationalism arose from Irish people's understanding of themselves as a group distinct from the English because of their different culture, language, and religious heritage, and because of their history together as a group. The English effort to settle Northern Ireland intensified the emergence of a unique Irish national identity that increasingly defined itself in opposition to the English intruders.

After 1920, the Protestants who governed Northern Ireland (known as Ulster Unionists) systematically discriminated against Catholics by restricting their access to economic, social, and cultural resources. A key turning point in these historical developments was the killing of 14 civil rights demonstrators in 1972 by the British military in Derry, Northern Ireland. This event, which came to be known as Bloody Sunday, escalated the conflict with clashes between the Catholic Irish Republican Army (IRA) and Protestant militias (Berkley Center, Northern Ireland, 2011, 3–5).

While the competing groups in Northern Ireland have been divided along denominational lines, the conflict did not explicitly revolve around doctrinal disagreements between Protestant and Catholic Christians. In fact, we could not effectively analyze the complexities of religious nationalism by thinking of religion as exclusively a belief in God or a set of commitments to theological doctrines. A person may identify himself or herself (and be identified by others) as Protestant or Catholic even if that person does not believe in God. If we reduced the Troubles to a religious conflict in simply theological or doctrinal senses, we would miss the complex intersections between religion and other social, political, and economic elements.

To account for the complex relationships between religion and other social and political variables, we must examine the multiple ways that religion produces and reproduces identity and community. We must analyze (1) institutional support, (2) social segregation, and (3) how ritual practices, symbol systems, mythic understandings, as well as theological concepts give meaning to, structure, and reinforce social and political identifications.

First, though the church and state are officially separate in Northern Ireland, churches were actively involved in the political processes by providing institutional support to the conflicting parties. Catholic religious leaders exercised far-reaching influence upon public opinion and were thoroughly engaged in public, community activities. Likewise, Protestant cleric-politicians and church leaders also became active in politics (Mitchell, 2006, 39–58). Second, the conflicting groups were socially segregated by religious affiliation. Catholics and Protestants were divided by separate schools, residential areas, and informal social networks. Religion constituted a marker that supported structures of discrimination and inequality—not necessarily through appealing to theological doctrines and formal beliefs, but by indicating communal boundary markers which served as bases of inequality, exclusion, and humiliating treatment (Mitchell, 2006, 59–68). Third, religious rituals and symbolic practices reinforced rigid community membership boundaries between Catholics and Protestants by embodying those identities in the present (Mitchell, 2006, 69–90). Ritual moments and holy days frequently became occasions for demonstrations and intergroup violence. In the next section, we examine how sacred times and spaces often provide occasions for the eruption of violence in order to identify specifically religious dimensions of nationalism.

Holy Places and Holy Times in Religious Nationalism

To understand the significance of sacred times and spaces, we must ask why holidays, holy places, and ritual enactments are often used to express national sentiments and generate nationalist activism. Independence days, memorial days, and other national symbolic times commemorate a group's history, as well as celebrate the events that led to its existence and the sacrifices it has made to perpetuate itself. In conflict-ridden contexts, these stories and commemorations often contain themes of the group's victimization, and sacrifices of martyrs who gave their lives for the greater good of the group. As we will see in the following case studies of Northern Ireland, Israel, and Serbia, such themes typically mix contemporary and historical events with religious practices, symbols, and mythical events.

Case Study: Northern Ireland and the Troubles

In the case of the Troubles in Northern Ireland, times of national and religious significance merged with one another, as has been evident in the Easter marches. These Catholic marches commemorated the Easter Rising of 1916, an event that inaugurated the Irish Republican Army's resistance against British rule. While subsequent Easter marches memorialized the resistance of 1916, we should ask why Easter was selected to inaugurate anticolonial resistance in Northern Ireland in the first place. Christians annually observe Easter Sunday to celebrate what they believe to be the resurrection of Jesus Christ some 2,000 years ago. As the holiest and most theologically significant of Christian holidays, Easter came to be interwoven with nationalist meanings and political resistance for Irish Catholics. Similarly, the official end of the Troubles was marked by the Good Friday Agreement (1998), which references the day in the Christian liturgical calendar that commemorates Jesus's passion and crucifixion. Such examples illuminate the uses of religion not only to mark collective boundaries, but also to construct and consecrate national symbolic times.

Case Study: Israel and Zionism

Similar to the Troubles of Northern Ireland, the case of Israel demonstrates why it is misleading to think of secular and religious varieties of nationalism as easily separable. In reality, the relationship between national and religious identities is far more complex and dynamic. A form of nationalism, Zionism supports the existence of a Jewish state in Palestine, the historic land of Israel. Zionism's account of Jewish history focuses on past catastrophes to justify its current political aims. From the destructions of the Temple (586 BCE and 70 CE) to recurrent persecutions of Jewish people and the Holocaust, the Jews have aspired to return to Zion. When Zionism emerged as a modern political movement in 19th-century Europe, it was framed as a secular, nationalist movement. However, even in its self-avowed secular form, the Zionist effort to return to the "holy land" of Israel referred to events narrated in the Hebrew Bible as historical evidence of the Jews' earlier possession of the land of Palestine. Zionists appeal to these narratives to support Jewish claims to a unique right to that land. According to biblical stories, Jews' presence there was forcefully interrupted by periods of exile and conquests by external invaders that dispersed them throughout the world.

Some Zionists explicitly identify themselves as religious Zionists. Religious Zionists have a religious interpretation of historical events and developments that might appear to be purely political from a nonreligious perspective. Such events include the establishment of Israel as a Jewish state in 1948, the arrival of Jews from around the world to that state, and the reclaiming of the ancestral sacred geography of Judea, Samaria, and Jerusalem as parts of Israel. Many Jewish settlers in the Occupied Territories of Palestine are motivated by explicitly religious Zionism, which perceives contemporary and historical events as the path to the messianic moment of redemption. This moment of redemption will occur when all the Jews return to the land of Israel, the Temple in Jerusalem is rebuilt, and the dead buried on the Mount of Olives are resurrected. According to religious Zionists, political developments are essential to the unfolding messianic saga and ultimate arrival of the Jewish Messiah. Moreover, these events are depicted as extraordinarily significant moments of history to justify an exceptional morality. Many religious Zionists claim, in effect, that the commandment to settle the land of Israel (as defined in biblical history) overrides all of the other 612 commandments.

This religious nationalist narration of extraordinary time also influences Israelis who identify themselves as nonreligious. Even in Israel's mainline secular educational system, the Tanach (the Hebrew Scriptures of Judaism) is taught as a book of national history. Such use of the Tanach draws direct links between the times of biblical figures—such as Abraham, Joshua, the Judges, and Jacob—and present-day Israelis. Even in the predominant mainstream of nonreligious Zionist mythology, the period of thousands of years during which Jews lived dispersed throughout the world outside of the land of Israel is portrayed as merely "empty time."

Though nationalist rhetoric often rigidly interprets group identity, in fact, religious traditions and sociopolitical units are internally diverse, plural, and multidimensional. Similarly, whereas religious traditions can be understood and embodied in ways that exclude those who are not members, they also contain many resources for inclusiveness and may accommodate people who are different. Religious leaders might be instrumental in conflict because they may be in uniquely high profile positions from which to challenge and reinterpret fundamental claims about how the texts and practices of a religious tradition appear to justify exclusivist conceptions of cultural and national identity. Importantly, the value of such flexibility should not be restricted to explicitly religious conceptions of a national identity. Rather, it invites rethinking secularist (and self-identified nonreligious) accounts of national identity, as well, and especially in so far as such secular accounts appropriate and employ symbols from religious traditions, histories, and memories (Omer 2013).

Like the case of Northern Ireland, elements of religious nationalism are interwoven in both religious and nonreligious Zionism. And yet many religious and nonreligious Zionists (both Israeli Jews and non-Israeli Jews) challenge elements of the Zionist mythology of religious nationalism. They argue, for instance, that the group referred to by the phrase "Jewish people" is thoroughly diverse. Rather than dismissing the periods between expulsion from and return to the land as "empty time," they attempt to reclaim and honor Jewish life during the periods of diaspora, when Jews were expelled from the land and dispersed throughout different regions of the world. Furthermore, they argue that life in diaspora has become itself an authentic form of Jewish existence. In other words, Israeli citizenship (which is automatically granted to every Jewish person around the world as a "birthright") and return to the land are not necessarily the ideal fulfillment of every Jew's life. This example demonstrates the complexities and diverse perspectives about religion and nationalism; even though religious events and places are often used to support the nationalistic aims of a particular group, religious and nonreligious members of the group may not support the nationalistic aims.

Ritual Practices in Religious Nationalism

Religions are not merely abstract ideas and beliefs. Rather, they are embodied in communities, practices, and institutions. In Northern Ireland, religion remains relevant to the formation of broad social networks, concrete events, and political organizing. Marches, parades, and other symbolic public performances often generate moments of tension and even violence. These rituals constitute and perpetuate a national narrative by focusing on tragic deaths, martyrdom, or miraculous heroic victories in the past.

Case Study: Marching Season (Northern Ireland)

Irish Protestants celebrate marching season on July 12 to commemorate King William of Orange's defeat of the Catholic King James at the Battle of Boyne (1690). This historical event is associated with the Protestant colonization of Ireland. As a public ritual, marching season involves intentional violations of typically segregated spaces. The marches of the Orange Order (a Protestant fraternal organization) are routed through streets in Catholic residential areas, where Protestants are normally prohibited. As a result, these actions provoke resentment and sometimes violent responses from Catholics. Though the act of marching in a parade itself is not essentially religious, its enactment in these circumstances is a symbolic assertion of Protestant identity across self-identified Catholic spaces and boundaries in Northern Ireland (Mitchell, 2006, 86).

Case Study: Ariel Sharon at the Dome of the Rock (Israel/Palestine)

Such symbolic provocations are not unique to Ireland. In a similar way, the second intifada or Palestinian uprising was ignited when former Israeli prime minister Ariel Sharon visited the contested site of the Dome of the Rock on the Temple Mount on the eve of the Jewish New Year (Rosh Hashanah) in September 2000. The Dome of the Rock is revered by Muslims as the site where

Muhammad ascended to heaven and by Jews as the location where Abraham prepared to sacrifice his son Isaac. Though he identified himself as a secular atheist, Sharon claimed, nonetheless, that he was simply exercising his eternal right as a Jew to visit the Temple, the holiest site in Judaism. As this example illustrates, religious and national identities are linked to particular times (e.g., holy days, historical events) and places, which may overlap with the interests of another group. Consequently, conflict often ensues when one group transgresses boundaries to assert its claim over a shared, mutually meaningful space.

Ariel Sharon's choice of space (*Haram al-Shari* or the Temple Mount in Arabic) and time (Rosh Hashanah) powerfully mobilized popular sentiments and sparked collective responses among Jews and Palestinians that led to rioting and violent resistance. This act exemplifies the important interconnections between religious, national, and ethnic identities. These interconnections are not easy to dismiss, even when nationalists define their commitment to national causes as nonreligious and their objectives as purely political. Of course, though it is widely acknowledged that political elites and activists manipulate religious symbols, narratives, and institutional frameworks, this fact does not explain *why* such acts are needed in the first place to consolidate power, mobilize popular sentiment, and confer legitimacy upon social structures and political arrangements. Does it matter that the symbols, rituals, and myths in the previous examples are selected from organized, historical religious traditions? Does that make them especially powerful, persuasive, or motivating? Or might any set of symbols or rituals be equally as effective?

Ethnoreligious Nationalism

In the previous discussions of Northern Ireland and Israel, we explored the multiple senses in which the Troubles and Zionism can be thought of as religious. We emphasized ways that religion was used to create boundaries for national identities. However, to gain a better understanding of the complexities of religious nationalism, we must expand our discussion of identity markers to include ethnicity and examine the interrelations between nationality, religion, and ethnicity.

The term "ethnonationalism" refers to forms of nationalism in which ethnicity or ethnic features of identity are used to forge national ties or determine membership in the group. Such ethnic features may include a shared language, belief in a common ancestry, as well as inherited cultural practices, customs, manners, attitudes, and sensibilities shared by (and constitutive of) a particular group. Sociologist Max Weber (1864–1920) defined ethnicity as a "subjective belief in common descent" (Weber, 1968, 389). Of course, such a belief need not be intentional or conscious. It might take the form of an emotional attachment or psychological bond. In addition, the impression that one's membership in a particular ethnic group is natural or given may even take the form of embodied sensibilities that are revealed in how individual group members behave and unreflectively live their daily lives. When we attempt to identify the basis for these underlying connections to the group, the boundary between ethnicity and religion often becomes blurred.

As we saw with Hibbard's account of communalism, groups frequently seek nationalistic aims based upon their common religious and ethnic identity. The following case studies illustrate how religious identity markers blur or merge with ethnic identity markers. When this is the case, it is necessary to expand the term "religious nationalism" to explicitly and intentionally include categories of ethnicity as well. To do this, we introduce the term "ethnoreligious nationalism."

Case Study: Jewish Elements of Zionism

We have discussed religious Zionism as an example of religious nationalism, but this concept alone does not fully account for the religious dimensions of the nationalist commitment of, for example, a Jewish atheist to Israel. We may approach this scenario by asking how an Israeli citizen can be both an atheist and Jewish. To answer this question, one might propose that the person is not Jewish in a religious sense because he or she does not believe in God and refuses to observe the religious practices of Judaism; nevertheless, the individual may be thought of as ethnically Jewish because he or she speaks Hebrew, identifies with events in Jewish history, and participates as a member of a Jewish community. However, this answer is problematic because it treats religion as a distinct facet that is easily separable from other markers of identity and spheres of social interaction. Moreover, such an answer suggests that if one does not believe in the existence of the God of Abraham, Isaac, and Jacob, one ceases to be a religious

Jew. Yet being religious means much more than intentional agreement with theological doctrines or holding to certain faith commitments. Religion is deeply embedded in institutions, societies, histories, and rituals.

For instance, if we grant the interrelation between religion and ethnicity, the question of what makes a Jewish state (i.e., Israel) Jewish appears more complex than a simple issue of demography (i.e., a state in which Jewish people constitute the majority of the population, or a state where citizenship depends upon identifying oneself and being certified by others—e.g., the religious authority—as Jewish). We may pose questions about the tangled links between ethnic and religious markers that define Jewish identity and the state. For example, why do the symbols of the Israeli state include traditionally religious symbols, such as the menorah? Why was modern Hebrew (a language based upon the biblical text and revived from an exclusively religious language of prayer for modern secular use in the 19th century) elected to be the national language of the State of Israel, instead of Yiddish, Polish, German, Russian, or any of the other languages that were actually in common use among Jewish immigrants to the Yishuv (the prestate Jewish society and institutional apparatuses in Palestine) and later to Israel? Why is the Sabbath (the weekly holy day of rest designated by God in the Hebrew Scriptures) the official day of rest in Israel? Why is every Israeli soldier given a copy of the Tanach (the Jewish holy Scriptures) upon their official induction into the military, regardless of whether they identify themselves as religious or nonreligious? Why is every Israeli Jew expected to be married and buried by the official orthodox rabbinate? In fact, there are ethnic, cultural, and national elements of Jewishness in Israel, and religious tradition, symbols, rituals, and history of Judaism permeate all of them.

Some claim that the religious dimensions of Judaism are simply a matter of personal belief in God and private ritual observance and thus are easily distinguishable from ethnic, cultural, and national senses of Jewishness; however, these claims are both factually inaccurate and conceptually inadequate. This conception reduces religion to simply a matter of personal choice and voluntary belief. It is too simplistic to serve as an analytical lens for understanding and intervening in complex problems that religious nationalism and ethnoreligious nationalism require.

Case Study: Serbian Nationalism in Yugoslavia

Serbian nationalism offers another example of how categories of ethnicity, religion, and nationalism are thoroughly intermingled. Again, as we saw in the cases of Zionism and Northern Ireland, the label "religious nationalism" does not necessarily mean that a particular form of nationalism is religious because its proponents demand that adherents practice religion (e.g., Judaism, Protestantism, or Catholicism), subscribe to particular theological truth claims or doctrines, or promote a theocratic regime. Nonetheless, when national boundaries and identity markers are framed in terms of religion, the language of *ethnic* purity often arises and is more appropriately described as *ethno*religious nationalism. In the cases of Zionism and Serbian nationalism, respectively, non-Jews and non-Serbs are classified as aliens and foreigners, even if they were born within the national territory in question and come from families that have lived there for several generations. To better grasp the concept of ethnoreligious nationalism and the questions it raises, we will explore the case of ethnocentric Serbian nationalism in greater depth.

After World War II, Yugoslavia consisted of a federation of six Balkan republics (Croatia, Montenegro, Serbia, Slovenia, Bosnia and Herzegovina, and Macedonia) all under the presidency of Josip Broz Tito. The populations within the Yugoslavian republics were a diverse mixture of ethnicities and religions. Under Tito, such areas as Bosnia and Herzegovina contained a multicultural coexistence of religions, ethnicities, and nationalities, and were characterized by a high degree of intermarriage across these identity markers. However, by the 1990s, the Yugoslavian federation had begun to split after the death of Tito in 1980 and the disintegration of the Soviet Union. Seeking to fill the power vacuum caused by the loss of Tito's charismatic leadership, several competing political agendas emerged and were divided along the lines of complex mixtures of religious, ethnic, and national affiliations. The most visible of these intermingled religious-ethnic identities were the Catholic Croats, the Orthodox Christian Serbs, and Bosnian Muslims.

Bosnia and Herzegovina boasted of tolerant and inter-religious coexistence among its diverse people. It heralded its rich diversity, in particular when its capital, Sarajevo, hosted the 1984 Winter Olympics. And yet this territory degenerated into bitter civil war and ethnic cleansing campaigns within just a few years. These campaigns were fought largely along the lines of rigid identities in which religion, ethnicity, and nationality were interspersed. Consider but one example, in 1995, when Bosnian Serb forces massacred more than 7,000 Bosnian Muslim men and boys in the town of Srebrenica, and expelled more than 20,000 civilians from the area.

In reflecting on these conflicts in the Balkans, political philosopher Michael Ignatieff observes that closely related (often inter-related) group identities became segregated along rigid collective boundaries that illustrate Sigmund Freud's psychoanalytical concept of the "narcissism of minor differences" (Ignatieff, 1997, 34–71). According to Freud, small differences between people become magnified and classified manipulatively and destructively, especially when those people are actually quite similar or live in close proximity to one another. In fact, according to Freud, the more similar or closely related people or groups are, the more likely they will be to amplify their small differences (Freud, 1985, 131, 305). This tendency is liable to assume the form of pathological self-love (narcissism) in which loving oneself (and one's people) becomes indistinguishable from loathing "the other" (i.e., those who are different from oneself and the members of one's group). Such self-love perceives the very existence of the other as a source of anxiety; it is perceived as harmful to—in some way, a judgment against—oneself and one's group. Typically, this narcissism results in explicit violence against the other who is perceived as perversely different but is, in the vast majority of ways, actually quite similar.

The wars in the former Yugoslavia indeed illustrate the devastating effects of the narcissism of minor differences. People who for many decades lived together peacefully as neighbors, friends, and relatives—who frequently intermarried and spoke the same languages—engaged in brutal acts of violence against one another. The differences in their religious, ethnic, and national identities were highlighted, magnified through the retrieval of mythical accounts of historical grievances, and manipulated in ways that resulted in mass violence and ethnic cleansing.

One key factor to the developments of civil war and ethnic cleansing in Bosnia and Herzegovina was Serbian president Slobodan Milošević, who mobilized an ethnoreligious nationalist ideology known as Christoslavism. This ideology blended both religious and ethnocentric interpretations of Serbian nationalism. Committed to realizing a Greater Serbia, this version of Serbian nationalism aimed to protect Serbians and to unify all of the Balkan regions where Serbs lived (Berkley Center, 2009, 4). Similar to the Troubles in Northern Ireland and Ariel Sharon's provocative visit to the Temple Mount, Christoslavism in Serbia merged religious and ethnic identifications to mobilize mass national support. This process selectively retrieved, reinterpreted, and manipulated myths, histories, memories, and cultural and religious symbols, as well as sacred spaces and times.

Like the case of messianic history for religious Zionists, Serbian Christoslavism emerged from a mythological interpretation of specific historical events. The Battle of Kosovo (June 28, 1389) marked a devastating defeat of the Serbian Prince Lazar and his military forces by the Ottoman Muslim armies under the command of Sultan Murad I. According to the legend, severely outnumbered, Lazar accepted total defeat in exchange for the promise that God would one day vanquish the Serbs' Muslim oppressors and raise the Serbian nation back to a unified and glorious condition.

The mythology of Prince Lazar is one of martyrdom in historical defeat, and resurrection as a saint in national imagination and memory. This mythology, combined with recollection of centuries of Ottoman rule that followed, became central components in Serbian national identity. In the late 1980s, these dimensions of Serbian nationalism were used by political elites to justify opposition to Muslim efforts to create an independent state in the Balkans and eventually to support purist anti-Muslim policies, including ethnic cleansing and mass killings (Sells, 1998a, xiii–xviii).

In Christoslavism, we again see the convergence of national and religious times and spaces. By the middle of the 19th century, scholar of religion Michael Sells explains, "Lazar was explicitly portrayed as a Christ figure in the art and literature, often surrounded by 12 knights disciples [including a traitorous Judas Iscariot figure, who supplied the Turks with battle plans], ministered to by a Mary Magdalene figure" (Sells, 2006, 147). The battlefield in Kosovo where Lazar and his men were martyred came to be known as the Serb Golgotha (Golgotha being the name of the place of Jesus's crucifixion according to Christian Scriptures). Slavic Muslims came to be referred to as "Christ killers." The region of Kosovo itself came to be commonly referred to as the Serbian Zion or Serbian Jerusalem (Sells, 1998a, 29–52; Perica, 2002, 7–8).

During the tumultuous period of the late 1980s after Tito's death, the portrayal of the Battle of Kosovo as an analogy to the passion of Christ (the story of Christ's suffering and crucifixion in Christian Scriptures) was revived in the commemoration of the 600th anniversary of Prince Lazar's death in 1989. That year, over 1 million people attended the sesquicentennial passion play (recounting the martyrdom and resurrection of Lazar as a national saint who was also beatified by the Serbian Orthodox Church), which was staged on the battleground in Kosovo. Sells's description highlights the significance of holy places and times in this Serbian nationalistic ritual: "Militant bishop-politicians and others took it over and used the passion play to affect a collapse of time. The audience—on site and around the Serb Orthodox world—were drawn through the power of the passion play into seeing themselves, not as spectators at a representation of a past event, but as living that event as original participants in the drama unfolding in an eternally present now." The event was held on June 28, a holy feast day of the Serbian Orthodox church known as Vidovdan (St. Vitus Day), which annually memorializes Saint Prince Lazar and the Serbian holy martyrs. This dramatic celebration was reproduced and reinforced by media campaigns and cultural productions that aimed to "militarize the 1989 commemoration by portraying the Slavic Muslims of contemporary Yugoslavia as bearing on their hands the blood of Lazar and other medieval Serb martyrs" (Sells, 2006, 147).

This event was part of a gradual process that intensified and radicalized Serbian nationalism. Over time, political elites—including Serbian president Milošević and Croatian president Franjo Tujman—promoted radical, chauvinistic, and ethnocentric interpretations of their peoples' ethnic, religious, and national identities. Motivated by these identities, the masses were mobilized to kill and die in order to defend themselves as a people. In short, the radicalization from 1992 to 1995 in Bosnia and Herzegovina occurred largely as a result of "marshalling of religious symbols as a way to create, define, deny, and eliminate a religious other" (Sells, 2006, 145).

It is important to note that the leaders who strategically drew on religious symbols were not necessarily religious practitioners themselves. Indeed, Sells explains, in the case of Serbia, "many militant religious nationalists had been lifelong communist secularists who became deeply effective at manipulating religious symbols." And yet it would be inaccurate to say that the religious tradition that the political elites drew upon was simply reduced to a set of tools and ornaments by which Serbian nationalist leaders carried out a purely political agenda. In fact, the irony is that in this case of ethnoreligious nationalism (as in many comparable cases), "the manipulator of the symbol becomes manipulated by the symbol. Those who start out using religious symbols instrumentally to gain power or other benefits end up becoming servants of those symbols psychologically" (Sells, 2006, 145). Leaders who used symbols and myths to tap into collective memory and captivate followers, and to mobilize them through ritual re-enactments, were themselves compelled to perpetuate and maintain the religious and cultural meanings that enabled the creation of the regime. Political elites derived much of their power from keeping those conflicts alive. However, the traditions of religious understanding, history, and practice through which they did this quickly took on significances of their own and produced results never intended at the time. Such unintended results included further and more expansive acts of ethnic cleansing and population displacement; Serbia's being chastised, sanctioned, even militarily bombarded by the international community; and later, Serbia's long-delayed entry into the European Union (EU).

As we argued above in our discussion of the religious dimensions of Zionism, on one hand, it is insufficient and inaccurate to think of religion simply as a set of subjective beliefs that a person (or people) voluntarily subscribes to. And though religious traditions are subject to different interpretations, on the other hand, it is insufficient to portray them simply as neutral collections of symbols, rituals, and narratives that take on whatever meanings a user ascribes to them at a given point in time. Religious traditions are socially embodied, manifest in culture, and extend over time. The meanings of religious symbols have histories. Rituals exert their power through social processes that reach beyond what a particular practitioner or leader might try to use them for. Mythical stories take hold and often assume a life of their own, especially in their capacity to captivate shared imagination, mobilize popular sentiments, or ignite passion. In precisely these ways, the religious significance and cultural power of Christoslavism overran the efforts of President Milošević, his colleagues, and Serbian Orthodox church leaders to use it to accomplish their own specific nationalist objectives. This insight is key for understanding how, in the case of Serbian ethnoreligious nationalism, the manipulators of the religious symbols, rituals, and stories themselves came to be manipulated by the symbols, rituals, and myths they used.

Case Study: Kosovo and the "Serbian Jerusalem"

Consider, for example, the mythical conception of the small region of Kosovo in southern Serbia as the Serbian Jerusalem. This image portrays the territory as uniquely sacred to Serbian history and national identity. It amplifies the significance of Kosovo as the homeland of the original Serbian Kingdom (dating back to the 13th century), the birthplace of the Serbian Orthodox Church (14th century), and a landscape that remains dotted by the oldest Serbian Orthodox churches, monasteries, and relics. It contains the battlefield of Prince Lazar's defeat at the hands of the Ottomans. These and many other associations contribute to the characterization of Kosovo as the cradle of the Serbian nation, a uniquely sacred soil that has been sprinkled by the blood of Serbian martyrs (almost always, the legends say, at the hands of Muslims). It was just these significances of the Kosovo territory that Milošević mobilized and radicalized during his famous visit to Kosovo Polje (the Field of Black Birds) on Vidovdan (June 28, 1989), at the field of the Battle of Kosovo.

Of course, the conception of Kosovo as the Serbian Jerusalem has a compelling history of its own. This history predates by centuries Milošević's manipulation of that mythology at the 1989 commemoration of the Battle of Kosovo. And importantly, the power of those symbols and mythic understandings has lived on in their capacity to justify and fuel ethnoreligious conflict in Kosovo well after the Dayton Peace Accords brought a truce to the fighting in Bosnia and Herzegovina in December 1995. In fact, the power of radicalized Christoslavism exerted itself even after Milošević was finally captured and put on trial for crimes against humanity at the International Criminal Tribunal of the former Yugoslavia at the Hague, Netherlands (he died during the trial in 2006).

In 1998, violent conflict erupted in Kosovo, again fueled by elements of Christoslavism. Kosovo had been home to a considerable ethnic Albanian population (historically Muslim, though largely repressed under communism) for several hundred years. Over the course of the 20th century, the Kosovar Albanians had come to constitute a vast majority of the population in that territory (as much as 80 to 90 percent, though estimates are inexact). Due partially to these demographic considerations, as early as 1974, Yugoslav leader Tito granted political self-determination to the region by engineering a constitution for the Socialist Autonomous Province of Kosovo. This granted Kosovo de facto autonomy (it had the same representation and voting rights as the six republics of Yugoslavia). Administratively, however, it remained officially part of Serbia within Yugoslavia. Kosovar Albanians sought autonomy as a full-fledged federal republic within Yugoslavia under Tito. They continued to pursue independence and sovereignty (sometimes militantly) through the 1980s and 1990s, after the splintering of the Yugoslav republics.

As Serbian ethnoreligious nationalism radicalized and surged in the late 1980s and early 1990s (greatly owing to the legacies and uses of Christoslavism described above), Milošević successfully revised the Serbian constitution. This revision returned Kosovo to its pre-1974 status as a province entirely under the sovereignty of the Republic of Serbia. As living conditions in Kosovo degenerated through the 1990s, Kosovar Albanian liberation efforts became increasingly militant. Serbia fought to defend Kosovo as the Serbian Jerusalem against continued attempts by separatist Kosovar Albanians to declare its independence. This resulted in further episodes of ethnic cleansing in which as many as 850,000 Albanian Kosovars were forcibly expelled from Kosovo and fled to Albania. These expulsions, along with thousands of murdered civilians and related atrocities, triggered a nearly three month long bombing campaign of Serbia by the member states of the North Atlantic Treaty Organization (NATO) in 1999. The bombing continued until Milošević withdrew his forces, and Kosovo was placed under temporary UN administration (Judah, 2000, 312–335).

Ethnoreligious nationalist tensions and separatist efforts simmered in Kosovo until, in 2008, Kosovar's Albanian majority unilaterally declared its secession from Serbia. The declaration was recognized by the United States and various other European countries. In response, Serbian nationalist protesters burned the U.S. and Croatian embassies in Belgrade. In 2009, Serbia challenged Kosovo's declaration of independence at the International Court of Justice at the Hague. The court ruled that the declaration of secession was not illegal according to international law, though Serbia (along with many other countries) persisted in its refusal to recognize Kosovo's independence.

The ethnoreligious dimensions of Serbian nationalism continue to echo amid even the most pragmatic of national interests. In recent years, Serbia has sought to become a member of the European Union, a goal that has motivated considerable cooperation with the international community. Serbian authorities have captured and handed over to the International Criminal Tribunal at the Hague, Netherlands, nationalist leaders who were indicted for acts of genocide and crimes against humanity during the Yugoslav wars. Such leaders include the former Serbian president Milošević (who was surrendered on the Serbian Orthodox holy feast day of Vidvodan, June 28, 2001), the Bosnian Serb politician Radovan Karadizc, and Bosnian Serb military leader Ratko Mladic (the latter two stand accused of planning and conducting the massacre of Srebrenica, among other mass atrocities, and were arrested in 2008 and 2011, respectively). In March 2010, the Serbian Parliament officially apologized for the massacre that occurred at Srebrenica.

In a 2010 interview addressing the possibility of Serbia's joining the European Union, the Serbian foreign minister was asked if Serbia was willing to officially recognize Kosovo's independence as part of its path to EU membership. The minister explained that Serbia's interest in maintaining its territorial unity, including Kosovo, could not be reduced to purely political interests. "Kosovo has deep historical and spiritual meaning for the people of Serbia," he recounted. "In a certain sense, it is our Jerusalem. We cannot accept unilateral decisions from those in power in Pristina [the capital city of Kosovo]. But we are prepared to negotiate and to work on compromises that guarantee the stability of the whole region. We would not reject any suggestion outright" (Jeremic, 2010). As of late 2012, Serbia and Kosovo continue to strike a tenuous and volatile truce, along with the presence of NATO peacekeepers. Violent outbursts continue along the jointly controlled border, as well as at the site of the Battlefield of Kosovo. To date, Serbia has qualified for candidate status in its bid for full membership in the European Union.

We have seen that religion pervaded nationalist and ethnic conflict in the Balkans through the selective retrieval and manipulation of symbols, ritual practices, and mythic histories by nationalist leaders and political elites. We have seen, as well, that religious associations and identities do not merely serve as instruments or superficial markers for divisions that are actually purely political. In fact, the complex and dynamic character of religious nationalism is evident in the ways that religious symbols and practices sometimes exert influences and meanings that reach well beyond the interests and intentions of those political elites who attempt to manipulate them.

In the Balkans, religion and ethnicity also fused with nationalism through institutional operations and religious leadership. Serbian religious leaders and institutions collaborated with political efforts to avoid the legal consequences of war crimes. Religious leaders and institutions denied that the atrocities against Bosnians and Albanians had ever occurred. In fact, they published documents declaring that genocide was being perpetrated against Serbians in Kosovo (claims for which no substantiating evidence was produced). In 1996, the Serbian Orthodox Assembly of Bishops carried further the elements of victimization and martyrdom that frequently characterize religious nationalist dynamics. They insisted that the International Criminal Tribunal at the Hague unjustly and unequally singled out Serbians as perpetrators of war crimes and crimes against humanity. In doing this, the Bishops insisted, they were "indicting an entire nation" (Sells, 1998b, 201–206).

Given the deep histories and prolonged conflicts in the Balkans, it may be tempting to claim that ethnic, nationalist, and religious divisions have always been the source of violent conflict in these regions, and that they always will be. It might be equally tempting for some to claim, by contrast, that sufficient political and socioeconomic incentives would make the ethnoreligious dimensions of these nationalist conflicts simply disappear. Both such approaches to understanding and addressing ethnoreligious nationalism in the Balkans are insufficient. The challenge, then, is to historically and culturally contextualize the religious dimensions of these conflicts and explore them thoroughly, rather than attempt to bracket them or filter them out, or assume that, under conditions of successful globalization, religion will secularize itself out of the picture.

Of course, Serbs were far from the only perpetrators of violence and atrocities in the Balkan wars, or in later conflicts over Kosovo. In many cases, Serbs were victimized at the hands of Croatian ethnoreligious nationalist efforts as well. In addition, the cultural and historical power of Christoslavism—its intersplicing religion, ethnicity, and nationality—is not the only analytical angle from which the religious nationalism in the Balkans can be understood. And yet Christoslavism provides a particularly instructive case study for demonstrating the necessity of taking seriously the religious and historical dimensions of these nationalist conflicts. As Sells points out, "the ideology [Christoslavism] that has constructed the notion of eternal hatred is not itself eternal" (Sells, 1998b, 197). The fact that Christoslavism has a history, that is, is a product of historical and social religious forces, makes it all the more indispensable to understand and address this instance of ethnoreligious nationalism on its own terms, and in concrete ways, *in addition to* understanding and addressing the socioeconomic and political dimensions with which those religious forces are interwoven.

The Serbian use of the martyrdom of Prince Lazar is comparable to how Jewish settlers in the Palestinian Occupied Territories interpret historical time in messianic terms. Both positions result from a framing that justifies ethnocentrism and chauvinism, and often leads to violence. In both instances, understandings of national identity interact with conceptions of ethnicity and religion in ways that cannot be fully comprehended without a careful examination of relevant mythologies, theologies, and historical events and memories.

Religion and the Emergence of Premodern Nationalisms

The case of Serbian nationalism is not unique in how political leaders manipulate religious, ethnic, and other collective identities. Indeed, scholars of nationalism have identified comparable patterns in early manifestations of modern nationalisms. In the previous sections, we have used case studies in the modern era to explore how religious and ethnic identity indices were used to mark communal boundaries and exclude others; now we will explore similar dynamics in the premodern era. In doing so, we seek to demonstrate that nationalism is not strictly a modern phenomenon and that premodern political leaders also used religion to strengthen communal identity for the sake of maintaining their own power.

In *Faith in Nation: Exclusionary Origins of Nationalism* (2003), scholar Anthony Marx argues that premodern and modern national identities were constructed through a process of excluding the "domestic other." To understand the emergence of tolerant, multicultural, modern liberal democracies, one must recognize the features of their origins and past that they exclude or misremember. For example, the United States sought to be a refuge from religious persecutions by drafting principles of tolerance and disestablishment of religion directly into the Constitution. However, U.S. history also involved processes of identifying domestic others, which resulted in the mass extermination of Native Americans and the enslavement of Africans; these events were pivotal to and inseparable from the nation-making process because they reinforced identity markers that determined who was entitled to constitutional rights.

In Anthony Marx's framework, state-making elites (early modern monarchs) relied on nationalism to generate social cohesion and to provide their regimes with legitimacy. Hence national identities were selectively consolidated for the purpose of establishing states and centralizing power; they were formed from previous stereotypes, symbols, and folklorist practices, including occasional pogroms or other violent acts directed at domestic others. Social cohesion and rigid definitions of identity were necessary to secure control over the centralized mechanism of the state.

Many premodern European monarchs realized that "their rule could not be protected or further consolidated without a corresponding popular allegiance that did not then exist" (Marx, 2003, 9). To create social cohesion, they selectively excluded others. In premodern Europe, religion constituted "the primary basis of mass belief and solidarity" and thus often provided the terms, symbols, and identity claims to include or exclude others (Marx, 2003, 25). But this process of erecting "pure" cultural boundaries and promoting a single religious or ethnic identity was neither automatic nor inevitable. Instead, it involved deliberate, and often strategic, efforts on the part of political elites.

Contemporary discussions of multicultural citizenship attempt to challenge the premises that lead to the conception of the modern nation as monocultural. According to Anthony Marx, modern liberal democracies seek to promote a model of equality that respects cultural differences and the collective rights of a group; however, it is often forgotten that the roots of liberal Western democracies originated from the exclusion of select groups. Moreover, Marx argues that exclusionary lines often drew upon and manipulated existing religious differences that had not been necessarily politicized up to that point. Marx emphasizes the role of political elites in the premodern era in his comparative study of Spain and France (2003).

Case Study: The Spanish Inquisition

In 1469, Isabella of Castile and Ferdinand of Aragon were married to unite the two crowns of the Spanish Empire. This act was intended to resist the regionalism of Hispania by centralizing power and consolidating a shared identity. Though the monarchs did not actively seek to construct a nation, they recognized the need to harness a certain degree of popular allegiance based on a common Catholic faith. During that time, Catholicism remained "more spiritually than politically cohering, even as it remained the strongest basis for any 'concessions to the common welfare'" (Marx, 2003, 2). Marx contends that the Spanish Inquisition consolidated a Spanish-Catholic identity by purging Jewish and Moorish elements in an effort to promote support for a nation that would be only for Spanish Catholics. Hence "Jews or converts were described as separate, alien, or enemy 'nations,' implying some unity of everyone else sharing 'blood relationship . . . habit or unity' or faith" (Marx, 2003, 80). "The imperative for unity through faith," Marx continues, "came to a climax with the single most dramatic episode of exclusion, the expulsion of Spain's Jews in 1492" (Marx, 2003, 85). The Inquisition sanctioned and institutionalized preexisting anti-Semitism by intentionally excluding Jews. Indeed, by the mid-16th century, this institution greatly enabled Spain's rulers to consolidate power and gain popular legitimacy (Marx, 2003, 86). The language of "purity of blood" was integral to the Inquisition; consequently, it provides a clear example of the important interconnections between religion, nationality, and ethnicity.

Case Study: France

In France, state centralization also led to a clear conception of nationhood. In the 16th century, "Catholicism within and international conflicts without did provide some basis for popular coherence, but this remained largely localized, abstract, and untapped" (Marx, 2003, 47). Like Spain, France had much earlier imposed restrictions on Jews (i.e., they segregated them from Christians, prevented them from certain occupations, and forced them to wear special clothing) before ultimately forcing them to leave the country in 1306. Due to the expulsion of the Jews and others, Catholic homogeneity had come to be taken for granted (Marx, 2003, 48). But with the spread of Protestantism in the early to mid-16th century, Catholic unity in France was challenged.

Religious sectarianism (or divisions) became one way that the French nobility resisted the increased consolidation of power by the French monarchy (Marx, 2003, 49). Despite some efforts by Catherine of Medici and other Catholic rulers to appease the Huguenots (French Protestants) and to accommodate multiple faiths in the interest of stability, anti-Huguenot violence erupted in 1562. And though that violence supposedly ended with the Edict of Amboise (1563), in reality, it fostered further resentment and fear that culminated in 1569 with the onset of "the bloodiest and most savage religious war yet" and continued until 1572 (Marx, 2003, 55). As Anthony Marx tells the story, these wars represented earlier instances of "self-serving elites" who deployed "religious propaganda to gain popular support." The result was that "religion quickly became politicized by elite conflicts and mass violence" (Marx, 2003, 56).

Challenging the Modern Secular Nationalism Model

Clearly, the manipulation of religious symbols, mythologized historical memories, and prejudices mobilized through ritual practices are not novel phenomena. In case studies from both the premodern and modern eras, we have seen that religion has been used as an identity marker to determine who should be excluded from the nation, even when such individuals may have seen themselves as integral to the social fabric of their places of residence. These examples, therefore, suggest some comparative reflections on the broader question of the interrelation between religion and politics in the modern and premodern eras.

Modern secular liberalism is often viewed as more tolerant and therefore better than the outdated irrationality and fanaticism that is associated with religious fervor. However, Anthony Marx has challenged this rosy view of modern secular liberalism by insisting that nationalism emerged on the back of exclusionary practices through religious distinctions. Marx's analysis provides an initial challenge to the assumption that religious nationalism constitutes an illogical, pathological form of nationalism. Instead of providing a cure for exclusionary violence, nationalism itself actually has exclusionary origins, and those lines of exclusions centrally involve religion (whether we discuss premodern Spain or more contemporary events in Yugoslavia). Furthermore, exclusionary lines pervade even the most liberal forms of nationalism. Thus we argue for the need to think of secular and religious forms of nationalism along a continuum of more to less exclusive, and more to less amenable to criticism, revision, and self-correction, rather than viewing the secular and religious as wholly separable and opposed to one another.

Political Elites and the Shaping of Identity

Similar to Marx's focus on political elites, Hibbard (2010) focuses on the role of leaders when conceptions of national identity shift from more liberal (and thus secular) interpretations to less liberal and more explicitly religious variations. In both analyses, the political establishment is the driving force behind the shifting conceptions of identity because such leaders manipulate and provoke the submissive masses but then become themselves coopted by religious agenda. As a result of these dynamics the national project is subverted, oscillating from greater to lesser inclusivity and liberality. Though this approach yields many important insights into the nature of religious nationalism, it does not present a complete picture and contains some flaws.

In contrast, Mitchell (2006) attempts to broaden the source of the transformation, crystallization, and reproduction of identities to include civil society. Her study of the Troubles in Northern Ireland focuses on the relationships between politicians and the church, as well as communities (housing patterns and social networks) and social institutions (marriage and education) that shape religious identity. In doing so, Mitchell's work challenges the elitist assumptions inherent in Marx and Hibbard's accounts. To understand the limitations of Hibbard's emphasis on political elites, we will examine in the following case study his attempts to explain the rise and fall of secularism in Egypt.

Case Study: Egypt

Under the regime of Gamal Abdel Nasser (1956–1970), secularist as well as socialist ideologies prevailed. However, Islamic conceptions of Egyptian identity reemerged and rose to the fore, even though they were occasionally brutally repressed by the police forces of the Anwar Sadat (1970–1981) and Hosni Mubarak (1981–2011) regimes. Hibbard (2010) seeks to explain how more religious exclusivist (what he refers to as illiberal) conceptions of identity appeared, especially since exclusivist and illiberal religious ideologies were criticized and marginalized by Egyptian political elites in the middle part of the 20th century. "In other words," Hibbard asks, "why has religion—and particularly a conservative and often illiberal rendering of religious tradition—remained so influential in the politics of these three ostensibly secular societies?" (Hibbard, 2010, 6).

After President Mubarak was toppled in 2011, the Muslim Brotherhood, which represents an exclusivist/religious ideology, rose to the foreground of the Egyptian political landscape. In fact, the Muslim Brotherhood candidate, Muhammed Morsi, won the Egyptian presidential election in June 2012. This reemergence of a religious political body further stresses the need to move beyond a secularist interpretation of nationalism (i.e., an interpretation that brackets religion as either a private belief or an increasingly irrelevant resource for cultivating national identity). Furthermore, reemergence of the Muslim Brotherhood challenges the assumption that a nation moves from an initial and necessary exclusivity to an increased inclusivity, even if this type of move may have occurred along such a trajectory in the histories of some Western liberal democracies.

Hibbard believes that national identity moved from secularist to more explicit religious interpretations because modern state elites co-opt religion to reinforce their own political legitimacy. Though Hibbard recognizes religion's prophetic capacity to criticize status quo conditions, he writes, "the effort of state elites to coopt an exclusive vision of religion and society—and otherwise to fan the flames of sectarianism for political gain—undermined earlier efforts to build an inclusive national identity. It also contributed to the communalization of public life and the corresponding polarization of society" (Hibbard, 2010, 12). To put it simply, Hibbard recognizes that separating religion (in both its positive and negative manifestations) from secular politics is not an easy thing to do. In fact, it may prove to be impossible.

If we closely examine historical events in Egypt, we find that the political elites in power were not the only actors who infused nationalistic aims with religious meaning. The legitimacy of

Nasser's regime and its ideologies was damaged by a variety of factors, not the least of which was the defeat associated with the Six Days War (1967) against Israel. Consequently, Sadat co-opted elements within the Egyptian landscape that held an Islamist vision of an Egyptian society. This shift was a drastic departure from Nasser's merely nominal commitment to the Islamic identity of the Egyptian state. Thus, Sadat cultivated alliances with those who criticized Nasser's secular regime, such as the Muslim Brotherhood. And yet, as we observed in the context of our discussion of Serbian nationalism above, the manipulators of the symbols typically come to be manipulated by the symbols that they co-opt. In Egypt, Sadat co-opted Islamic vocabularies to legitimize his authority, but his rule ended with his own assassination by an Islamist activist. The use of religious systems to support and articulate the language of purity and authenticity often backfires and leads to uncompromising, vindictive, and even unexpected acts of "purification."

Language, Literature, Texts, and Claims of Authenticity

The language of authenticity and purity often appear as ideas that are constructed to support ethnoreligious nationalisms. Unsurprisingly, purist conceptions of nationality that portray other inhabitants of the land as "foreigners" and "invaders" (regardless of long centuries spent living together as fellow citizens, friends, and relatives) constitute a form of cultural and structural violence that can lead to direct violence. The messianic Jewish settlers rationalize the uprooting of the Palestinians, for instance, by dismissing the validity of their rootedness in the actual land of Palestine. More broadly, secular and religious Zionists alike have invoked the Jews' "right of return" and their claim of being native to the land (based on biblical narratives) to justify the displacement of Palestinians.

Case Study: Hindutva and India

The ideology of Hindutva, or Hinduness, in India provides another example of an ethnoreligious conception of identity; this conception mixes Indian national identity with Hinduism. This conception of identity categorizes, by definition, non-Hindus as aliens of the nation of India (even if they are, in fact, legal citizens of India). Moreover, this language undergirds and justifies violent incidents, such as violence between the Hindu and Muslim communities in the western Indian state of Gujarat. The ideology of Hindutva was born in the context of resistance to Western (primarily British) colonialism in India. The word was first coined in 1923 but came into political fruition in the late 1980s, especially due to the controversy surrounding the Babri Mosque, which was allegedly built on the birthplace of the Hindu god Rama. In 1992, Hindutva activists destroyed the Babri Mosque because they believed that Muslims had violated the holy site; more than 1,000 people died in the subsequent riots. As in the case of Christoslavism in Serbia, purist conceptions of Indian identity were not invented out of nothing. In part, their construction involved various symbolic acts and manipulations by political and religious leaders. Hindutva has exerted a wide-ranging influence, beyond merely marginalized sectors of the population. For example, the Bharatiya Janata Party (BJP) has been influential in Indian politics and espouses the Hindutva ideology to varying degrees.

Hindutva literature projects themes of sacredness and purity, which are prevalent in nationalist ideological formations. Indian scholar Rajmohan Gandhi explains that Hindutva literature "defines good Indians as those to whom India is both their homeland and their holy land, a criterion that makes India's Muslims and Christians unpatriotic by definition" because they follow different religions (Gandhi, 2004, 50). Used to justify the demolition of the Babri Mosque, this ideology stands in striking contrast to the inclusive and pluralistic Indian national identity that was advocated by Mohandas Gandhi (1869–1948), the renowned leader of resistance to British colonialism. Instead, Hindutva's historiography tells a story of repeated "destruction of temples, forcible conversions, massacres" committed by Muslim "invaders" (Gandhi, 2004, 53). This mythology is similar in many ways to the religiously themed stories of victimization, heroic deaths, and martyrdom that we explored in Northern Ireland, the former Yugoslavia, and Israel/Palestine. In the case of Hindutva, the Bhagavad Gita (a sacred Hindu Scripture, whose title translates as "The Song of God") and specifically the stories of revenge contained in the Mahabharata (the larger body of Scripture that contains the Bhagavad Gita) are deployed selectively to legitimate violence and thus portray Hindu nationalism as a religious phenomenon.

Like the increasing influence of Islam in Egypt during the latter part of the 20th century, India experienced a shift from secularist to ethnoreligious conceptions of national identity in the latter part of the 20th century. Similar to Sadat's Egypt, Hibbard states, India's Congress Party selectively co-opted "the themes of Hindu nationalism," which resulted in the "communalization of Indian politics" (Hibbard, 2010, 175). Despite conscious efforts to project a "secular veneer," this political practice of co-optation "belied a majoritarian strategy of right-wing populism." A study of Indian politics in the 1980s and the 1990s therefore illustrates that BJP's rise to power did not so much signify a paradigm shift, but rather an expression of the long process of transforming the political landscape altogether. Hibbard writes to this effect: "It was not a matter of secular versus religious but rather of competing claims to speak for the nation" (Hibbard, 2010, 176). While the secular Congress Party did not condone violent eruptions, such as the demolition of the Babri Mosque or the Gujarat massacre, it nonetheless contributed to the "communalization of the public sphere" and to a significant move away from Mahatma Gandhi's vision of multireligious and pluralist Indian secularism (Hibbard, 2010, 176).

Case Study: Sri Lanka

Sri Lanka presents another case of ethnoreligious nationalism. Since British colonial rule, tensions have existed between the Buddhist Sinhalese majority and the predominately Hindu Tamil minority. Sri Lanka (known as Ceylon during and immediately following the colonial era) gained the right of self-rule through the Solbury Constitution (1947) and by the 1950s, the Sinhalese gained political dominance. The government declared Sinhalese the official language, provided state support for Buddhism, and promoted Sinhalese culture. In response to growing marginalization, the Tamil minority rebelled. From 1983 to 2009, civil war was fought between Sinhalese-led government forces and Tamil rebel groups, resulting in the deaths of more than 70,000 and the displacement of tens of thousands. Again, an observer might be tempted to conclude that the conflict was not *really* religious because religion functions merely as an ethnic and national marker. Clearly, the observer may conclude, this conflict was not about beliefs or about "winning converts to Buddhism or Hinduism" (Little, 1999, 41).

However, it is problematic to dismiss the relevance of religion in such instances because it limits our capacity to offer an adequate explanation of difficult cases. In the case of Sri Lanka, David Little writes, a narrow view that reduces the cause of conflict to mere ethnicity "ignores or distorts historical realities" (Little, 1999, 41). Religion, ethnicity, and nationality are closely intertwined; after all, in Sinhalese, "the words for nation, race and people are practically synonymous" and "the emphasis on Sri Lanka as the land of Sinhala Buddhists carried emotional popular appeal, compared with which the concept of a multiethnic polity was a meaningless abstraction" (K. de Silva quoted in Little, 1999, 42–43). As in the case of Zionism, this mingling of identity markers and the appeal to the concept of sacred territory may give rise to an ethnocratic political agenda (Little, 1999, 43).

As in the case of Hindutva, the Sinhala Buddhists have used religious literature both to justify and magnify the significance of their nationalist claims. Ancient Buddhist sources have been used to substantiate the perception of Sri Lanka as "the land of Sinhala Buddhists"; in particular, a series of sacred texts written by Sri Lankan Theravada Buddhist monks between the fourth and 14th centuries portray the Sinhala people as "a people destined with a sacred mission" (Little, 1999, 43). A scriptural text composed in the sixth century, the Mahavamsa is another key source that draws on the ethnoreligious aspects of Sinhala Buddhist entitlement to the land. This chronicle tells the story of "a supposed visit to the island by the Buddha himself in order to secure a place where his doctrine could be defended and advanced." The arrival of the Buddha to the island entailed ethnically cleansing the island of its natives to make room for "a group of immigrants from north India led by Vijaya, the father of the Sinhala." Vijaya, the offspring of a lion and a human, becomes the progenitor of the Sinhala people ("the people of the lion") "whose primary obligation ever after is to preserve Buddhism, by violent means if necessary" (Little, 1999, 43). Additionally, the Mahavamsa tells the story of Duttagamani, the Buddhist king of the second century BCE. Duttagamani reportedly gave up his monkhood only to be reborn as a king whose only goal was to overcome Tamil domination, perceived as alien to the island, and to establish Buddhist domination over the sacred Sinhalese territory (Little, 1999, 44).

This story vindicates and sanctifies the claims of Sinhala Buddhists to exclusive control of Sri Lanka.

At the same time, analysis of the emergence of Sinhala ethno-religious nationalism should not be reduced to these violence-justifying myths. "Despite the abiding symbolic power of these ancient chronicles and crucial place in defining an ideal Buddhist Sinhala social order," Little writes, "they are only a part of what constitutes the modern understanding of the idea of Sri Lanka as the land of the Sinhala Buddhists" (Little, 1999, 44). Little consequently identifies "four critical intervening or proximate causes of the rise of modern Sinhala Buddhist nationalism," all specific to the 19th and the early 20th centuries, and reactions to British colonialism in the form of what came to be called "Buddhist revivalism" (Little, 1999, 45).

According to Little, the first proximate cause is preferential policies during British rule. Like the previous Portuguese and Dutch colonial administrations that inflamed intolerance in Sri Lanka, the British system played favorites to pit one group against the other. The Buddhist Sinhalese grew resentful of Hindu Tamils, who they believed were receiving preferential treatment from the British in education and civil service jobs. The Buddhist revivalism gained momentum in the context of colonialism and as a reaction against aggressive Christian missionary work in the 19th century (Little, 1999, 45–46). Hindu Tamils were also targets of Buddhist Sinhalese nationalism because they were viewed as allies of the colonial power.

A second proximate cause is an awareness of racial distinctions introduced by British colonialists, who viewed the Sinhala people as somehow connected to the "Aryan race" and thus superior to other inhabitants of the island. Though this racial categorization was never translated into full equality under British control (at best, the Sinhala were considered "second class Aryans"), this account of ethnic superiority worked in tandem with "the element of Sinhala racial self-consciousness as superior to other ethnic groups on the island, particularly the largest minority, the Tamils" (Little, 1999, 46).

The third proximate cause involves the Sinhalese "reaction to the perceived threat and unfair advantages represented by the Tamil community." Despite a position of relative privilege as the political majority after Sri Lanka gained independence, the Sinhalese feared the threat of "being swamped by the millions of Tamils living so close to their shores in the south Indian region of Tamil Nadu" because of Mahavamsa's stories of repeated Tamil invasions (Little, 1999, 48). These concerns led to hostile exclusionary policies against Tamils. For instance, the Sinhala-only language policy (1956) replaced English as the official language but did not recognize the language of the Tamil ethnic group. As a result, many Tamils were forced out of official posts as civil servants due to their lack of fluency in the Sinhala language.

The fourth proximate cause resulted from the mechanism put in place to ease the transition from British rule to self-rule. Though the Soulbury Constitution (1947) was designed to ensure decolonization and to establish the foundations for multiethnic democratic polity, there was a strong inclination toward majoritarian dictatorship, also called ethnocracy (Little, 1999, 38–51). The move toward an ethnocratic regime typically involves the amplification of an existential fear of being overwhelmed by an other (in this case, Tamils) who is not only contained within the geopolitical borders, but who also constitutes a broader regional demographic threat.

The cases of Sinhala Buddhism and Indian Hindutva illustrate how religious literature and texts, as well as historical events, intermingle to produce exclusivist national historiographies, which are then used by political, religious, and cultural leaders to vindicate ethnocratic state infrastructures.

Nationalism: A Replacement for Religion?

We have presented several case studies that exemplify important interrelations between religion and the construction of national identities. On one level, the perception of, and desire for, group purity exposes the intricate connections between ethnicity, nationality, and religion. Indeed, the ways that ethnicity, nationality, and religion may intermingle and mutually reinforce one another produce a form of nationalism that appears to be a "religious" one. Theorist Anthony Smith (2003) offers yet another approach to examine the internal logic of these forms of nationalism. Smith examines how nationalism resembles, and may even be considered a form of, religion.

Through historical comparative analysis, Smith shows that the nation is a collective identity that may be viewed as "a form of communion that binds its members through ritual and symbolic practice. . . . But nationalism also operates on other levels,"

Smith concludes. "It is best seen as a form and a type of belief-system whose object is the nation conceived as a sacred communion" (Smith, 2003, 18). This depiction of the nation as a sacred communion is appropriate since the word origins of the Latin *natio* and *religio* imply a communal orientation and commitment. This idea of the sacredness of a community (as well as the unique sanctity of its territory) often justifies the rhetoric of group purity and may result in destructive consequences for excluded groups. According to this idea, authentic Indian identity is equated with Hinduism, authentic Sri Lankan identity with Buddhism, authentic Israeli identity with Judaism, and so forth. Smith writes: "At the centre of the nationalist belief-system stands the cult of authenticity, and at the heart of this cult is the quest of the true self" (Smith, 2003, 37). Smith believes that the cult of authenticity implies a sense of reverence and significance to group identity; that it bears a striking family resemblance to the traditional concept of "holiness" in religious traditions (Smith, 2003, 38).

Smith focuses on ethnosymbolism, which he defines as "the sacred sources of nationalism and national identity, and their subjective relationship to certain traditional religious beliefs, motifs, and practices" (Smith, 2003, 5). He explores not only the question of the origins of nations, but also the reasons for their long-term persistence. While the issue of origins may relate to ethnicity and language, a nation's ability to survive may relate to culture and religion. Smith writes that the "strength of national identities can be understood only by exploring collective beliefs and sentiments about the 'sacred foundations' of the nation and by considering their relationship to the older beliefs, symbols, and rituals of traditional religions" (Smith, 2003, 3–4). In Smith's ethnosymbolist approach, he also seeks to move away from the focus on elites found in modernist analyses of nationalism, such as Anthony Marx's comparative study (2003). Marx views the "nation" as an entirely new social reality that emerged in premodernity due to shifting patterns of political systems. In contrast, Smith does not think that the nation is a product of modernity or premodernity. Instead, he argues that nationalisms (broadly construed) have existed and persisted for millennia and are thus not merely the result of changing power configurations.

Principally, Smith's ethnosymbolist approach analyzes the emergence of nationalism within preexisting landscapes of collective ethnic identities. This approach tries to explain "why nationalists so often seek to rediscover and appeal to cultural and symbolic repertoires within the antecedent populations with whom they claim a deep cultural continuity" (Smith, 2001, 58). To account for the interrelation between religion and nationalism, Smith disagrees with the conventional modernist view that nationalism is a product of the modern state as a political entity by which a group exercises self-determination. Nor is nationalism simply a social phenomenon replacing traditional religion. Based on Smith's account, these views are too shortsighted and beholden to a particular misinterpretation of modernity as liberating society from religion. Smith also denounces the "neo-traditional" position that views religion as a condition or structure that has persisted into modernity and subsequently as a natural ally of nationalism by sharing populist and messianic features as well as techniques of mass mobilization.

In contrast, Smith views nationalism as a "heterodox religion," or a form of religion that is "opposed to conventional, traditional religions," while also "inheriting many of their features—symbols, liturgies, rituals and messianic fervor—which now come to possess new and subversive political and national meanings" (Smith, 2003, 13). This interpretation of nationalism as heterodox religion is helpful, Smith contends, in order to understand "the predominantly secular content but religious forms of so many nationalisms." Likewise, this understanding can account for the ability of nationalisms to transform "the values of traditional religion into secular political ends" (Smith, 2003, 14).

In short, rather than being simply opposites, Marx's and Smith's approaches might actually complement each other. Marx's attention to the functions of religion is consistent with Smith's ethnosymbolist view of nationalism as a heterodox religion. Their combined approaches enable one to scrutinize the view that says religious nationalism is a pathological version of an otherwise secular nationalism. Marx's focus on state-making and power complements Smith's focus on the ethnosymbolic motifs of nationalisms, along with their ability to survive and evolve across time.

And yet holding Marx's and Smith's approaches together does not produce a complete understanding of religious nationalism since neither theorist focuses on the individual actors who are shaped and formed within the collective bodies that rally behind these forms of nationalism. Smith's and Marx's works do not address the specific processes on the ground that result in historical change; Marx emphasizes political elites, and Smith is not interested in the combination of power and the mechanisms of state-making. To understand how individuals are captivated by nationalism, we may revisit Mitchell's work (2006), which examines how national identities are reproduced and cultivated through rituals, along with the account of ethnoreligious nationalism captured in its multilayered complexity by the work of Sells (1998, 2006). This approach helpfully expands the discussion of nationalism to include embodied identity practices and therefore views the masses as more than merely "subjects" for manipulation in this or that direction.

To conclude, the primary objective of this chapter was to demonstrate why it is both analytically inadequate and factually incorrect to claim that secular and religious forms of nationalism are clearly and distinctly separable and stand as opposites to each other. To challenge this claim, we discussed the religious dimensions of secular forms of national identities, and examined the parallel ways that traditional religions, ethnicity, and modern nationalism have been used to build allegedly authentic group identities by excluding others.

We have presented and assessed the work of various scholars to demonstrate that a multidisciplinary combination of approaches is necessary to understand the complexities and dynamic character of religious nationalism. This kind of analysis is crucial because it brings to the fore related discussions concerning the connections between religion and violence, religious fundamentalisms, and the "resurgence" of religion in contemporary contexts around the globe.

References

Berkley Center for Religion, Peace, & World Affairs at Georgetown University. "Bosnia: Ethno-Religious Nationalism in Conflict," *Case Study Series* (June 2009). http://repository.berkleycenter.georgetown.edu/110811Bosnia[FINAL].pdf (accessed May 4, 2012).

Berkley Center for Religion, Peace, & World Affairs at Georgetown University. "Northern Ireland: Religion in War and Peace," *Case Study Series* (February 2011). http://repository.berkleycenter.georgetown.edu/110811NorthernIreland[FINAL].pdf (accessed July 2, 2012).

Douglas, Mary. "The Effects of Modernization on Religious Change," *Daedalus* 117, no. 3 (Summer 1988).

Freud, Sigmund. *Civilization, Society and Religion*, Pelican Freud Library, vol. 12 (Harmondsworth: Penguin, 1985).

Gandhi, Rajmohan. "Hinduism and Peacebuilding," in Howard G. Coward and Gordon S. Smith, eds., *Religion and Peacebuilding* (New York: SUNY Press, 2004).

Hibbard, Scott W. *Religious Politics and Secular States: Egypt, India, and the United States* (Baltimore: Johns Hopkins University Press, 2010).

Ignatieff, Michael, "The Narcissism of Minor Differences," in Michael Ignatieff, ed., *The Warrior's Honor: Ethnic War and the Modern Conscience* (New York: Henry Holt and Company, 1997).

Jeremic, Vik. "Kosovo Is Our Jerusalem," *Spiegel Online* (May 31, 2010). http://www.spiegel.de/international/europe/serbian-foreign-minister -vuk-jeremic-kosovo-is-our-jerusalem-a-697725.html (accessed July 17, 2012).

Judah, Tim. *The Serbs: History, Myth, and the Destruction of Yugoslavia* (New Haven: Yale University Press, 2000).

Juergensmeyer, Mark. *The New Cold War? Religious Nationalism Confronts the Secular State* (Los Angeles: University of California Press, 1994).

Little, David. "Religion and Ethnicity in the Sri Lankan Civil War," in Robert I. Rotberg, ed., *Creating Peace in Sri Lanka: Civil War and Reconciliation* (Washington, D.C.: Brookings Institution Press, 1999).

Marx, Anthony. *Faith in Nation: Exclusionary Origins of Nationalism* (Oxford: Oxford University Press, 2003).

Mitchell, Claire. *Religion, Identity and Politics in Northern Ireland: Boundaries of Belonging and Belief* (Burlington, VT: Ashgate Publishing Company, 2006).

Omer, Atalia. *When Peace Is Not Enough: How the Israeli Peace Camp Thinks about Religion, Nationalism, and Justice* (Chicago: University of Chicago Press, 2013).

Perica, Vjekoslav. *Balkan Idols: Religion and Nation in Yugoslav States* (Oxford: Oxford University Press, 2002).

Sells, Michael. *The Bridge Betrayed: Religion and Genocide in Bosnia* (Berkeley and Los Angeles: University of California Press, 1998a).

Sells, Michael. "Serbian Religious Nationalism, Christoslavism, and the Genocide in Bosnia, 1992–1995," in Paul Mojzes, ed., *Religion and the War in Bosnia* (Atlanta: Scholar's Press, 1998b).

Sells, Michael. "Pilgrimage and 'Ethnic Cleansing' in Herzegovina" in David Little and Donald Swearer, eds., *Religion and Nationalism in Iraq: A Comparative Perspective* (Cambridge, MA: Harvard University Press, 2006).

Smith, Anthony. *Chosen Peoples* (Oxford: Oxford University Press, 2003).

Smith, Anthony. *Nationalism: Theory, Ideology, History* (Cambridge: Polity Press, 2001).

Videmsek, Bostian and Dan Bilefsky. "Protestors Attack U.S. Embassy in Belgrade," *New York Times*, February 22, 2008.

Weber, Max. *Economy and Society,* edited by G. Roth and C. Wittich (New York: Bedminster Press, 1968).

2

Nationalism: A Religion?

Introduction

In the previous chapter, we explored many of the ways that religious nationalism can be thought of as religious. This chapter continues that conversation by asking whether nationalism itself can be analyzed as a form of religion. Specifically, we explore a concept known as civil religion.

The scholarship on nationalism tends to focus on "bad" nationalism, that is, nationalism that is explicitly ethnocentric or religiously centered. This body of scholarship usually views religious and ethnic forms of identity, when mixed with nationalism, as likely to promote violence. "Good" nationalism in this view must therefore be secular, pluralistic, and liberal.

On the other hand, scholars of civil religion focus on the lasting influences of religious symbols, stories, rituals, and beliefs that articulate national identity within civil society. The scholarship on civil religion examines the broad array of characteristics and functions of such religious features even in societies that have formally separated religious institutions and the state, and identify themselves as liberal and pluralist. Our discussion will connect theories from the sociology of religion with theories of nationalism. We will review and expand upon the debates surrounding the terms "secularism," "modernism," and "religion." For the ways these terms are conceptualized, defined, and used affects how forms of religious nationalism are understood.

Constructing and Conceiving Nationalism

The nation is a construct whose reality and continuity depends on a shared *belief* in its objective reality. A nation becomes null and void if it loses its legitimacy and sense of authenticity in the eyes of its people. Although nations emerge from contingent, histori-cal, and social processes, they ultimately become social facts. In other words, they are not simply imaginary, and they cannot sim-ply pass out of existence at any moment. Thus we should examine how societies construct basic assumptions about the objectivity of the national community, what the effects of those assumptions are, and how they are perpetuated in the daily life of a group of people.

Forms of nationalism that identify themselves as "nonreli-gious" are not devoid of cultural, religious, and ethnic elements. In fact, as Max Weber pointed out, even "secular" forms of nationalism selectively use cultural, religious, and ethnic re-sources to build, sustain, and protect collective identity. Known as selective retrieval, this dynamic demonstrates the ineffective-ness of dividing forms of nationalism into mutually exclusive cat-egories of secular versus religious. Recognizing this allows us to ask questions that can illuminate the complex character of nation-alism. How do groups construct nationalism? What do they intend to achieve? What problems and challenges arise through the process?

These queries may lead to specific questions about seemingly insignificant religious aspects of rituals, beliefs, and symbolic practices that make up nationalism in the United States. For example, why is the motto "In God We Trust" printed on every piece of U.S. currency? Why does the Pledge of Allegiance include a vow of loyalty to the flag, the Republic, and "one nation under God"? Do these features of U.S. culture and civic life express religious elements of an otherwise secular nationalism? Do Americans continue to share early views of American destiny as providential (e.g., that Americans are a people specially chosen, whose history is uniquely directed by God, or a people understood to fulfill a unique role in history)? More importantly, to what extent do such ideas affect how Americans understand themselves and their society in the present and, consequently, in-fluence current policies and laws?

Both secular and religious nationalisms rely on mythic narratives and sacred texts to justify their "undeniable" and "undisputable" claims to their homeland; national spaces are considered sacred (unique or set apart in their meaning and value). For example, Hindu nationalists imagine the topography of India as a sacred space or a holy land; Sinhala Buddhists consider the island of Sri Lanka as holy; and both Jewish religious settlers and secular Zionists venerate the lands of Palestine as sacred. When spatial borders and boundaries are compromised, members of the violated territory are called on to defend not only the sovereign control of the state over its territory, but also what is perceived to be a unique significance of the spaces encompassed within its borders.

An extreme form of space violation, ethnic cleansing is a policy by which one group (ethnoreligious, or national) uses violence and intimidation (e.g., killing, torture, rape, expulsion) to forcibly remove another ethnic or religious group from a geographic area. When the violation of a group's alleged homeland occurs in the form of acts of ethnic cleansing, such violations are not perceived by the threatened group as merely a disregard for the value of human life. Rather, the ethnic cleansing of a homeland is seen as the violation of something of unique value. Similarly, acts of ethnic cleansing are frequently motivated not only by defense of territorial integrity and sovereignty, but by the belief that the sanctity of a nation's territory and/or culture is threatened (or polluted) by the presence of some group of contrasting ethnic and religious identities (we examined an example of this in Chapter 1 in the case of Serbian nationalist treatment of Kosovo as the "Serbian Jerusalem"). Conflicts erupt and persist because homeland boundaries are often subject to interpretation and are disputed; sometimes they overlap. And as we will see, the sacredness of a space is not fixed and unchanging, but rather dynamic and elastic.

In the case of the state of Israel, secular Zionists accept a different territorial definition than the one embraced by religious Zionists. Yet even secular Zionists would be willing to make profound sacrifices to maintain the country's 1948 borders (the territory demarcated at the state of Israel's founding) and the demographic conditions necessary for maintaining a Jewish democracy. Israeli nationalism of both self-identified secular and religious varieties ascribes some sense of sacredness to the social experiment itself, investing the social construct of a Jewish state with a reverence, prestige, and even an exceptional role in history. Frequently, nonreligious (even antireligious) Zionists consider "the land" on which the state of Israel is founded (the land known biblically and historically as Palestine) to have a unique and non-negotiable status.

In the United States, many people take for granted the ways that North America has also been transformed from mere geography to sacred topography. Virtually every schoolchild is taught to sing of their country as the "sweet land of liberty" ("land where my fathers died / land of the Pilgrims' pride"). Among the first to settle the New World in the 17th century, the Puritans sought to establish a "city upon a hill" as an exemplary community and way of life. Over time, this vision of the exceptional role that America was to play within world history contributed to the conception of Manifest Destiny. Emerging as a formal doctrine in the mid-19th century, Manifest Destiny was the belief that it was the destiny of the United States to expand across the North American continent. This idea justified polices to displace and contain, and in many cases to eliminate, Native Americans in order to expand the United States "from sea to shining sea."

Like the perceived sacredness of a territory, national identities are not fixed or static. For example, the meanings of American identity have been repeatedly contested. Debates often involve the presence of religion in the public sphere in both its prophetic and priestly capacities. The prophetic capacity refers to the ability to criticize the status quo and to question and challenge established meanings. The priestly capacity relates to religion's institutional functions, which may be deeply entangled with the mechanisms by which the status quo is maintained.

To shed light upon the subtle interconnections between religion, nation, and state, we may ask such questions as why Christmas is observed as an official holiday in the United States and other North and South American as well as European contexts, but Rosh Hashanah and Eid al-Fitr are not. Is it significant that President Barack Obama's 2008 inaugural address departed from historical conceptions of American civil religion (which remained suspicious of the absence of religious faith) by explicitly welcoming nonbelievers? While they may appear trivial at first, such questions further reveal the limitations in thinking about secular and religious nationalisms as easily compartmentalized or mutually exclusive.

Nations as Imagined Communities

Like nationalism, the nation itself is a shared idea that people have constructed. In *Imagined Communities: Reflections on the Origin and Spread of Nationalism* (1991), Benedict Anderson defines the modern nation as "an imagined political community." "It is *imagined*," he writes, "because the members of even the smallest nation will never know most of their fellow-members . . . yet in the minds of each lives the image of their communion" (Anderson, 1991, 6).

Anderson wishes to draw important distinctions between his understanding of nationalism and Ernest Gellner's portrayal of nationalism as an invention that is functionally necessary for securing consent and social cohesion in postagrarian contexts. Anderson agrees with Gellner's point that "nationalism is not the awakening of nations to self-consciousness." This kind of a "sleeping beauty" approach is often held by nationalists themselves and assumes that the nation is a given. However, Anderson rejects Gellner's further claim that nationalism is an invention *ex nihilo* (Latin for "out of nothing"). Anderson writes that "Gellner is so anxious to show that nationalism masquerades under false pretenses that he assimilates 'invention' to 'fabrication' and 'falsity,' rather than to 'imagining' and 'creation'" (Anderson, 1991, 6). Anderson's analysis reinforces the role that processes of selective retrieval and appropriation play in constructing national identity, namely, that nationalism is imagined and constructed out of its cultural and religious roots and resources.

Anderson views nationalism as a uniquely modern development. He claims that nationalism first emerged in late 18th century after the collapse of religious empires and the disintegration of religious authority. Anderson specifically identifies three conditions that made it possible for people to imagine themselves as nations. First, people began to doubt the given and comprehensive character of the religious tradition in which they found themselves. This was spurred by the increasingly widespread belief that the language of their religious texts, worship, and practices was not, itself, uniquely sacred, and therefore did not provide privileged and exclusive access to unique and ultimate religious truth. Second was the gradual diminishment of widespread belief in the "divine right of Kings," the divinely sanctioned political order, and hierarchical conception of the created order that held that divine right

in place. Third, people slowly lost a sense of the origins and significance of the creation of the world (cosmology) as indistinguishable
and inseparable from their own day (history). These three ideas
had oriented the ways that people had understood their world
since antiquity. Anderson (1991) writes:

> Combined, these ideas rooted human lives firmly in the
> very nature of things, giving certain meaning to the
> everyday fatalities of existence (above all death, loss,
> and servitude) and offering, in various ways, redemption
> from them. The slow uneven decline of these interlinked
> certainties, first in Western Europe, later elsewhere . . .
> drove a harsh wedge between cosmology and history.
> No surprise then that the search was on, so to speak, for
> a new way of linking fraternity, power and time meaning-
> fully together. Nothing perhaps more precipitated this
> search, nor made it more fruitful, than print-capitalism,
> which made it possible for rapidly growing numbers of
> people to think about themselves, and to relate them-
> selves to others, in profoundly new ways. (36)

Anderson's account may be classified as modernist because he
views modernity as a radical break with premodernity on all of
the levels identified above: the loss of privileged access to onto-
logical truths through a particular script language (Latin); the dissolution of monarchical dynasties and of divine and/or
cosmological legitimacy of monarchs; and the changing conceptions of time, particularly the divergent interpretations of cosmology and history.

Though it echoes Gellner's equally modernist approach,
Anderson's notion of nationalism as an imagined community
concedes that the modern nation was neither imagined simply
out of nothing, nor devised by elites merely to control a con-
senting populace. Rather, this social construct emerged out of
prior cultural and religious building blocks. Thus nationalism
may have constituted a break from the premodern due to the collapse of dynasties and drastic changes in religious authorities;
nevertheless, nationalism emerged out of, and was imagined in
reference to, these earlier contexts and carried forward structural
and thematic dimensions of its religious past.

Like many religious traditions, the secular modern nation
offers promises of salvation and regeneration. The modern nation

promises the "transformation of fatality into continuity, contingency into meaning" (Anderson, 1991, 11). In the context of nationalism, giving one's life on behalf of the nation is portrayed as a sacrifice that supported the continuity of the community across history, vindicated the greater significance of group identity, and defended and perpetuated the group's values and way of life. When nationhood becomes interwoven with the institution of the state, such sacrifices become an essential responsibility of every citizen. As subjects of the state, citizens are urged and often required either to serve or to send their children to defend "our way of life," "our people," or "our values," lest that way of life be endangered and its most sacred values be compromised or lost.

Anderson's thesis has been criticized because his work does not sufficiently question *whose* imagination brings the nation into being. Anderson does not address those whose narratives and identities have been pushed to the margins in the process of imagining the nation as a unified unit. The nation is an imagined community or a social construct with coercive force that enabled its own perpetuation; nevertheless, individuals and groups have imagined and attempted to construct alternative visions of the community. Indeed, at various moments, these alternative visions have gained momentum and popular traction in contexts ranging from the United States to Egypt, India, Israel, Northern Ireland, and the former Yugoslavia.

Civil Religion as a Form of Nationalism

Civil religion is neither a modern phenomenon nor a particularly novel concept. In fact, the French philosopher Jean-Jacques Rousseau theorized an early version of the concept in his text *The Social Contract* (1762). More recently, in his groundbreaking 1967 essay "Civil Religion in America," sociologist Robert N. Bellah argued that Americans hold certain common beliefs, values, rituals, and sacred days in spite of the disestablishment of religion (separation of church and state) in the United States as well as their individual religious convictions and practices. Bellah dubbed this phenomenon "civil religion" (1–21). While civil religion is composed of commonplace mechanisms that aim to ensure the nation's continuous legitimacy, it is something much more like a variant of religion in the ways that it functions rather than something opposite or outside of religion.

As Max Weber explained the concept, at its heart, nationalism is largely about a sense of "chosenness" (i.e., its members are a chosen people), cultural prestige, and a providential mission (the group's divine purpose or unique role in world history)—motifs clearly evident in the conception of civil religion in the United States (i.e., the "city upon a hill," American exceptionalism, and Manifest Destiny). According to Weber, nationalism shares an elective affinity with (may gravitate toward, interact with, and mutually reinforce) notions of ethnicity, culture, and religion. There are important conceptual connections between the basic elements of nationalism, ethnicity, and religion (Weber, 1968, 387–398).

The root of the word "nationalism" (the Latin *natio*) means "that which has been born," suggesting that one belongs to one's people (nation) naturally or by birth. In this view, membership comes innately through biological relation. It is an understanding of nationality that shares many similarities with the concept of ethnicity. The term "ethnic" means "origin by birth or descent." And, in fact, Weber influentially identified "ethnicity" as a "subjective belief in common descent" (Weber, 1968, 389). According to this definition, whether common descent is based on objective realities is largely beside the point. What matters is the shared *belief* in, or basic perception of, the "naturalness" of shared membership in the group as well as the origin that is common to the community. Religion is far from simply a matter of what an individual believes or feels. Etymologically, the word "religion" conveys a general conception of communal belonging. The word "religion" derives from the Latin root *religare*, which means "binding or linking together again." At a general level, this root gestures toward a social entity bound together by shared obligations, encompassing commitments, the constraints of lived practices, institutions, and traditions that codify, enforce, and transmit those practices and obligations over time. Like the words "ethnicity" and "nationalism," "religion" is a term with a rich history and wide variety of context-specific applications. However, to assert that "religions" are socially constructed and manifest themselves in a broad diversity of ways in no way denies that they are socially real. Nor does it contradict the accuracy of applying the term "religion" across a breadth of cases and contexts (Schilbrack 2010).

In sum, as is the case with religion, both nationality and ethnicity are historically produced or constructed. And comparable to the way that shared religious identity might cohere, in part, through a shared myth of origin, both nationalism and ethnicity derive, in part, from a group's unifying belief in its "common descent" (Weber, 1968, 395). The concepts of nation and ethnicity differ in that nations and national identities tend to be intricately linked to political agendas and desires for self-rule; moreover, nations are more self-conscious and committed to a defense of their "cultural prestige" (Little, 2012). Self-identified ethnic groups might not think of themselves as a nation, nor desire political self-determination as a group. The desire for political self-determination and cultural prestige are apparent in our descriptions in Chapter 1 of American exceptionalism, Zionism, Christoslavism, and Sinhala Buddhism.

Markers of Civil Religion: Rituals, Myths, and Symbols

According to Jason Springs, "[C]ivil religion broadly refers to the practices, symbols, myths, rituals, and consecrated spaces and times that serve to unify and integrate the disparate parts and individuals of a society into a cohesive whole" (2012a, 29). This definition reflects a functionalist understanding of religion because it identifies the components of a civil religion, in part, by how they function in society. These components help to bind a society together. They do this by representing the values that society claims to be based on and to which it holds itself collectively responsible. These ideals bind members of a society together through a set of commonly shared stories, rituals, festivals, commemorative occasions, and consecrated spaces. These practices and resources function to symbolically express and justify the legitimacy of the society's authority, amplify its significance, and defend the integrity and sovereignty of its political institutions. Through them, citizens are socialized into a more or less coherent and unified way of life. Ideally, the civil religion of a society will generate enough solidarity to facilitate the smooth operation and continuation of that society.

The elements of civil religion typically take the form of symbols, mottos, narratives, holidays, and festivals that recall the origin or founding of the society, commemorate the sacrifices and achievements by which it has sustained itself, and reenact the journey that led to its current state. Such rituals can be as mundane as standing to salute the flag and sing the national anthem at the opening ceremonies of athletic competitions. Other examples include pledges of allegiance; ceremonies for presidential inaugurations; monuments to memorialize dead soldiers and epic battles; and holidays to commemorate great leaders, exemplary citizens, or personal sacrifices for the society or nation.

Of particular importance is that civil religion manifests itself through symbols, ritual practices, and stories that are often taken for granted. Springs (2012a) has characterized this symbolic power as follows:

> A common paradox of the practices of civil religion in everyday life is that the deeper and more pervasive the hold by which such rituals, symbols, and stories bind together and unify a society, the more inconspicuous they tend to be. They may appear ordinary, unimportant, or even trite, making it easy for practitioners to be unaware of the influence that they exert. . . . [And yet] because anthems, pledges, and flags function as identity markers for a group or society, they quickly can become charged with conspicuous political significance as objects of patriotic zeal or even nationalist fanaticism. (30–31)

To illustrate an "ordinary" ritual of civil religion, Springs describes the observance of the national anthem at a baseball game; this practice is often viewed as incidental to the event as singing "Take Me out to the Ball Game" during the seventh inning stretch or visiting the concession stand. And yet part of the power of civil religion lies in the way its practices become so commonplace that they are seen as unimportant. In this case, however, they signify the shared allegiances against the background of which more regional attachments play out on the field of athletic competition.

Under certain circumstances (e.g., times of war, shared fear of an external threat, a national tragedy) rituals and symbols that are otherwise ordinary quickly become pronounced in their larger meaning. They can mobilize an emotionally and psychologically powerful sense of "who we are" as a group. So, for instance, on the afternoon and evening of September 11, 2001, following the terrorist attacks on the World Trade Center and Pentagon, the retail store Wal-Mart reported national sales of 116,000 U.S. flags, and an astounding 250,000 flags sold on the following day. These quantities contrasted starkly with the 6,400 and 10,000 U.S. flag sales recorded by Wal-Mart for the same dates the previous year (Huntington, 2004, 3–4). Along similar lines, for the remainder of the baseball season following the terrorist attacks of September 11, 2001, the Major League Baseball commissioner replaced the standard practice of singing "Take Me out to the Ball Game" during the seventh inning with the singing of Irving Berlin's anthem "God Bless America" in every major league baseball stadium in the United States.

The national anthem may also provide an object of dissent, as it did in the days leading up to the 2003 U.S.-led invasion of Iraq. In protest, a stadium of Montreal Canadien hockey fans controversially booed throughout the playing of the U.S. national anthem (Caldwell, 2003). Such was famously the case at the 1968 Mexico City Olympic Games, when African American U.S. sprinters Tommie Smith and John Carlos, Gold and Bronze medalists in the 200-meter race, bowed their heads and raised their black glove-clad fists in the form of the Black Power salute while standing on the medal podium as the U.S. national anthem played. In doing this, Smith and Carlos expressed their refusal to endorse the ideals that the flag and the anthem purported to symbolize, given that the social realities in U.S. society were characterized by white supremacy, economic injustice, and violent unrest. The four months leading up to the 1968 Olympics had witnessed some of the most tumultuous political and social events in U.S. history—the assassinations of Martin Luther King Jr. and Senator Robert Kennedy, and widespread rioting in protest of racial discrimination and the Vietnam War at the 1968 Democratic National Convention in Chicago (Gerstle, 303–305; Springs, 2012a).

Numerous examples exist of how seemingly commonplace or "merely patriotic" rituals and symbols that signify and celebrate a group's identity have been used for purposes of criticism and protest. Sometimes, these transform into frenetic moments. They lead to violent expressions of nationalism, as we saw in Chapter 1 in the commemorations for Prince Lazar in Serbia and the annual marches of the Orange Order in Northern Ireland.

At the same time, the sacredness ascribed to such rituals and symbols can manifest in their legally enforced consecration, and thus laws criminalizing demonstrations of contempt or disrespect, or using them as objects of dissent. For instance, "flag desecration" (desecration meaning, literally, "to violate the sacredness of") in the United States was legally banned for most of the 20th century. The U.S. Supreme Court upheld the nationwide statutes that prohibited desecration of the U.S. flag in 1907 (*Halter v. Nebraska*), and Congress passed a Federal Flag Desecration law in 1968 in response to many instances of flag burning in protest of the U.S. war in Vietnam. In 1989, the Supreme Court ruled (*Texas v. Johnson*) that flag desecration in the form of flag burning was, in fact, a form of political speech that is protected by the First Amendment of the U.S. Constitution. The ruling overturned laws prohibiting flag desecration in 48 states. Since that ruling, however, the U.S. Congress has attempted to pass a constitutional amendment that would permit banning flag desecration, thus overruling the Supreme Court's 1989 decision, on seven different occasions. In its most recent attempt in 2006, passage of the amendment fell short by one vote in the Senate after passing the House of Representatives (Goldstein, 1996; Hulse and Holusha, 2006).

Even without being legally banned, aversion to flag burning exerts itself like a taboo in many places in the United States (i.e., an illicit action that threatens to defile or endanger the group identity if it is committed) (Freud 1950, 33). Thus Carolyn Marvin and David Ingle write:

> In civilian and military protocols the flag must not touch the ground, it must hang in proper alignment, it must not be lower than other flags, it must appear in the place of honor on the right, it must not be used as a receptacle or covering. Crisis triggers obligatory ritual exceptions. The flag is the only proper casket covering in funerals with military honors. . . . [N]o public outrage accompanies burning an effigy of George Washington or Abraham Lincoln. Generations of tourists to the Statue of Liberty have not been religiously discouraged from adorning it with discarded chewing gum. Even igniting copies of the Constitution probably would not produce the level of outrage that accompanies flagburning, though flags exist in hundreds of thousands of "copies" just as the Constitution does. The desecratory taboo applies to the flag alone, for only the flag signifies the sacrificed body. (Marvin and Ingle, 1999, 30–31)

Self-Conception of Civil Religion: Origins, Identity, and Values

Civil religion is not only embodied in a series of symbols and social practices, but also reflects certain understandings about "who we are" as a nation or a society. As with many organized religious traditions, civil religion is often preoccupied with a myth of origins. In the case of the United States, this origin myth involves a story of redemption: the first Puritan settlers fled religious persecution in Europe to a land that they believed was promised to them by God as a "new Israel." This narrative echoed the biblical story in Exodus in which God led the Israelites across the Red Sea and out of slavery in Egypt to the Promised Land. These biblical narratives invested the Puritans' journey with a sense of fulfilling God's divine will. Despite its origins in distinctly Christian—and particularly Puritan—interpretations of biblical narratives, civil religion in the early United States gradually expanded to embrace principles of religious freedom and the separation of church and state. This expansion enabled it gradually to enlarge its definition of the nation beyond Christianity and Anglo-Saxon identity. And yet this gradual inclusionary inclination cannot be permitted to hide the wretched forms of exclusion and subjugation of slaves and the near extermination of indigenous populations that, in many ways, made possible the gradual expansion of the American nation and American national identity.

Even though American civil religion can be inclusive, it is not immune from tendencies to link national membership to particular ethnic and religious identities; as a result, xenophobic outbreaks are not uncommon. Under the right circumstances, forms of nationalism can be exclusivist, as was evident in the over 700 confirmed violent incidents directed at Muslim Americans and Arab Americans (or those perceived to be Arab Americans) in the nine weeks following the terrorist attacks of September 11, 2001 (Ibish, 2003, 47–48). Likewise, in 2010, many Americans vehemently opposed plans to build a Muslim cultural center a few city blocks from the site of the World Trade Center in New York City (Pew, 2011). In both cases, Muslims and Arabs who were U.S. citizens—in many cases, who were born in the United States and lived all their lives there—were nonetheless treated with suspicion. In some cases, they were viewed as enemies and foreigners because of their ethnicity and religion, and subjected to acts of exclusion and violence. Such incidents demonstrate patterns of xenophobia and chauvinism that we identified in Chapter 1 in other seemingly more explicit instances of religious nationalism. During times of national crisis and conflict, political and religious leaders often revive exclusivist Christian (or Judeo-Christian) interpretations of American identity.

On one hand, civil religion assumes that a conception of American identity exists. At the same time, civil religion perpetuates that identity by selectively retrieving religious and cultural images and practices. Typically, the religious and cultural elements form a set of civic practices. For instance, sacred spaces in civil religion are venerated memorials to the dead who sacrificed their lives for the good of the society or in defense of American values. Sacrifice for the defense of American values is a concept that assumes the sacredness of America's founding principles, as demonstrated through the country's myth of origins.

The Puritan "city upon a hill" myth of origins later contributed to another facet of American civil religion: American exceptionalism. American exceptionalism is the idea that the United States of America has a unique role in the political and social history of the world. This understanding is famously represented in the Statue of Liberty. Depicted as "Liberty Enlightening the World," the statue symbolizes new forms of liberty and justice that the social, political, and legal life of the United States is understood to embody. Engraved in bronze and attached to the statue's pedestal, the poem "The New Colossus" expresses American exceptionalism by describing the United States' extraordinary role in world history.

"The New Colossus" was composed by Emma Lazarus, a daughter of Sephardic Jewish immigrants from Portugal. In the poem, Lazarus contrasts the Statue of Liberty with the ancient statue of Colossus of Rhodes, erected in the third century BCE at the harbor entryway to the island of Rhodes in Greece. The 100-foot Colossus represented the Greek Titan, Helios, and was considered one of the seven wonders of the ancient world. Lazarus's sonnet alludes to the ancient ideals that the Colossus represented ("brazen fame" and "storied pomp" of conquest in battle and god-like grandeur), only to reject those as outdated and surpassed by the conceptions of justice, freedom, and equality realized in the new world of the United States.

In contrast to Colossus, Lazarus portrays the statue at the entryway to New York City's harbor as silently announcing a new set of values and way of life. Liberty enlightens the world by welcoming the "tired, poor, huddled masses yearning to breathe free," thereby suggesting that the promise of freedom and justice in the United States belongs equally to all people (Lazarus, 1888, 202–203). In other words, in principle, this promise does not depend upon any person's rank or station in society, their religion, or ethnicity, but applies in virtue of their common humanity. Like the Puritans' journey from repression to freedom, despised, persecuted, and disenfranchised people who fled from their homelands would gain freedom on the shores of the United States.

Lazarus's sonnet suggests that this new world embodies a revolutionary departure from ancient, feudal, and aristocratic conceptions of freedom and justice. These values lay the foundation for an increasingly diverse society of immigrants. The United States was called—in many minds, by God—to play this exceptional role in history as a beacon of freedom and a haven for the oppressed from around the world. This narrative has been central to American exceptionalism since its earliest emergence. Of course, as we will see in the following chapter, even though American exceptionalism has proclaimed important values, it has also inspired and justified U.S. policies that led to violent conflict, injustice, and imperialist practices around the globe.

The Sacred Canopy: Unifying Society around Civil Religion

The idea of the sacred canopy is an important concept that helps us to understand both civil religion and religious nationalism. In *The Sacred Canopy: Elements of a Sociological Theory of Religion* (1967), Peter Berger suggests that religion results from purely human and historical processes. Likewise, society is not a given, but rather a human creation. According to Berger, the socially defined reality is held together under a sacred canopy, or a constructed worldview based on common assumptions that gives meaning to life and is perpetuated through various social institutions and practices.

Berger advances a human-centered theory of religion. "Religion," he writes, "implies the farthest reach of man's self-externalization, of his infusion of reality with his own meanings. . . . Put differently, religion is the audacious attempt to conceive of the entire universe as being humanly significant" (1967, 27–28). Humans use religion to make sense of their significance in the universe. Religion presents itself as factual in the same way that a society presents itself as given. Yet society and religion are produced by the same kind of processes; consequently, society and religion are linked and influenced by each other. Building on this reciprocal relationship between society and religion, Berger argues that the

social order needs to be legitimized through the process of socialization, and "religion has been the historically most widespread
and effective instrumentality of legitimation" (1967, 32).

Combined with the concept of the sacred canopy, civil religion
may be seen as a mechanism that ensures the basic acceptance and
perpetuation of certain conceptions of society. Civil religion, therefore, is not all that different from nationalism, particularly when
nationalism is viewed as a means to legitimize the political and
social orders, and to consolidate power and influence of the people
to whom those orders belong. Similarly, nationalism often presents
the nation and national identity as givens, concealing their nature
as historical constructions. The belief in the nation as an objective
and fixed reality in turn functions as a means of communicating
the nation's authenticity and inevitability.

Civil Religion: Debunking the Myth of Religion as Antimodern

Nationalism is an expression of the belief in the nation's objective
reality. Although the sense of a group's legitimacy and authenticity
emerges from social processes and shared imaginings, it does not
exist merely as a matter of *subjective* belief. These imaginings
become social facts. Nor is it the case that the perceived reality of
the nation emerges only in the presence of external threat, shared
tragedy, or national crisis. To take an example considered earlier in
this chapter, the U.S. flag is presented and saluted, and the national
anthem is sung, before virtually every formal athletic event in the
United States, not just during times of war, or in response to perceived threat, or in the wake of national tragedy. In other words,
the elements of ritual and symbol that embody and perpetuate a
group's belief in itself as a nation typically take the form of seemingly small details and everyday operations of a group's life
together.

In his essay "What Is a Nation?" written in 1882, Ernst
Renan, a 19th-century French scholar, argued influentially that a
nation is based upon a two-dimensional spiritual principle. The
first dimension is a common history and shared sense of the past,
particularly of the labors, sacrifices, and devotion that made possible the present solidarity of the people. The second dimension is
the persuasiveness of the idea of the nation in the present. In other
words, the conception of the shared past must have sufficient

solidity and weight in the present to capture and consolidate the collective imagination of a community. It is this second spiritual dimension of the nation that generates an encompassing willingness to participate in the nation in the present, and to make that willingness and participation seem natural, even necessary. This dimension of the nation takes the form of what Renan called a daily referendum (usually translated as a "daily plebiscite," i.e., daily practices of consent by the people) (Renan, 1995, 154). By this, Renan meant that the nation lives in the present to the extent that the idea of that nation encompasses and enfolds its members in sufficiently compelling, yet sufficiently simple, daily truths of its reality. This conceptualization of nationalism is intricately related to civil religion.

As we saw in the preceding examples, civil religion occurs in the commonplace social practices and mechanisms that represent and perpetuate the historical significance, legitimacy, and coherence of a civil society; its political systems; and its sense of "who we are." We have argued that it is in and through its familiar, seemingly trivial operations that civil religion most exerts its influence. Rituals that typically seem inconspicuous, commonplace symbols, and narratives often taken for granted can promote solidarity and a sense of continuity. They can generate forms of reverence and commitment, recollect past sacrifices, and call for future sacrifices; mark venerated spaces and times; commemorate the past through monuments, museums, holidays, and observances; and mythologize a group's story of origin, destiny, and world-historical significance. Understood in this way, civil religion is not a phenomenon categorically distinct from nationalism. It is the very stuff of nationalism. If we think of it as distinguishable at all, it is as a version or type of nationalism. It is in, and through, the commonplace workings of civil religion that the recurring "daily referendum" upon the persuasiveness and power of national solidarity is lived out.

We have described civil religion as a variety of nationalism in order to challenge the assumption that religious nationalism is uniquely antimodern. We argue that religious nationalism should not be regarded as intrinsically more fanatical or pathological than any other form of nationalism. Such judgments should be made on a case-by-case basis. As we have seen, even forms of nationalism that self-identify as secular or antireligious (those that aggressively strive to keep organized religion out of public, political life) selectively depend on religious and cultural rituals and symbols to maintain social unity and commitment to the group.

At the same time, nationalism is not a modern replacement for religion. Rather, it draws upon and intermingles with elements of established or organized religious traditions. It is unhelpful to regard religion as a generic category that is antimodern and uniquely prone to violence. Such a view ignores the reality that religion is used to construct and maintain modern forms of political and social identifications, often in self-reflective and self-critical ways. Moreover, once we recognize that civil religion and the nation's historical narratives are always highly selective, we may critically examine religious nationalisms as a complex conceptual, social, and political phenomena in which religion is selectively appropriated and applied for the sake of constructing and maintaining the nation.

A False Dichotomy: Ethnic Nationalism versus Civic Nationalism

The study of nationalism often distinguishes between ethnic and civic forms of nationalism. Ethnic nationalism is typically understood as membership in the nation or group based upon the ethnicity with which one is born. By contrast, civic nationalism bases membership in the nation upon one's status as a citizen, a legally recognized participant in the civic life of the society, or agreement with a political creed, regardless of one's race, color, religious creed, ethnicity, or language (Ignatieff, 1993, 5–9).

Ethnic nationalism is often associated with violence, intolerance toward other ethnicities, and human rights violations. Civic nationalism is associated with individualism, tolerance, and human rights. In this view, the principles of civic nationalism further suggest a commitment to secularism. The ethnic versus civic model resembles the misconception of the religion versus secularism model that we examined in Chapter 1. Consequently, it wrongly assumes that religion is necessarily an obstacle to the values celebrated by the civic nation.

Political theorist Bernard Yack expresses skepticism about this civic versus ethnic division and other types of dichotomy parallels (i.e., rational/emotional, voluntary/inherited, Western/Eastern, good/bad, liberal/illiberal). Yack writes as follows:

> Designed to protect us from the dangers of ethnocentric politics, the civic/ethnic distinction itself reflects a considerable dose of ethnocentrism, as if the political identities *French* and *American* were not also culturally inherited artifacts, no matter how much they develop and change as they pass from generation to generation. The characterization of political community in the so-called civic nations as a rational and freely chosen allegiance to a set of political principles seems untenable to me, a mixture of self-congratulation and wishful thinking. (1999, 105)

Yack exposes the assumptions and problems of the civic/ethnic dichotomy through an approach called discourse analysis. In particular, Yack evokes the reliance of this dichotomy on the discourse of orientalism.

Discourse Analysis of Orientalism

To define discourse, we draw on philosopher Michel Foucault's understanding of knowledge as intricately connected to power. According to Foucault, one's view of the world is guided and defined by a set of historical and conceptual lenses which are produced by complex systems of disciplinary structures and social practices. A different set of lenses would change how one views the world and what one knows about it. Thus a discourse frames one's field of vision, and positions one within that field. A discursive analysis attempts to unmask the emergence of the field that is viewed, and expose the lenses through which this viewing is made possible. Discursive analyses are used to debunk sacred canopies. The late Palestinian scholar and critic Edward Said provides an example of a discourse analysis in his description of orientalism (Said 1978).

Orientalism refers to assumptions and biases that have shaped Western attitudes toward, and conceptions of, the Orient ("the East"). The West has regarded the Orient as backward, violent, superstitious, sexualized, intolerant, and disrespectful of individual autonomy and liberties. Viewed as the opposite of the Orient, Western civilization is seen as civilized, liberal, tolerant, and individualistic.

This set of ideas presupposes the superiority of the West and has authorized many imperialist and colonial efforts. A concept related to orientalism, eurocentrism assumes the basic superiority of European political and cultural norms.

Eurocentrism and orientalism are reflected in the civic/ethnic dichotomy that Yack calls into question in the preceding quotation. He points out that civic nationalism often behaves like or assumes characteristics typically ascribed to ethnic nationalism, a dynamic that is evident in the United States and France. As we noted in our discussion of American civil religion, the identity markers of American nationalism are often subtly based on conceptions of group membership that are distinctly European and Judeo-Christian. Consequently, Arabs, Latinos, Asians, and other minority groups may be viewed as foreigners or aliens as opposed to Americans.

The ethnic aspects of civic nationalism are also evident in France's ban on Muslim headscarves. In 2004, France passed a law that prohibited Muslim women from wearing the *hijab*, or headscarf, in public schools and state-affiliated settings. In fact, it banned all religious symbols that could be identified as "conspicuous" or "assertive." The assertiveness of a symbol was determined primarily by its size and visibility. Thus the ban included, for example, large crosses, Jewish yarmulkes, and Sikh turbans. Small crosses, Stars of David, and Hands of Fatima worn as necklaces or bracelets were not banned. The religious symbol most broadly affected by the ban, and most consistently the focus of intense controversy surrounding the law, was the Muslim headscarf (Bowen, 2004).

Some have argued that the ban was motivated by deep-seated orientalism and even racism in an attempt to defend a particular interpretation of French identity (Scott, 2007, 42–89). Proponents of the ban appealed to France's tradition of secularism, which is grounded in both the legal history (its historic separation of church and state in 1905), as well as deeply engrained French cultural sensibilities that seek to protect individual freedom of choice and equality between men and women against all forms of religious coercion and inequality. For many Muslim women wearing a headscarve is an obligation of religious piety and obedience to Allah. Clearly, it is an act that distinguishes women from men. From the perspective of French *laicite* (or secularism), the headscarf indicates treatment of women that is obviously unequal and assumed to be coercive (especially with regard to school-aged girls). Even when some Muslim women claim that they participate in this practice "of their own free will," many proponents of the law banning headscarves allege that, most likely, those women have internalized their own oppression. That is, they have come to believe that the practice of wearing headscarves as an act of religious devotion is something that they desire to do. However, in reality, it is demeaning to them and an act of self-discrimination.

The values that motivate this French civic nationalist understanding of religion are deeply ingrained in French history and culture. These portray "good" or acceptable forms of religious belief and practice as matters of free, personal choice kept quietly in the private sphere (Weil, 2004, 1–2). They understand expressions of religious identities that do not cleanly conform to their conception of acceptable religion as personal and private to be "communalist," that is, assertive markers for membership in, and allegiance to, some particular community that stands in contrast (or opposition) to the more fundamental, encompassing identity of French citizenship (O'Brien, 2005, 14–60). These dimensions of French civic nationalism reflect distinctively French interpretations of the values of liberty, equality, and fraternity, which are understood to hold together and unify the public, civic life of French society. As such, these values serve as elements of civic nationalism in French society.

And yet the law banning headscarves (and other obvious religious symbols) reinforces the suspicion that France's civic nationalism is not so benignly civic after all. For in its effort to protect against the prejudices and chauvinism that it considers likely to come from prevalent and persistent religious commitments and practices, this nationalism itself becomes deeply prejudicial and chauvinistic toward religious identities and practices. In attempting to prohibit inequality and coercion in religious symbolic and ritual practices, it restricts or forbids even voluntary participation in those practices as genuine expressions of one's religious identity. In seeking to protect against the dangers of religious fundamentalism, it makes itself into a form of secular fundamentalism. As such, the law banning the public wearing of religious symbols is an example of the selective uses of religious resources and themes to construct and reproduce national identities—even if, in this case, the sacred or non-negotiable principle of French national identity is a principle of antireligion itself.

Religion and Modernity—Compatible, Not Contradictory

The civic versus ethnic nationalism model raises the questions of whether religion is antimodern and whether religious nationalism should be analyzed as a rejection of modernity. Many scholars have attempted to illustrate that religion and modern values are compatible. Specifically, for example, secularism and Islam can be constructively compatible; Islam can exist within a society that claims that secularism is indispensable for fostering pluralism and accommodating minority and gender rights as well as a vibrant civil society. Despite those who argue that Islam is antithetical to secularism, a careful historical study of Muslim contexts illustrates that Islam and the state are, more often than not, functionally separated. Furthermore, Islam is amiable to values of human rights and democracy. In fact, some have argued that the idea of an Islamic state is actually foreign to Islam and derived from European conceptions of state and law (An-Na'im, 2008).

The Challenge of Reductionism for Understanding Nationalism

Many believe that religious nationalism appears in different global contexts as political movements with explicit religious claims about their identities and national aspirations. In this view, religious nationalism is typically linked to a broader conversation about the supposed rise—often dubbed a resurgence—of religious militancy in the post–Cold War era. In the following two sections, we will address two reductionist viewpoints—essentialism and materialism—that reduce the complexities of religious conflicts to overly simplistic explanations in the context of what is perceived to be a global resurgence of religious militancy in the late 20th and early 21st centuries.

Essentialist Approaches

In his landmark article "The Clash of Civilizations?," the late Harvard political scientist Samuel Huntington argued that with the end of the Cold War, the basis of conflict in the international arena would shift from the ideological differences between communism and capitalism, to cultural values and civilizational identities. According to Huntington, civilizational identities are defined "by common objective elements, such as language, history, religion, customs, institutions, and by the subjective self-identification of people" (Huntington, 1993, 24). Civilizational identities, for Huntington, coincide with religious ones, and Huntington sees these identities and the values associated with them as profoundly incompatible. He most provocatively describes Islam as especially involved in bloody conflicts with non-Islamic religions and cultures. Thus, according to Huntington, where Islamic civilization touches the edges of other civilizations, violent conflict typically results. In short, Huntington infamously wrote, Islam has "bloody borders" (Huntington, 1993, 33). Huntington's essentialist approach to conflict is not only orientalist with respect to religion, but also reductionist because it reduces a highly complex and internally diverse phenomenon (i.e., religious identities and practices) to what is allegedly the basic, simple essence of that phenomenon. Put simply, Huntington views religion as essentially a source of conflict.

Materialist Approaches

Instead of viewing religion as essential in conflicts, another reductionist approach to religion marginalizes the role of religion in conflicts. According to the materialist approach, conflicts may appear to be caused by religious differences or motivations but actually result from more genuine causes that have nothing to do with religion. In other words, causes that appear to be religious can (and must) be reduced to their true, more basic, nonreligious essence. The materialist approach claims that at the root of any conflict one can identify real material causes such as economic deprivation or political grievances. For example, Paul Collier, a World Bank economist, explains the eruption of national civil wars as the result of "greed, not grievance." While including religious and ethnic claims as a form of grievance, Collier concludes that violent rebellions and conflicts erupt only if they appear to be financially feasible. Thus religious or ethnic grievances carry no causal capacities in and of themselves (Collier, 2001, 143–162).

Collier's materialist argument is problematic because it is internally inconsistent with its own central claims and includes fairly sweeping exceptions and qualifications. For example, even Collier concedes the potential influence of grievances in multiethnic contexts where one ethnic group institutes ethnic domination

(Little and Swearer, 2006, 7). Since Collier's concession accounts for most of the cases of ethnoreligious nationalism, the argument that conflict erupts *only* as a function of greed and economic calculation is significantly weakened.

The materialist approach to the question of religion and politics suggests that failed (or untried) strategies of economic development and global trade, or struggle for resources and against savage inequalities, are the basic causes of conflicts, and are simply masked by apparently religious motivations. According to this account, the failures of global trade and development are the true causes of conflicts that, on the surface, may appear to be religious in nature. In other words, when development strategies and globalization fail to improve socioeconomic, health, and quality of life conditions in developing countries, the developing world's response typically appears to take the form of resurgent religion, and fanatical and fundamentalist forms of resurgent religion, in particular. However, the true causes are either primarily, or exclusively, material.

The materialist approach can be applied to the September 11 attacks on the United States by al-Qaeda—an incident widely understood as being motivated by fundamentalist and fanatical Islamic jihadism. A materialist might argue that while the Pentagon in Washington, D.C., was an example of an explicitly military target, the terrorists, targeting of the World Trade Center in the financial district of New York City reflect that the towers represented the exorbitant wealth, economic power, developmental dominance, and prestige that fuel the global influence and the economic imperialism of the United States. On this explanation, the September 11 attacks were not really about religion (i.e., destroying the infidel or combating "the great white Satan," i.e., the United States). Rather, the Twin Towers were targeted in response to the failure of global development strategies, the exploitative effects of global trade, and other forms of domination that globalization often brings with it (such as military activism that protects global economic interests). Such an explanation is but one example of how the materialist approach to religion and conflict reductionistically interprets violent militant forms of religion as, at bottom, a response to changes that are actually social, economic, and political.

By discussing reductionist approaches to religion, we seek to demonstrate that any attempt to examine religious nationalism must consider the ideas behind the study of the role of religion in conflict. As we have seen, for instance, the analysis of religious nationalism is related to the discussion of religious fundamentalism. Thus we need to examine and identify the biases that lead to assumptions that nationalism and religion are essentially in opposition to each other, and that religious nationalism is an especially violent and pathological variation of nationalism.

The Myth of Religious Violence

Both the essentialist (as in Huntington) and the materialist (as in Collier) explanatory frameworks result in counterproductive misconceptions about religious nationalism. The assumption that religion is simply or uniquely a cause of violence is not only flawed, but also seems to justify the legitimacy of secular and/or rational violence.

One important work that dismantles the reductionist arguments about religion and violence is Christian theologian William Cavanaugh's *The Myth of Religious Violence*. Cavanaugh suggests that the myth of religious violence is an overly simplistic view of a complex historical development. Cavanaugh describes the myth of religious violence as the "migration of the holy from church to state in the establishment of the ideal of dying and killing for one's country" (Cavanaugh, 2009, 10). This insight resonates strongly with our overall argument that nationalism constitutes a political theology (Omer 2013). It is important to see how nationalism functions as a form of religion; this approach will help us to understand the phenomenon of religious nationalism beyond the secularism thesis and the myth of religious violence that results from it. This approach makes religious nationalism much more complex than simply rendering religious nationalism as an aberration of secular modernity.

Secular Western modernity has relied on the myth of religious violence to affirm its superiority. In the triumphant narrative of secular Western modernity, the bloody religious wars of premodern Europe allegedly ended with the birth of secular tolerance and the rise of the institutional separation of religion and the modern state. The myth of religious violence has been used to expose how the religious wars in 16th- and 17th-century Europe are misrepresented in the narrative of secular modernity. In fact, such narratives constitute a myth of origin in which Catholics and Protestants violently fought one another over doctrinal differences. This mythology expresses the supposed inherent violent nature of religion and portrays the birth of the modern state as an antidote to the brutal, intolerant tendencies of religion. However, closer historical study shows that many of the 16th- and 17th-century wars in Europe involved Catholics and Protestants fighting their coreligionists. In fact, the motivations for conflict were far from doctrinal differences and theological controversies alone. Similarly, the transfer of power from the church to the state was not the novel solution to the problem of religion, as the myth of religious violence claims. State-building processes preceded the Protestant Reformation, the development that led to the Catholic and Protestant schism. And, in fact, these state-building political processes contributed to the bloody wars of the 16th and 17th centuries, wars that are often mischaracterized as simply wars of religion.

In contemporary debates, the myth of religious violence marginalizes religion in domestic contexts. At the same time, this myth authorizes militancy against non-Western—especially Muslim—people who are perceived as unable to tame their wild religious passions. One can immediately detect the traces of eurocentrism and orientalism that undergird this mythology. This myth is also apparent in attempts to understand religious nationalism as antithetical to secular nationalism. The myth also assumes that religious violence is different from secular violence because it is supposedly more passionate and fanatical.

Drawing on the origin story of liberal modernity as a supposed antidote to the legacy of the European Wars of Religion, the myth of religious violence claims that religion is a wholly unique and especially volatile cause of violence in modern contexts. We have exposed this myth to disrupt the equally defective claim that religious nationalism is the opposite of—and resurgent reaction against—secular modernity. In fact, both secular and religious nationalisms are thoroughly modern and interwoven with the histories and resources by which they are constructed. Rather than easily compartmentalized opposites, they might better be analyzed along a spectrum and better understood through a detailed exploration of how various features of religious traditions inform, critique, and might aid in constructive engagement with conceptions of national identities. We conduct just such an investigation in Chapter 3.

A Society Worshipping Itself?

Berger's sacred canopy (the shared worldview that gives meaning to social and political life) resonates with the concept of nationalism as a quasireligion and a secular replacement for the religious worldviews that preceded it. It is also consistent with other social-functionalist thinkers like Emile Durkheim. Durkheim identified the inevitable role of the sacred in social life.

Durkheim's theory is another example of reductionism and of treating religion as secondary, similar to the materialist approach. Yet he acknowledges that religion is a thoroughly social phenomenon that cannot be separated from social realities. For Durkheim, religion is always the expression of a society worshiping itself. In his influential *The Elementary Forms of Religious Life* (1912), Durkheim defined religion as "a unified system of beliefs and practices relative to sacred things, that is to say things set apart and forbidden—beliefs and practices which unite into one moral community called a Church, all those who adhere to them" (Durkheim, 1995, 44).

Studying Australian aborigine religious practices, Durkheim identified totems, that is, concrete symbols and visible images that represent a clan. He concluded that totemism is not a mere representation of a basic religious experience, but rather it constitutes the basis for every form of religious practice. "The god of the clan, the totemic principle, can therefore be nothing else than the clan itself, personified and represented to the imagination under the visible form of the animal or vegetable which serves as totem" (Durkheim, 1995, 206). Durkheim argued that religion is thoroughly and basically social, and its main purpose is to perpetuate social sentiments through symbol and ritual practices. Berger would refer to such acts of perpetuation as socialization and legitimization.

Hence, unlike those theorists who celebrate the end of religion as an inevitable outcome of modernity and progress, Durkheim concludes that religion—or some substitute for it, like nationalism—would inevitably endure. With respect to the French Revolution, Durkheim wrote: "Under the influence of the general enthusiasm, things purely secular in nature became transformed into sacred things: these were the Fatherland, Liberty, Reason. A religion tended to become established which had its dogmas, symbols, altars and feasts" (Durkheim, 1995, 215–216). Durkheim affirms the relationship between nationalism and civil religion, as well as construction of sacred ideas and rituals to legitimize their shared identity. While revolutionary enthusiasm was short lived, Durkheim claims, the French Revolution attempted "to give a kind of authoritative fulfillment" to "the

Cult of Reason" (Durkheim, 1995, 216). Indeed, Durkheim's sociological reduction of religion echoes Benedict Anderson's observations that nationalism offers the promise of salvation and meaning through communal identity. The sacredness of the religious communities and the dynastic realms was displaced and redirected toward the idea of the nation, understood as a cultural creation and artifact (Durkheim, 1995, 12–36).

The belief in the sacredness of the community empowers the kind of sacrifices necessary to maintain the continuity of the community. In their *Blood Sacrifice and the Nation: Totem Rituals and the American Flag*, Carolyn Marvin and David W. Ingle ground their analysis of American patriotism and civil religion in a Durkheimian framework. They write: "In American civil religion, the flag is the ritual instrument of group cohesion. It transforms the bodies of insiders and outsiders who meet a border of violence. This is the kernel of the totem myth, endlessly re-enacted in patriotic life and ritual, and always most powerfully in the presence of the flag ... The totem secret, the collective group taboo, is the knowledge that society depends on the death of its own members" (Marvin and Ingle, 1999, 2). The nation amounts to "the shared memory of blood sacrifice, periodically renewed" (Marvin and Ingle, 1999, 4). These memories are powerfully present in a range of contexts; as we discussed in the previous chapter, Serbian nationalists memorialize the martyrdom of Prince Lazar, Zionists recall the expulsion of the Jews from their ancestral lands, and Irish Catholics bitterly remember the violent legacy of Protestant British colonialism in Northern Ireland.

Modernist Misconceptions of Religious Nationalism

Modernism is another concept that deserves more extensive attention because it conveys a particular attitude toward religion. Modernism underpins much of the discussion of religious fundamentalisms broadly, and of religious nationalism more specifically. Modernists view nationalism as a recent and "qualitatively novel" phenomenon (Smith, 2003, 46). They believe that the advent of the modern nation represents a radical break between premodern and modern epochs. As such, it represents another example of modernity's progress.

Types and Forms

Gellner attributes nationalism's origins to changing sociocultural conditions; he believes it became functionally necessary to construct a "standardized culture" within the nation during the transition to modernization (Gellner 1997). In contrast, Anderson's modernist approach is classified as constructionist because it underscores the constructed nature of the nation—a political community imagined as the secular replacement for previous religious conceptions of time and space (Smith, 2003, 48–49). Marx's account constitutes a revision to the modernist account in that he pushes the roots of nationalism back to premodernity. Yet, like other modernists, he still believes the emergence of nationalism constitutes a novel functionalist social consciousness that is unique to the modern era (Marx, 2003).

Assumptions and Misconceptions

As illustrated in the previous discussion of the myth of religious violence, modernism is a constructed worldview that is intricately related to the discourse of orientalism. While certain features associated with modernization (e.g., the development of scientific methods, industrial production, technological innovation, and the rise in standard of living) are uncontroversial, modernity is a contested cultural and historical construct. It portrays itself as possessing the traits of capitalism, the state, secular culture, liberal democracy, individualism, and rationalism—features that also characterize the ideal-type of the civic nation. These traits of modernism, typically portrayed as essential features of the West (i.e., Europe and North America), are then compared with the antithetical construct of the Orient. But, as Lawrence Cahoone argues, modernity as a sociological construct is indeed controversial because "the positive-self-image" of Western modernity is not shared by all:

> The positive self-image modern Western culture has often given to itself . . . is of a civilization founded on scientific knowledge of the world and rational knowledge of value, which places the highest premium on individual human life and freedom, and believes that such freedom and rationality will lead to social progress through virtuous, self-controlled work, creating a better material,

political, and intellectual life for all. This combination of
science, reason, individuality, freedom, truth, and social
progress has, however, been questioned and criticized
by many. Some critics see modernity instead as a movement of ethnic and class domination, European imperialism, anthropocentrism, the destruction of nature, the
dissolution of community and tradition, the rise of
alienation, the death of individuality in bureaucracy.
(Cahoone, 1996, 12)

The discourse of modernity contains structures of power and
forms of domination. Along the lines of this discursive critique,
the secularism thesis is intricately related to concepts of modernity that view progress as leading to the eventual elimination of
religion from the public and political spheres of social relations.
This account of modernity informed the works of the founding
fathers of modern social thought. It still exercises great influence
over how political, social, and religious phenomena are understood and analyzed today. It involves the presumption that religion inhibits progress and modernity, portraying science as the
pinnacle of human rationality and knowledge.

As we discussed earlier in this chapter, material reductionism insists that religion is never a reality on its own terms, but
rather a mere appearance and expression of something more
basic (what some political scientists refer to as a "dependent var-
iable" and some social theorists term "epi-phenomenal"). To take
another example, the inventor of psychoanalysis, Sigmund Freud,
explained religion as a form of neurosis (a mental or emotional
disorder that involves a distorted perception of reality) that
resides deep in the infancy of civilization. This neurosis needs to
be exposed as pathological and subsequently overcome in order
to attain civilizational maturity. Freud's approach is reductionist
because it analyzes religion as a mere by-product of psychological
distress. Once its real roots are exposed, Freud argues, religion is
nothing more than an illusory wish fulfillment generated by the
unconscious (Freud 1989 [1927]).

Karl Marx similarly rendered religion as a form of false consciousness that compensates for the real material interests of the
working classes (Marx, 1964 [1843], 41). He viewed religion as
an illusory invention used to maintain social and economic hier-
archy. It is the most efficient ideology (Berger would call it a
sacred canopy) that has legitimated the oppressive conditions

caused by economic realities. We have discussed various reductionist approaches to the study of religion and conflict in order to demonstrate that such approaches pose problems when they are applied as comprehensive explanations of the nature and basis of religious conflict. They also tend toward more orientalist and Eurocentric conceptions of religion.

Religion as a Force for Change

Scholar of religion Daniel Pals introduces an important critique of the economic reductionism found in Karl Marx's work, which centers on class struggle. He explains that Marx's treatment of religion as an ideology fails to engage with the materialist-essentialist dilemma: Where can one identify the origins of change? Can we be sure that economics changed religion? Or could it be that religious developments actually changed economics?

The Protestant Ethic

Max Weber framed an influential argument to address the issue of religion as a force for change. He claimed that the Protestant ethic generated the spirit of modern capitalism, rather than the opposite; in Weber's explanation, Protestants were driven to work hard and efficiently because they believed that, however mundane the task, would be a sign of their salvation. Indeed, Weber is a key thinker in connecting the theories of modernism and secularism. Weber observed that modernism led to the decline of religion and the rise of secularization, which resulted in what he called the "disenchantment" of the world (the replacement of spiritual and traditional beliefs with scientific and instrumental forms of rationality). Moreover, Weber believed that human beings were trapped in an "iron cage" of the modern secular capitalist order because their lives had come to be driven by cold rationality, bureaucracy, and efficiency. In Weber's account, this order grew out of a particular ascetic Protestant worldview and ethic, but it eventually acquired a logic of its own. More importantly, it came to present itself as independent from—and without any reference to—the religious formations that contributed vitally to its emergence in the first place.

Weber famously concluded his *The Protestant Ethic and the Spirit of Capitalism* with the possibility of "re-enchanting" the "iron cage" of modernity. He wrote: "No one knows who will live in this cage in the future, or whether at the end of this tremendous development entirely new prophets will arise, or there will be a great rebirth of old ideas and ideals, or, if neither, mechanized petrifaction, embellished with a sort of convulsive self-importance" (Weber, 1992, 124). Weber suspected that it might be mere wishful thinking to conceive of modernity as the pinnacle of human progress and development (i.e., in terms of the triumph of reason, science, and bureaucracy). In the minds of some scholars, the "resurgence" of religion in the latter 20th century consists of attempts to forcibly and fanatically challenge the rigidity imposed by the iron cage and to overturn the structures of disenchanted, secular modernity. Others explain what appears to them to be the very recent global resurgence of activist and militant religions as an example of what Weber called the emergence of "new prophets" and charismatic and religious worldviews, the possibility of which had been suppressed and pushed to the margins in the Cold War geopolitical frameworks, but since then have surged back with a vengeance.

Weber's insight concerning the relationship between the Protestant ethic and the emergence of modern capitalism complicates reductionist accounts of religion. It problematizes exclusively materialist theories that attribute the emergence of nationalisms solely to changing power configurations. Weber's approach challenges attempts to explain the rise of religious nationalism as a mere reaction to the failure of secular regimes; as an outcome of changes in the geopolitical condition (e.g., a power vacuum resulting from the death of a leader); or as a tool for manipulation by the elites. Such analyses overlook the actual substance of religious ideas and beliefs, and how they may also produce an effect or change.

The Protestant Reformation and the Sovereign Nation-State

Recognizing the potential for religion to bring about change, political theorist Daniel Philpott has suggested that the ideas of the Protestant Reformation influenced the international system of nation-states. In his book *Revolutions in Sovereignty: How Ideas Shaped Modern International Relations*, Philpott argues that ideas have a causal capacity to influence political change. Initially, ideas may shape popular identities, which in turn may eventually materialize through the exercise of social power upon political elites. The elites in question then act to bring about change and reconfigure political realities, locally and globally. Of course, Philpott does not propose a monocausal explanation, in which all change can be attributed to a single idea. However, Philpott focuses on the causal power of ideas during the Protestant Reformation, a movement in which Protestants rejected the rituals, doctrines, and authority of the Roman Catholic Church. In the case of early modern Europe, Protestant beliefs eventually enabled dissenters to struggle against the powers of the Roman Catholic Church, which provided legitimacy for the Holy Roman Empire. According to Philpott, this opposition to the Roman Catholic Church facilitated the end of medieval Christendom (the Holy Roman Empire) and the rise of secular sovereign states. These processes culminated with the Peace of Westphalia in 1648, which, Philpott argues, laid the basis for the international system of nation-states and redefined the role of religion therein.

Establishing a new political order in Europe, the Peace of Westphalia enabled individual states to gain sovereignty and eventually absolute authority apart from the Holy Roman Empire. While individual states were expected to minimally tolerate religious minorities in their midst, Philpott writes, religion ceased to be a justification for acts of war (Philpott, 2000, 213). If it were not for the Reformation, Philpott argues, "persistently medieval features of Europe—the substantive powers of the Holy Roman Empire and its emperor, the formidable temporal powers of the church, religious uniformity, truncations of the sovereign powers of secular rulers, Spain's control of the Netherlands— would not have disappeared when they did, to make way for the system of sovereign states" (Philpott, 2000, 214). "Protestant ideas," Philpott continues, "challenged all temporal powers of the church and the empire. Sweeping causes produced sweeping effects" (Philpott, 2000, 99). If it were not for the ideas that emerged from the Reformation, therefore, state and nonstate contestants would have continued to compete for institutional sovereignty long after the Treaty of Westphalia.

Philpott further argues that the ideas of equality and colonial nationalism also revolutionized sovereignty and brought about the final collapse of colonial empires around the 1960s. Philpott recognizes that material factors (including changing economic and military conditions) contributed to these developments; however, he argues that material factors do not provide the only explanatory factors that led to the restructuring of authority into the international system of nation-states. Westphalia not only created the international system of sovereign nation-states, it also established the "territorialization of religion," defined as the association of a particular religion with a state's territory (e.g., Catholic Spain, Lutheran Germany, Anglican Britain); subjected religious institutions to the authority of the secular state; and confined religion to the private sphere. While highlighting Westphalia as a key turning point conforms to the conventional myth of religious violence, Philpott's account otherwise powerfully corroborates Cavanaugh's argument about the "migration of the holy" from church to nation-state as key to understanding modern political and religious developments.

The breakup of medieval Europe, as Benedict Anderson argues, was one of the factors that brought about the emergence of the national imagination as a replacement for religion's promise of "fatality into continuity" (e.g., resurrection of the dead, life after death, rebirth) (Anderson, 1991, 11). To reiterate, however, nationalisms were not imagined out of nothing and have continued to be selectively interwoven with previously existing religious and cultural narratives, symbols, and communal prejudices. However, Anthony Marx's analysis further highlights those interrelations by locating the emergence of nations in premodernity. His account illustrates that long before the Treaty of Westphalia, tensions within and against the centralized authority of the Catholic Church played a pivotal role in changing the patterns that generated social cohesion and political authority.

Even so, Philpott's argument exemplifies why Westphalia signals a key turning point in the narrative of secular modernity. The concept of sovereignty presented by the Peace of Westphalia changed the location of religion in public and political life. It carved out secular and political spaces that were not beholden to the authority of religious institutions. It moved religion to the private and nonpublic realms of social life. According to the secularist discourse, the unruly, irrational, and violent tendencies of religion had to be domesticated or made safe for liberal democratic political contexts. This discourse has contributed to the perception that the principles of modernity and secularity are violated by religious ideas or expressions that push beyond the private sphere. Of course, proponents of this view believe that religion in the private sphere is irrelevant or harmless to political configurations in the modern nation-state. This view fails to consider that nationalism is a kind of religion. Moreover, this view does not take into account civil religion and its relations to prior or existing cultural and religious roots and narratives, as we discussed in previous sections.

Religion in the Public Sphere

A widely held view among popular and scholarly circles, some versions of secularist discourse presuppose that a hallmark of modernity is the diminishing significance and eventual decline of religion. However, this thesis has been challenged by religion's obvious publicity or presence around the globe, as described by José Casanova.

According to Casanova, historicism (an approach that focuses on specific historical contexts) gave rise to secularism as a worldview (Casanova, 1994, 30–35). This historicist angle views secularism as a symptom of Enlightenment's critique of religion, which valued human reason over faith, superstition, and tradition. Casanova stresses the importance of recognizing the ethnocentric biases in the historicist's study of secularism. Such biases favor subjective Protestant forms of religion and the containment of religion in the private sphere; liberal conceptions of politics and the public sphere; and the sovereign nation-state as the basic systemic unit of analysis. Even though it is important to recognize and grapple with the weaknesses of secularism, Casanova argues, it is not necessary to eliminate everything it represents. In fact, Casanova affirms civil society when it allows religious voices to participate unapologetically in debates concerning the meanings of that society.

Anthropologist and cultural critic Talal Asad praises Casanova for breaking away from the approach that views secularism as symptomatic of modernity. In *Formations of the Secular: Christianity, Islam, Modernity,* Asad writes, "The argument [of Casanova] is that whether religious deprivatization threatens modernity or not depends on *how* religion becomes public" (Asad, 2003, 182). In other words, not all forms of religion in public life are equally dangerous, and in fact, some may be quite edifying to modern, liberal, democratic politics. Asad then highlights the liberal bias in Casanova's acceptance of public religion, which he refers to as the deprivatization of religion in modern political life. He argues that Casanova welcomes only those public expressions of religion that are seen as "compatible with modernity . . . Only religions that have accepted the assumptions of liberal discourse are being commended, in which tolerance is sought on the basis of a distinctive relation between law and morality" (Asad, 2003, 183).

Asad then exposes the power dimensions integral to Casanova's view of public religion and asks about the religious actors who substantively challenge the ground rules of modern and secular public life: What about their rights? Might they be allowed into the conversation? What of their objective to utterly transform societal structures? If they are not allowed, then, how does Casanova's critique of an unrevised secularism avoid the result that "good" religion is ultimately domesticated and willing to behave according to the rules of liberal civil society?

Asad explains that the public space is not a given, but rather "a space *necessarily* (not just contingently) articulated by power" (Asad, 2003, 184). This proves to be a critical point for the analysis of the resurgence of religion, a phenomenon often depicted as negative because it is perceived as a threat to the enduring liberal presuppositions that religion should be public only when it is tolerant and abides by liberal values. Asad asks: "If the adherents of religion enter the public sphere, can their entry leave the preexisting discursive structure intact?" (2003, 185). This becomes a critical question when religious voices seek to change social and political structures (including even the curtailing of free speech and religious pluralism) (Springs, 2012b). It follows, then, that only a particular range of religious expressions is acceptable within the liberal framework. And yet the liberal framework is largely unaware of its own cultural, historical, and religious particularity, as Yack demonstrated in his criticism of biases in the civic versus ethnic dichotomy. "The public space," Asad adds,

> is not an empty space for carrying out debates. It is constituted by the sensibilities—memories and aspirations, fears and hopes—of speakers and listeners . . . Thus the introduction of new discourses may result in the disruption of established assumptions structuring debates in the public sphere. More strongly, they may have to disrupt existing assumptions to be heard. Far from having to prove to existing authority that it is no threat to dominant values, a religion that enters political debate on *its own terms* may on the contrary have to threaten the authority of existing assumptions. (2003, 185)

In response, Casanova claims that Asad incorrectly characterizes his account as too tightly linked to liberal discourse. He argues that respect for freedom of conscience as a condition for the deprivatization of religion is not necessarily grounded in secular liberal values (Casanova, 2008, 13–14). Furthermore, Casanova claims that the notion of public space is not solely regulated by rational debate (Casanova, 2008, 14). He does, however, recognize the need to develop a comparative global perspective to analyze secularism, particularly one that highlights important distinctions between European and American types of secularism. Casanova suggests the need to move beyond a Eurocentric view (which assumes that specific European developments are universal) because European secularism is not the rule but the exception (Casanova, 2008, 18–19). Yet despite historicizing and deconstructing its premises, Casanova continues to argue that the secularism paradigm is still a useful one:

> not only as a way of reconstructing analytically the transformations of modern European societies, but also as an analytical framework for a comparative research agenda that aims to examine the historical transformation of all world religions under conditions of modern structural differentiation, as long as the outcome of this transformation is not predetermined by the theory, and as long as we do not label as religious fundamentalism any countersecularization, or any religious transformation that does not follow the prescribed model. (2008, 19)

In short, Casanova concedes that depictions of religion as antimodern and antisecular are tied to discourses and misconceptions of orientalism, eurocentrism, and modernism. Moreover, it is inaccurate and unconstructive to frame the secular and the religious as easily distinguishable and separable categories, especially when used to think about the resurgence of religion—a phenomenon that is widely associated with religious nationalism around the globe.

Exposing the Discourses of Secularism

Elizabeth Shakman Hurd is another political scientist who criticizes approaches that regard resurgent religion as a challenge to and/or a failure of the process of secularization. Hurd exposes the assumptions that undergird the term "religious resurgence." This term, Hurd writes, "refer[s] to activities, movements, and processes that challenge authoritative secularist settlements of the relationship between metaphysics, politics, and state power" (2008, 135). In other words, any public manifestation of religion that seems to violate Casanova's liberal conception of the public space of civil society is identified as pathological and threatening. Hurd differentiates two similar, but subtly different, discourses of secularism: laicism and Judeo-Christian.

Laicism Discourse

Laicism is a system that excludes religious involvement in government affairs and the government's involvement in religious affairs. This discourse is similar to the antireligion critiques and sentiments which view religion as something to be overcome in the march toward modernity and progress. Laicism, Hurd explains, "presumes that metaphysical [e.g., spiritual, religious] traditions of all kinds have been exhausted and transcended." Critically, laicism constitutes "the founding principles of modern political thought and one of the practical pillars of the separation of church and state" (2008, 29). Borrowing from Scott M. Thomas, Hurd identifies the "Westphalia presumption" as the belief that religion was and/or should be privatized. Drawing on Philpott's account, Hurd alludes to the Peace of Westphalia as the supposed moment in which the international system of modern nation-states came into being (2008, 30–31)—a historical development that Philpott situates in the broader development of European Christianity.

Echoing Casanova's historicist approach and Asad's deconstructive critique, Hurd maintains that laicism is deeply indebted to Christianity in spite of its attempt to describe itself as a "universalizable discourse" and "a solution to the 'wars of religion'" (2008, 31). By assigning religion to the private domain, the Westphalian framework marked the end of the religious violence that defined the supposed wars of religion. Within this perspective, "laicism succeeds in positing itself as public, neutral, and value-free, while assigning religion the role of its private, affective, and value-laden counterpart. Religion becomes the domain of the violent, the irrational, the undemocratic, the 'other'" (Hurd, 2008, 37). In the narrative of laicism, religion has alienated humanity from itself; this material reductionist narrative renders religion as a form of "false consciousness" or something that masks the true nature or cause of a phenomenon.

Hurd's account highlights the strong orientalist elements within laicism. Moreover, her criticisms are consistent with those of Yack (discussed previously), which demonstrates that civic nationalism is viewed positively as rational, secular, and modern, while ethnic and religious nationalism is negatively viewed as fanatical, intolerant, and antimodern. Indeed, in examining the discourse of laicism, Hurd shows that Islam and the Orient, by definition, came to be associated with the nonsecular. They are "represented as impediments to the rationalization and democratization of modern society" (2008, 54). These assumptions justified the colonization of North Africa, the Middle East, and the East Indies. Hurd elaborates on this point: "In French interventions . . . the expulsion of religion from politics was identified with progress and civilization, while Islam was associated with Oriental despotism" (2008, 54).

The French civilizing mission authorized domination, colonization, and military intervention, similar to the global entanglements authorized by American exceptionalism. In both instances, it is important to scrutinize the specific cultural and religious themes that inform French and American perceptions of orienting values, national prestige, and providential mission. For instance, the concept of "oriental despotism" was initially developed by Charles de Secondat (the Baron de Montesquieu) in his *Persian Letters* (1773), which was written from the perspective of a Persian who observed French culture, society, and politics. These letters illustrate how images of the Orient were used to support critiques of religion in France. The image of the modern West was made possible by depicting the Orient as "the other" or the opposite of modernity and the West, thus morally vindicating the civilizational mission known as colonialism.

Judeo-Christian Discourse

Hurd identifies a second discourse of secularism that she classifies as Judeo-Christian. While the laicist model aspires to overcome religion as an obstacle for an enlightened modernity, Judeo-Christian secularism, as exhibited in the case of the United States, "connects contemporary Western secular formations to a legacy of 'Western' (Christian, later Judeo-Christian) values, cultural and religious beliefs, historical practices, legal traditions, governing institutions, and forms of identifications" (Hurd, 2008, 38).

While laicism finds its roots in Greek and Roman democratic institutions and values, the Judeo-Christian discourse holds that modern democratic values came from the Christian (and, to some degree, Jewish) pasts of Europe and North America. In other words, "Christianity . . . led to secularism" (Hurd, 2008, 42). This Judeo-Christian discourse assumes that "religion (singular) is ultimately good for democratic politics, because a *shared* adherence to a common religious tradition [i.e., the Judeo-Christian tradition] provides a set of publically accessible assumptions within which democratic politics can be conducted" (Hurd, 2008, 42). In this context, the idea of a civil religion is a variation on previous cultural and religious traditions (again, the Judeo-Christian tradition), in that it facilitates cohesion.

The Judeo-Christian discourse produces a version of orientalism that is similar to the one we identified in Huntington's argument, namely that the sources of conflict in the post–Cold War era are religious or civilizational. As we saw, Huntington predicted that wars would erupt along what he called civilizational fault lines and that the borders of Islam are especially bloody. Huntington's thesis views various eruptions of religious nationalisms as a symptom of broader civilizational struggles. In Huntington's account, Catholicism and Protestantism provide the foundation for the value system of the West and subsequently the civic nation: tolerance, individualism, constitutionalism, democracy, human rights, and so forth. Because these values are rooted in the particularities of Western Christian history, proponents of this account would argue, they tend not be present in the same way in other civilizational contexts; consequently, non-Western Christian civilizations are potentially more prone to violent conflict and civilizational confrontation.

Unlike Hurd's view of laicist orientalism, Huntington does not position Islam as a "surmountable though formidable stumbling block to the rationalization and democratization of societies." Rather, Islam is represented "as a potential threat to the cultural, moral, and religious foundations of Western civilization that must be successfully defused" (Hurd, 2008, 47). In short, according to Huntington, Islam simply must either be fully domesticated—"made safe" for liberal democracy—or combated and excluded altogether.

Secular-Orientalist Discourse

These different accounts of orientalism—one criticized by Hurd, the other championed by Huntington—convey subtle differences in their views of how religion relates to political and social frameworks. However, as we mentioned earlier in this chapter, the two quickly become conflated in heated political and cultural controversies such as the veil controversy in France and the protest against building a Muslim cultural center near where the World Trade Center towers once stood in New York City.

In the case of the ban on the veil in France, the debate conjured up orientalist representations of Islam not as a surmountable identity, but of Muslims (even third- and fourth-generation French Muslims) as utterly foreign and unable to assimilate to French culture. While there are examples of more accommodating forms of French nationalism, Muslim assimilation into French national identity would require them to rid themselves of their collective identity or at least the aspects of identity that are perceived to infringe upon the public and neutral space, which is essential to French society's understanding of itself. In other cases, however, French civic-national identity is underpinned by elements of explicit—even severe—ethnocentrism. These forms of French nationalism deny Muslims the possibility of genuine assimilation, even when the offending features of Muslim religious identity are cast off or one denies being a practicing Muslim altogether (Scott, 2007, Chap. 2).

In the controversy surrounding the proposed plan to construct a Muslim cultural center near the site of the former World Trade Center in 2010, the rhetoric similarly rendered Islam as the "other" or someone outside of a certain conception of an American identity. Some commentaries on the controversy observed that Catholicism used to be represented as a threatening and inassimilable other but gradually accommodated itself to and became encompassed by American civil religion (Appleby and McGreevy, 2010, 48). In other words, in the cases of both France and the United States, the construction of a national identity has entailed "negative appropriations of Islam" (Hurd, 2008, 58). This orientalist tendency is pivotal for the analysis of the modern era and the birth of the nation-state as an entirely modern phenomenon, as argued by the modernist model of nationalism.

Modernism assumes that once the previous structures of authority and legitimacy (both religious and imperial) have dissolved, a national identity must emerge in order to maintain social cohesion. This view implies certain (re)arrangements of social spheres. In the discourse of laicism, once religion is pushed to the private sphere, it will eventually cease to be a relevant factor in political life. The Judeo-Christian discourse recognizes religion's continuous effectiveness and relevance, and understands secularism as grounded in a particular cultural and religious landscape. The Judeo-Christian discourse of secularism resonates with the tradition of civil religion because it recognizes religion as a particularly strong means to maintain legitimacy and social cohesion.

Of course, the Judeo-Christian discourse does not provide a constructive approach to understanding religious resurgence. Like laicism, the Judeo-Christian discourse presumes the superiority of Western interpretations of the proper place of religion. As a result, Hurd underscores, it marginalizes "non-Western and non-Judeo-Christian perspectives on religion and politics" (2008, 44). Hurd exposes how the discourses of secularism constrain the ways religious resurgence is analyzed and how enduring orientalism limits the scope of international relations.

Conclusion

This chapter addressed how the discourses of secularism conceal the ways religion continuously relates to conceptions of nationhood. To recognize the full depth and complexity of religious nationalism, we need to closely examine secular concepts, each of religious nationalism's related parts, and the possibilities for constructive engagement. To that end, we must question how these phenomena are constructed and framed. In short, this recognition requires what we described earlier in this chapter as a discourse analysis.

This chapter explained what discourse analysis is and explored certain discursive analytical moves. We identified the ways that several basic presuppositions about religious nationalism rely on normative, historically, and culturally particular commitments and orientations. Specifically, we pointed out that orientalism, reductionist approaches to religion, and biases toward civic forms of nationalism (i.e., civic nationalism as good, ethnic nationalism as bad) are harmful because they not only obscure critical and constructive possibilities, but also hold unquestioned prejudices and presuppositions in place.

Furthermore, we demonstrated that we must deconstruct the myth of religious violence and understand why this myth is central to conventional accounts of religious nationalism. Both of these approaches are necessary to expose the mythology of the modern West and to think constructively about the question of religion, conflict, and the transformation of conflict in the context of the nation-state and nationalist struggles. We must rethink the presuppositions that inform the discourses of secularism in the modern world so that we can think differently about "resurgent religion." Moreover, when we deconstruct and understand the historical context of secular discourses, we can view religious nationalism as a way to renegotiate secularity and cultural religious identities and histories, instead of simply dismissing religious nationalism as a pathology.

In the chapter that follows, we use these theoretical insights to comparatively examine two cases of religious nationalism: contemporary Israel and the contemporary United States. Our aim is to illustrate how it might be possible to think critically and constructively about persistent forms of religious nationalism and the challenges they present.

References

Anderson, Benedict. *Imagined Communities: Reflections on the Origin and Spread of Nationalism* (New York: Verso, 1991).

An-Nai'im, Abdullahi Ahmed. *Islam and the Secular State: Negotiating the Future of Shari'a* (Cambridge, MA: Harvard University Press, 2008).

Appleby, Scott R. and John T. McGreevy. "Catholics, Muslims, and the Mosque," *New York Review of Books* 57, no. 14 (September 30, 2010), p. 48.

Asad, Talal. *Formations of the Secular: Christianity, Islam, Modernity* (Stanford, CA: Stanford University Press, 2003).

Bellah, Robert N. "Civil Religion in America," *Journal of the American Academy of Arts & Sciences* 96, no. 1 (Winter 1967), pp. 1–21.

Berger, Peter. *The Sacred Canopy: Elements of a Sociological Theory of Religion* (New York: Bantam Doubleday Dell Publishing Group, 1967).

Bowen, John R. *Can Islam be French?: Pluralism and Pragmatism in a Secularist State* (Princeton, NJ: Princeton University Press, 2010).

Bowen, John R. "Muslims and Citizens," *Boston Review* (February/March 2004).

Cahoone, Lawrence. "Introduction," in Lawrence Cahoone, ed., *From Modernism to Postmodernism: An Anthology* (Malden, MA: Blackwell Publishers, 1996).

Caldwell, David. "Canadiens Issue Apology for Fans' Booing Anthem," *New York Times*, March 22, 2003.

Casanova, José. *Public Religions in the Modern World* (Chicago: University of Chicago Press, 1994).

Casanova, José. "Public Religions Revisited," in Hent DeVries, ed., *Religion: Beyond a Concept* (New York: Fordham University Press, 2008), pp. 101–119.

Cavanaugh, William. *The Myth of Religious Violence* (Oxford: Oxford University Press, 2009).

Collier, Paul. "Economic Causes of Civil Conflict and Their Implications for Policy," in Chester A. Crocker, Fen Osler Hampson, and Pamela Aall, eds., *Turbulent Peace: The Challenges of Managing International Conflict* (Washington, D.C.: U.S. Institute of Peace Press, 2001) pp. 143–162.

Durkheim, Émile. *The Elementary Forms of Religious Life*, translated by Karen E. Fields (New York: Free Press, 1995 [1912]).

Freud, Sigmund. *The Future of an Illusion* (New York: Norton, 1989 [1927]).

Freud, Sigmund. *Totem and Taboo* (New York: W.W. Norton, 1950 [1913]).

Gellner, Ernest. *Nationalism* (London: Weidenfeld & Nicolson, 1997).

Gerstle, Gary. *American Crucible: Race and Nation in the Twentieth Century* (Princeton, NJ: Princeton University Press, 2002).

Goldstein, Robert Justin. *Desecrating the American Flag: Key Documents of the Controversy from the Civil War to 1995* (Syracuse, NY: Syracuse University Press, 1996).

Hibbard, Scott W. *Religious Politics and Secular States: Egypt, India, and the United States* (Baltimore: Johns Hopkins University Press, 2010).

Holusha, John and Carl Hulse. "Amendment on Flag Burning Fails by One Vote in Senate," *New York Times*, June 27, 2006.

Huntington, Samuel P. "The Clash of Civilizations?" *Foreign Affairs* 72, no. 3 (Summer 1993), pp. 22–49.

Huntington, Samuel P. *Who Are We? The Challenges of America's National Identity* (New York: Simon and Schuster, 2004).

Hurd, Elizabeth Shakman. *The Politics of Secularism in International Relations* (Princeton, NJ: Princeton University Press, 2008).

Ibish, Hussein, ed. "Report on Hate Crimes and Discrimination against Arab Americans: The Post-September 11th Backlash, September 11, 2001–October 11, 2002." American-Arab Anti-Discrimination Committee, Washington, D.C., 2003.

Ignatieff, Michael. *Blood and Belonging: Journeys Into the New Nationalism* (New York: Farrar, Straus, and Giroux, 1993).

Lazarus, Emma. "The New Colossus," *The Poems of Emma Lazarus, Vol. 1* (New York: Houghton, Mifflin and Company, 1888), pp. 202–203.

Little, David. "Belief, Ethnicity, and Nationality," http://www.crvp.org/book/Series01/I-7/chapter_i.htm (accessed July 5, 2012).

Little, David and Donald K. Swearer, eds. *Religion and Nationalism in Iraq: A Comparative Perspective* (Cambridge, MA: Harvard University Press, 2006).

Marvin, Carolyn and David W. Ingle. *Blood Sacrifice and the Nation: Totem Rituals and the American Flag* (New York: Cambridge University Press, 1999).

Marx, Anthony. *Faith in Nation: Exclusionary Origins of Nationalism* (Oxford: Oxford University Press, 2003).

Marx, Karl. "Critique of Hegel's Philosophy of Right: Introduction," in *Karl Marx and Friedrich Engels on Religion*, introduction by Reinhold Niebuhr (New York: Schocken Books, 1964 [1843]).

O'Brien, Robert. *The Stasi Report: The Report of the Committee of Reflection on the Application of the Principle of Secularity in the Republic* (Buffalo, NY: William S. Hein & Co., 2005).

Omer, Atalia, *When Peace Is Not Enough: How the Israeli Peace Camp Thinks about Religion, Nationalism, and Justice* (Chicago, IL: University of Chicago Press, 2013).

Pals, Daniel. *Seven Theories of Religion* (New York: Oxford University Press, 1996).

Pew Research Center. "Controversies over Mosques and Islamic Centers across the U.S.," Pew Forum on Religion and Public Life, September 29, 2011. http://features.pewforum.org/muslim/controversies-over-mosque-and-islamic-centers-across-the-us.html (accessed July 25, 2012).

Philpott, Daniel. "The Religious Roots of Modern International Relations," *World Politics* 52 (January 2000), pp. 206–245.

Philpott, Daniel. *Revolutions in Sovereignty: How Ideas Shaped Modern International Relations* (Princeton, NJ: Princeton University Press, 2001).

Renan, Ernst. "What Is a Nation?" in Moar Chabour and Micheline R. Ishay, eds., *The Nationalism Reader* (New York: Humanities Press, 1995).

Said, Edward W. *Orientalism* (New York: Pantheon Books, 1978).

Schilbrack, Kevin. "Religions: Are There Any?" *Journal of the American Academy of Religion* 78, no. 4 (December 2010), pp. 1112–1138.

Scott, Joan Wallach. *The Politics of the Veil* (Princeton, NJ: Princeton University Press, 2007).

Springs, Jason A. "Civil Religion," in Richard Hecht and Vincent Biondo, eds., *Religion and Culture: Contemporary Practices and Perspectives* (Minneapolis: Fortress Press, 2012).

Springs, Jason A. "On Giving Religious Intolerance its Due: Prospects for Transforming conflict in a Post-Secular Society," *The Journal of Religion*, Vol. 92, No. 1 (Jan. 2012): pp. 1–30.

Smith, Anthony. *Chosen Peoples: Sacred Sources of National Identity* (Oxford: Oxford University Press, 2003).

Thomas, Scott M. *The Global Resurgence of Religion and the Transformation of International Relations: The Struggle for the Soul of the Twenty-First Century* (New York: Palgrave Macmillan, 2005).

Weber, Max. *Economy and Society,* edited by G. Roth and C. Wittich (New York: Bedminster Press, 1968).

Weber, Max. *The Protestant Ethic and the Spirit of Capitalism*, trans. Talcott Parsons (London: Routledge, 1992 [1930]).

Weil, Patrick. "A Nation in Diversity: France, Muslims, and the Headscarf," *Open Democracy*, March 25, 2004. http://www.opendemocracy.net/faith-europe_islam/article_1811.jsp (accessed July 25, 2012).

Yack, Bernard. "The Myth of the Civic Nation," in Ronald Beiner, ed., *Theorizing Nationalism* (Albany: State University of New York, 1999).

3

Reimagining Religion and Nation: The Cases of Israel and the United States

Introduction

This chapter studies two cases of nationalism, one in the United States and the other in Israel. As we saw in the previous chapter, the "religious dimensions" of nationalism refer to ways that various symbols, narratives, myths, rituals, and consecrated spaces and times are selectively retrieved or appropriated, adapted, and deployed to imagine, mobilize, and perpetuate conceptions of national identity and membership. Over the course of the preceding chapters we have argued that, to varying degrees and in various forms, such elements are constitutive features of nationalisms. The constitutive roles that they play resist analytical efforts to simply segregate and compartmentalize "the religious" from "the secular" when engaging varieties of nationalism.

Recognizing the deficiencies of an ironclad secular/religious dichotomy overturns certain widely held presumptions. Perhaps the most widespread presumption it overturns is the idea that "nationalisms" that are somehow "religious" are uniquely antimodern, parochial, and thus prone to intolerance and violence in ways that "nonreligious," or secular, varieties of nationalism are not. As we argued in Chapter 1, approaching the study of nationalisms with such analytical opposition leaves too many complexities obscured from view, forecloses crucial avenues for assessment, and pre-empts the possibility of constructive analytical engagement of nationalisms.

At the same time, the religious dimensions of nationalism here also refer to how and why structural and legal configurations (e.g., a constitutionally grounded separation of church and state) enable certain roles for religious traditions and religiously moti-vated actors in constructively shaping or challenging national identities, and conceptions of the nation. Such structural factors, in turn, carry significant ramifications for the degree to which conceptions of nation may fluctuate along a spectrum from more to less ethnocentric and religiocentric visions of a national iden-tity. Generally speaking, the closer one is to the pole representing chauvinistic interpretations of identity (i.e., those that, in the case of religious nationalism, tend to deploy myths, symbols, rituals, and sacred times and spaces in exclusionary ways), the greater is the likelihood for discriminatory and violent practices on domestic and international levels.

It is important to keep in mind two key points. The first is that actors and institutions that explicitly identify with religious traditions, as well as religious ideas, themes, practices, and imag-inings can, and do, play roles all across the spectrum that stretches between a more chauvinistic and exclusivist pole to a more intentionally and self-critically inclusive pole. The public, political impact of political theologies and religious features of nationalism can both occur in either conceptions of a national identity that are chauvinistic as well as resistant to criticism and correction, or in conceptions that are more accountable to the dif-ficult processes of criticism, self-correction, and continuing revi-sion, reconceptualization, and expansion.

The second key point to keep in mind is that these opposing poles that stand at either end of the spectrum (exclusionary on one end, inclusionary on the other) are *ideal types*. To call them ideal types is to say that they are conceptual models that are con-structed for some specific analytical purpose at a given point in time. They are "types" because they are composed by drawing together a set of selected characteristics that are shared by a range of actually existing, related items. The types are "ideal" because the models, themselves, do not actually exist anywhere in the world. They are, rather, analytical constructs used for some spe-cific comparative, critical, and/or organizational purpose (Weber, 1904; Weber, 1917).

To better understand a type in this sense, imagine a portrait of a single person whose image has been composed as a composite representation of several different members of a family. In other words, the single figure in this portrait is a synthesis of the family resemblances shared by the different members of the family. No single member exhibits all the features that appear in the composite portrait, but each member has some (one or more), and some have more than others. So composed, the image presents a type that is ideal in that the figure depicted in the portrait does not, itself, actually exist anywhere in the world. And yet it is a composite of features that do actually exist somewhere, though separately (they appear in various combinations and to various degrees in the different family members). Once composed, the ideal representation in the portrait can then be used to identify, compare, categorize, and critically assess particular instances (in this case, immediate and extended family members) that do share some of these features, identifying which of the features they exhibit, the degree and extent to which they exhibit those features, and the different and unique ways that each may exhibit those features.

In the case of our present analysis, because it is ideal types that stand at either end of the exclusivist/inclusivist spectrum, all actually existing cases will contain some mixture of both exclusivist and inclusivist tendencies and elements. In other words, even the most intentionally inclusivist examples will have exclusivist elements and tendencies, and vice versa. Once this is recognized, the objective of an ethical analysis of religious nationalism cannot be to propose or to achieve a version of nationalism from which all elements of exclusivism have finally been rooted out once and for all (that would be cosmopolitan utopia, which suffers limitations of its own) (Yack, 2012, 253–285). The objective becomes, rather, to identify and critically assess actually existing instances of religious nationalism for the purpose of illuminating which inclusivist and exclusivist tendencies each case exhibits. This permits interrogating the potential for, or actual presence of, direct, structural, and cultural forms of violence in each case. It aids in identifying the degree to which each instance of nationalism may be (or might become) self-reflective, self-critical, accountable to claims about justice, and open to revising tendencies toward injustice.

The usefulness of exploring the cases of Israeli and U.S. nationalisms, with specific attention to their religious dimensions, is that despite their profound differences, comparing them brings important, but often overlooked, similarities into analytical view. As we demonstrate, the cases are similar in how vocabularies, symbols, ritual practices, and myths from traditional conceptions of Judaism and Christianity are recruited and interlaced in the construction and reconstruction of civil religion. The religious dimensions of what results are not limited to the religiously self-identified citizenry who characterize the United States as a "Christian" or "Judeo-Christian" nation, or who insist upon the integrity of a "Jewish democracy." Certain religious dimensions are also operative in the ways they function among self-identified "secular" citizenry.

When assessed through the analytical lenses of religious nationalism that we have developed throughout the preceding chapters, striking similarities become apparent. Similarities are evident in the history and character of their myths of origin as well as the exceptionalist role that each understands itself to play in world history; in addition, their providential conceptions of destiny echo one another. Both reflect Max Weber's description of nationalism as generally cohering around a sense of "choseness" and "cultural prestige." Choseness, a sense of providentially ordained mission, and unique world-historical role are three typical features of nationalism that reflect what Weber termed the "elective affinities" between religion, ethnicity, and nationality. Of course, while the ways that one qualifies for citizenship in the United States and Israel differ (the United States grounds its citizenship primarily on the principle of *jus soli*—Latin for "right of the soil"—and Israel's principle of citizenship is *jus sanguine*, Latin for "right of blood"), assessing this thread of these two instances of nationalism shows that they are anything but opposites. U.S. nationalism, we will see, is not devoid of ethnocentricity and exclusivist conceptions of the meanings of inherited American identity.

Not a Sleeping Beauty: Anti-Semitism and the Negation of Exile

One of the greatest fallacies of nationalist fervor is representing one's cause as constituting the awakening of consciousness that had existed since time immemorial. This understanding views national identity as essential and not subject to historical change and variation. The nation, in this view, is a constant and unchanged entity—even if it is perhaps unrecognized or suppressed—to which its members finally awaken to the reality of. This fallacy represents one of the paradoxes of nationalism: a nation is perceived to be, and is heralded as, ancient, but in actuality it is recent or modern (Gellner, 1983, 47–48). This insight helps in our effort to understand the story of Zionism, that is, Jewish nationalism.

Zionism emerged as a modern movement for political self-determination in the late 19th century. It appeared in a European context that had witnessed the emergence of other nationalisms. It is important to keep this context in mind, despite the recurring inclination to analyze Zionism (Jewish nationalism) as representing a consciousness that has persisted throughout centuries since biblical times, until the right historical conditions enabled the Jewish people to return to its homeland. To adequately understand Zionism as a political movement, we must identify the particularities of its contexts of origin and the discourses out of which it emerged.

One of these discourses is that of anti-Semitism. The 19th century witnessed the rise of new forms of anti-Semitism, a wave that culminated with the events of the Holocaust in Nazi Germany. What was new about this form of anti-Semitism? With the development and popularization of racial theories, classical anti-Semitism, whose origins can be found in Christian teachings about the Jews, was transformed. Classical anti-Semitism viewed conversion as a channel of change. However, the biologically racial basis of modern anti-Semitism perceived being Jewish as a permanent attribute one could never rid oneself of, not even through religious conversion or cultural assimilation. One's Jewishness was not merely a "religion," it was now rendered as "race."

The rise of this new form of anti-Semitism also coincided with the emergence of national movements in Europe and their language of "purity," a recurring characteristic of nationalist imaginings. While Jews were highly integrated and assimilated into European cultures, they became the target of anti-Semitic pogroms and other types of attacks. Various thinkers and public intellectuals pondered why Jews would never be able to fully integrate into European societies and framed the discussion as one concerning the "Jewish question." Interestingly, this framing has also impacted intra-Jewish conversation and led many notable Jewish thinkers to find a "solution" to the Jewish question (Meyer, 1990).

In some respects, the language of early political Zionism reflects the internalization of the anti-Semitic discourse in that Jewish existence in the "diaspora" (in areas outside its "homeland") was viewed as "sickly" and "inauthentic." This predicament could be resolved only by returning to the land of Palestine and reassuming a fully authentic existence, where Jews could tend their own soil, and not be restricted to their stereotypical occupations in the diaspora as bankers and money lenders.

This conception of the diaspora as inauthentic and sickly provides the backbone for one of the most prominent recurring themes in Israeli national mythology and the civil religion to which it contributes—the "negation of exile." On this understanding, the nation of Israel can become whole and complete only through the ingathering of Jews from all across the world into the land of Israel, a state of affairs understood to be the *telos* (the "goal") of Jewish history. By contrast, the diasporic (period of time during which Jewish people were "dispersed" throughout other lands) is understood as an empty, undifferentiated time, when the Jews had to reside outside the land of Israel, as if in a holding pattern waiting for their opportunity to return to the homeland. The "teleological" (or goal-directed) understanding enabled the dismissal of millennia of Jewish flourishing in a wide range of diasporic contexts. It glossed over cultural and contextual differences between an array of Jewish communities that were sometimes radically different. It tended to universalize and homogenize Jewish experiences, as if Jews had one voice, a singular experience, and a unified destiny.

In the contexts within Palestine prior to the formal establishment of the state of Israel (what we will refer to as the "prestate"), as well as in the modern Israeli context, the negation of exile has also translated into active rejection of the character of "the diasporic Jew." The "new Hebrew" (the eventual Israeli) represented the antithesis of the passive, pale, learned, and religious Jew in the shtetels (Jewish ghettoes and enclaves) of Europe. The modern Hebrew was heroic, sun kissed, and normal.

The "negation of exile" came to inform various policies and practices in Israeli society. For instance, in the secular educational system of modern Israel, students study the Tanach (or Hebrew Bible) as a purely historical text that connects directly to present-day events. What is not incorporated into the mainstream educational system, however, is the Oral Torah or the midrash and Mishnah—the texts of Jewish wisdom and interpretation. These texts were written in the diaspora and are deemed to reflect those contexts. They are held aside as insignificant to the project of cultivating new Hebrews (Israelis) who bear direct links to the biblical character of Joshua and the story of the conquest of the land of Canaan. Likewise, in the early days of the Zionist project in Palestine, the new city of Tel Aviv held a greater significance in contrast to Jerusalem. Jerusalem represented the "pathologies" of the pre-Zionist Jewish existence since the Jews of Jerusalem subsisted on donations and thus were not self-reliant.

As an organizing motif of national identity, the negation of exile has elastically changed over the years. Sociological works on the dynamic properties of civil religion in Israel suggest that Zionist socialization shifted from its initial emphasis on heroic events related to the Holocaust (e.g., the Warsaw Ghetto Uprising) to Jewish victimhood in European contexts, to the interpretation of the constant existential threat experienced by Jews in Israel. In various ways, life in Israel echoes those familiar themes of Jewish history. Jerusalem has now become a point of fixation for secular and religious Zionists alike. As we discussed in Chapter 1, it was the visit of the former prime minister Ariel Sharon (a self-declared atheist and secular Zionist) to the Dome of the Rock or the Temple Mount, exercising what he referred to as his "eternal right to the eternal Jerusalem," that ignited the second Palestinian intifada. On the occasion of his visit to the contested site, Sharon remarked: "The Temple Mount is in our hands and will remain in our hands. It is the holiest site in Judaism and it is the right of every Jew to visit the Temple Mount" (Goldenberg, 2000).

The discourse of anti-Semitism went a long way in fueling the development of Zionism as a political movement for national self-determination as a likely solution to "the Jewish question." It also aided in cultivating the Zionist conception of the negation of exile. And yet the negation of exile represents a complex and paradoxical element of the character of Zionism as it changes and fluctuates within the realities of nation-statehood. Israeli heroism in the face of imminent death and destruction was also exemplified through the retrieval and celebration of the story of the Bar Kokhba Revolt and the suicidal defense of Massada. These are events that date back to the first century BCE.

The Massada story, as told by Josephus Flavius in his *The Jewish War*, narrates the story of Jewish resistance to the Roman

Empire in the aftermath of the destruction of the Temple (70 CE). Jewish rebels escaped to the fortress of Massada (built by Herod the Great and located in the Judean Desert), overcame Roman forces, and turned the fortress into their base, attracting various zealots who were escaping Jerusalem. Confronting the accumulating Roman artillery in 73 CE, the Jews of Massada committed collective suicide. The Bar Kokhba Revolt (132–136 CE) against the Roman Empire enabled the establishment of an independent Jewish zone over parts of Judea over the course of a couple years, until this effort was finally crushed by the Roman military machinery. In modern Israeli culture, these stories are retrieved and interpreted as the ideal for contemporary heroism, and the lessons are framed with the mantra "Never Again" (or "Massada will not fall again"). That the narratives of Bar Kokhba and Massada became elevated over and against counternarratives that viewed heroism, for instance, as the resilience of the Jews in sustaining their religious tradition and practices in various diasporic contexts—despite the constant possibility of persecutions—highlights the selectivity involved in the construction and reproduction of a national way of life.

Colonialism

Colonialism is another discourse that facilitated the cultivation of Zionism as a viable political movement. Zionism came into being as a nationalist movement for political self-determination under the initial vision and leadership of an assimilated Jew by the name of Theodore Herzl (1860–1904). Being immersed in a colonial context, Herzl was not opposed to shopping the Jewish problem among various imperial powers such as the Ottoman Empire or Great Britain. He sought, in effect, to settle the Jews in any territory that might be made available to them, as long as settlement was accompanied by political autonomy. In other words, the territorial settlement of the Jews did not need to be restricted to Palestine. In fact, as a result of Herzl's discussions with Joseph Chamberlain, the British colonial secretary, and other influential figures within the British colonial framework, Uganda was proposed as a possible territorial context for establishing a national home for the Jews. What came to be known as the Uganda Proposal was ultimately rejected by the delegates to the Seventh Zionist Congress in 1905. In short, for Zionism to materialize as a national movement with popular appeal, its territorial fixation needed to be the land of Palestine, or Zion.

For millennia, Jews the world over have recited the words "Next year in Jerusalem" as part of their daily prayers. Indeed, the *return* to Jerusalem was mostly perceived as an event that would take place outside of, or at the end of, human history, in a messianic moment. This redemptive return to the land also entailed the "ingathering of the exiles" (an idea originating in Deuteronomy 30:1–5) and rebuilding the Temple. The distinction between this messianic conception of return and the political vision of Zionism is of critical importance for the analysis of Israeli and Jewish nationalisms because secular Zionism has entailed physical and historical—what we referred to in Chapter 2 as "embodied"—interpretations of redemption.

In his revolutionary pamphlet Excerpts from Herzl's *The Jewish State* (published in 1896), Herzl's words capture this notion of physical and political redemption and its interrelated conception of Jewish exceptionalism (linking the redemption of the Jewish people with the redemption of humankind). He writes:

> We have sincerely tried everywhere to merge with the national communities in which we live, seeking only to preserve the faith of our fathers . . . In our native lands where we have lived for centuries we are still decried as aliens . . . Oppression and persecution cannot exterminate us. No nation on earth has endured such struggles and sufferings as we have . . . Palestine is our unforgettable historic homeland . . . Let me repeat once more my opening words: The Jews who will it shall achieve their State. We shall live at last as free men on our own soil, and in our own homes peacefully die. The world will be liberated by our freedom, enriched by our wealth, magnified by our greatness. And whatever we attempt there for our own benefit will redound mightily and beneficially to the good of all mankind.

For Herzl, the redemption of the Jewish people was to take place within history rather than at the end of history. This redemption is physical rather than metaphysical or messianic. In this context, the ingathering of the exiles is viewed literally as the need to reconvene the dispersed community back in the homeland. The redemptive qualities of Zionism and of the political project of self-determination in the modern state of Israel were motivated by the catastrophic Holocaust of European Jewry and justified by a shared conception of "near extinction" that has narrated Jewish history as a series of similar catastrophes: the destructions of the Temples in Jerusalem, the exiles, the pogroms, and now the fear of extinction by Israel's neighboring Arab countries and the poisonous effects of the new tide of anti-Semitism.

This dominant Zionist account that focuses on the perception of near extinction selectively appropriates theologically laden motifs such as the ingathering of the exiles and the return to Zion while, for the most part, insisting on the secular character of Israel. It portrays Zionism as an essentially political rather than a religious movement. Notably, Zionism has taken many forms and threads that interlace the aspiration for political self-determination and self-reliance within an autonomous context with other ideological currents, from socialism to free-market capitalism. The Zionist project, in its early days, was also a movement that aspired to create a social utopia with the kibbutz as its symbol of communal living. In the late 1990s, the dominance of neoliberal Reagan-Thatcherite ideological orientations displaced the prominence of the kibbutz and of the social welfare state in favor of privatization, echoing and mirroring the overwhelming logic of free market capitalist global trends.

The Zionist case exemplifies Anthony Smith's analysis of modern nationalism as involving particularly this-worldly redemptive qualities—the gaze of a national movement is upon physical, political, and social redemption within historical time (Smith, 2003). While nationalisms are sometimes anticlerical and even antireligious, they draw selectively on religion in the process of imagining, constituting, and perpetuating themselves. The selective retrieval of religious and cultural imageries, symbols, rituals, and narratives attests to the relevance of religion to the imagining of national consciousness. It also hints as to why religion so often becomes critical to processes of reimagining and reinterpreting the boundaries of a national identity. As we show in detail later in this chapter, the emergence to the fore of religious Zionism does not need to be analyzed as antithetical to secular Zionism, but rather as amplifying some of the basic tenets of secular Zionism, and in some instances, carrying those tenets to their full conclusions. In many respects (and as in the case of the Canaanite movement), the religious Zionism that fuels efforts to settle the biblical lands of Judea, Samaria, and Galilee (the settlement movement) is resolving the many conceptual inconsistencies of secular Zionism.

Orientalism

We have argued that it is insufficient to assess Zionism as a purely political movement with a secular agenda and thus a movement that can compartmentalize conceptions of Judaism as a set of religious beliefs, and Judaism as nationality, ethnicity, history, and culture. That the territorial destination of the state of Israel had to be Zion (or Palestine) rather than Uganda, and Zionism's reliance on the biblical and theological motifs of dispersion, return, and the ingathering of the exiles, indicates both the particular ambiguities of Zionism as a form of allegedly secular nationalism, and the power of the dynamic affinities between ethnicity, nationality, and the religious imaginations.

The Uganda Proposal (forwarded at the Sixth Zionist Congress at Basel, Switzerland, on August 26, 1903) failed in large part because the imagining of a modern Jewish national consciousness necessitated conjuring selectively from antecedent cultural and religious motifs that resonated powerfully in the popular imaginations. The desire to be recognized in the truest sense as "a people" overrode the value of being collected together as a geographically unified population. Thus while intense discussions surrounded the Uganda Proposal, primarily due to the urgency presented by pogroms against Eastern European Jews and rising anti-Semitism throughout Europe, Zion had to be the destination for implementing the idea of Jewish political and territorial autonomy. An opponent of Herzl's political Zionism, Ahad Ha'am, countered that once Judaism ceased to be a "supernatural religion" (as it must, he claimed, since supernatural belief was no longer tenable in a modern world characterized by reason and science), Judaism would achieve its fulfillment as a national culture. As such, it would hold on to its various religious concepts, symbols, and stories as well as revive Hebrew as a national language. However, it would transform all of these into allegedly nonreligious (cultural and national) senses. As such, the Jewish people would have to return to Palestine itself, which would enable "the spiritual rebirth of the Jewish nation." The nation would thereby live out its choseness (understood as a purely historical legacy, rather than a divine appointment) (Batnitzky, 2011,

155–160). Whether this Jewish autonomy was to be established in Palestine or Uganda, the Zionist leadership recognized that the process entailed dealing extensively with colonial and imperial powers. That leadership gave a lesser amount of thought to how Jewish colonization might affect and displace local communities, whether in Palestine or in Uganda.

A minority of Zionist leaders and thinkers did acknowledge this as a problematic issue that had to constrain and challenge the Zionist agenda (e.g., Martin Buber, 1983). But the general tenor of the Zionist movement is captured in the Zionist slogan "A Land without People to a People without a Land." This slogan reflects Zionism's enmeshment within the colonial imagination. Additionally, this image of Palestine as a land without people is not only silencing the Palestinian presence as the collateral damage of the process and imperative of Jewish return to the land, but also this image resonates with representation of the biblical land as if it were frozen in time. This inclination is reflected in travelers' representations of Palestine in the 19th century (Christison, 1999). Those representations depicted the biblical landscape as sacred geography, glossing over the concrete realities of its actual inhabitants. Often, travelers' accounts would represent the Arab inhabitants of Palestine as idealized biblical figures (a version of the colonial motif of the "noble savage") blending into the topography of the Bible. This glossing over the concreteness of Palestine can be understood in the context of the discourse of orientalism which, as we showed in previous chapters, involves deciphering how knowledge production about, and representation of, Islam and the Orient are related to the power of empire as well as to religious and cultural imaginations.

Thus in many respects, the discourses of colonialism and orientalism enabled Zionism to materialize as a viable national movement focused on a particular territory as its destination. Those discourses oriented Zionism by a teleological conception of Jewish destiny, thereby silencing the diversity and multilocality of Jewish diasporas. This amounted to universalizing Jewish history, turning diversity into uniformity. The term "universal" here refers to the portrayal of Jewish people as constituting one body or one People whose diasporic condition could be likened to a dismembered body. This unifying logic, we show later in this chapter, came under strong criticism from Mizrahi (Arab Jews; i.e. , Jews who trace their ancestry to Arab and Islamic countries) and by non-nationalist Jewish critics of Zionism.

The fixation on Palestine as the destination for Jewish political redemption was similarly aided by the emergence of Christian Zionism in Europe and the United States, and the active support of influential people associated with this movement of the Jewish Zionist project. The support of Christian Zionism has remained a critical aspect for any attempt at analyzing the dynamics of the Israeli-Palestinian conflict (Merkley, 1998; Clark, 2007; Spector, 2009). In the theological imagination of Christian Zionists, the end-time drama (as Christians understand it) involves the ingathering of the Jews in Palestine. While this understanding has translated into overwhelming support of the Zionist project, and later of the state of Israel, this form of philo-Semitism—one that celebrates the Jewish state and its exclusionary and territorially maximalist practices—turns into blatant anti-Semitism when, upon the Second Coming, all Jews will either have to convert or perish.

Christian Zionism is not merely a fringe movement; rather, it has influenced the perception of cultural affinity between Americans and Jews in Israel (McAlister, 2001). The *Left Behind* series of 16 fictional novels based on the biblical book of Revelation—and the unique role their stories ascribe to the state of Israel within a Christian evangelical account of the apocalypse (the divinely determined end of the world)—has sold over 63 million copies. Five of the titles in the series held the top spot on the *New York Times* bestseller list, and altogether the series generated two feature films and further book series (Frykholm, *Rapture Culture*, 2004). Many key figures in the U.S. Congress are thoroughly influenced by Christian Zionist currents. A perception of cultural affinity with the Jewish state is also aided by how it resonates with the American way of life and in particular, the perceived mythological origin of the United States in the form of a Puritan settlement that would be a "city upon a hill" and a "new Israel." This perception is further aided by the discourse of orientalism that positions American identity as Judeo-Christian.

Domestically, this account of the character of American national identity has facilitated the emergence of Islamophobia in the United States, especially in the aftermath of the September 11, 2001, terrorist attacks upon the United States. In terms of foreign affairs, it has enabled some to frame the Israeli-Palestinian conflict as exemplifying the "clash of civilizations" argument that we discussed in Chapter 2. Israel is often depicted as a democratic stronghold in the midst of a region that is hostile to individual rights and liberties, democracy, and religious freedom. To this extent, Israel is rendered as a part of "the West" even if it is located geographically in the Orient. Clearly, this logic has been increasingly scrutinized with the phenomenon known as the Arab Spring, one that not only marked democratic and nonviolent revolutions, but also exposed the problematic nature of U.S. support of authoritarian regimes across the Middle East and North Africa.

Many Americans' deep dedication to Israel also came under scrutiny with the publication of the controversial book *The Israel Lobby and U.S. Foreign Policy* by John Mersheimer and Stephen M. Walt (2007). The thesis of these coauthors is that, in its persistent support of Israel, the United States has acted against its own political interests in the regions of the Middle East and North Africa. This argument necessitated a probe into why this has been the case—a line of questioning that brings to the fore what usually is bracketed in political science, namely a cultural and social analysis of the patterns and reasons of cultural and social formations. In other words, to adequately understand why the United States persists in acting against its geopolitical interests by aiding Israel, one must engage in a cultural and discursive analysis.

The orientalist and colonialist discourses that enabled the privileged support of Jewish Israeli claims and interests over and against Palestinian ones were also deeply internalized by Zionists themselves. We demonstrated earlier in this chapter how the discourse of anti-Semitism is integral to the articulation of Zionism as a political project, and how it relates to the ethos of the negation of exile, an ethos that homogenized and universalized Jewish history and identity. Orientalism and eurocentrism further facilitated these processes. The dominant Zionist leadership also cultivated the self-identification of Israel as a Western country, enlightened and democratic, attributes that allegedly contrast starkly to Arab and Islamic cultural contexts. Orientalist brushstrokes were also deployed to depict the Arab Jews (Jews who could trace their ancestry to Arab and/or Islamic regions). With the realization of the extent of the catastrophe of European Jewry (i.e., the Holocaust), Arab Jews became a group necessary for the fruition of the Zionist dream. They became assimilated into a Zionist account as a necessary demographic group, though of a lesser quality. The processes by which they were incorporated into the Zionist project largely humiliated them. On many occasions they were segregated into camps, sanitized, and systematically discriminated against (Omer, 2013, Chapter 7).

A variety of Israeli scholars and critics have shown that the Eurocentricity and orientalism of the early Zionist establishment overwhelmed internal diversities. Ironically, despite its secularity, this establishment prioritized Judaism as the entry ticket to an Israeli society. This also meant that for Arab Jews, assimilation into a Zionist frame required that they, in effect, split their Arab and Jewish identities, identities that were previously interwoven, or interrelated, without any sense of oxymoronic contradiction.

Arab Jews and Mizrahim: Challenges to Monolithic National Identity

Arab Jews (the Mizrahim), compared with European Jews, took a different approach to religiosity, an approach born out of their peculiar experiences in Arab and Islamic contexts. Unlike Jews in European contexts, they did not experience the same kind of pogroms and the antireligion critique and assimilationist pressures associated with the emergence of secularization in Europe and the European Enlightenments. In the Israeli context, the Mizrahim became closely associated with militant approaches to the Palestinian conflict and with ethnocentric interpretations of Israeli identity. This does not mark something about their "essence" as a sector within Israeli society. Rather, it is indicative of the overwhelming pressure to amplify their Jewishness over and against their Arabness (Shenhav, 2006). This inclination can partially explain the emergence of Shas to the political foreground in the 1980s.

Shas

Shas is an acronym for the political party Shomrei Torah Sepharadim (observant Sepharadim, or Jews of "Oriental" or Spanish origin). This party was formed in 1984 to increase Sephardic and Mizrahi representation politically and religiously within the Israeli framework. Accordingly, the Shas movement directed its attention to exercising political pressure in order to secure funding for its alternative religious educational system, and for ensuring representation of Sephardic traditions and mores as part of the Israeli religious establishment. To this extent, Shas has dissented from the dominant Ashkenazi (i.e., central and eastern

European Jewish) interpretations of Judaism which informed the official rabbinate (Lehmann and Siebzenhner, 2007).

On the social justice front, Shas has capitalized on the experiences of disenfranchised Mizrahim who have been struggling with the systemic implications of their disadvantaged location within Israeli society. Shas has provided social services as well as an antiestablishment rallying cry. The religiosity of this movement has not constituted a deterrent to its popular base due to the Mizrahi inclination to be more accepting of tradition than are mainstream secular Ashkenazi Israeli citizens; in addition, Arab Jews see that it was their Judaism that granted them a ticket for full participation in the Zionist framework. Notably, however, the leadership of Shas is Haredi (ultraorthodox). This profile is an interesting and unique feature of Israeli religiosity. The leaders of Shas were incubated in European yeshivas, thereby assuming the Haredi lifestyle that is a distinct import from Eastern Europe.

Shas has gained momentum politically because of the particularities of the Israeli parliamentary system. The party managed to gain sufficient mandates or seats in the Knesset (the Israeli parliament) to enable it to exert pressure with a focus on channeling funds to its schools and social infrastructures. This has been a movement with a significant popular momentum that has changed the political landscape in important ways. As is the case in other contexts (e.g., Hizb'allah in Lebanon and the Hamas movement in Palestine), the networks and infrastructures of social services and their overlaps with religious learning and worship centers (madrasa and mosques in Islamic contexts, yeshivas in Jewish contexts) also provide a ready infrastructure for mobilization and recruitment.

It is now hardly shocking to see political leaders vying for photo opportunities with and endorsements of Shas's spiritual leaders. One may wonder why self-described secularists and even atheist Israeli Jews are compelled to seek out the endorsement of rabbinic authorities. This peculiarity is especially acute when we contrast such efforts with early prestate ethos and Israeli civil religion that heralded the image of the new Hebrew as not only physically liberated from the threat of near extinction that comes with landlessness and deterritorialization, but also liberated from the shackles of tradition. Recall that the early decades of the Israeli nation-state were dominated by Ashkenazi worldviews and experiences, which were interlaced with broader Eurocentric and orientalist undertones as well as a strong critique of religion born out of particularly European experiences. Shas gave an outlet for counter voices and counternarratives, and has offered an important critique of the hegemony of Ashkenazi religiosity and antireligiosity.

While its adherents tend to support territorial maximalism and chauvinistic trends, this can be explained as a function of internalized orientalist discourses that dichotomized "Arab" and "Jew" and positioned these identities as if they were antinomies. Importantly, Rav Ovadia Yoseph, the spiritual leader of the movement, supported the withdrawal from Sinai, grounding his reasoning on the religious principle of *pikuach nefesh* (i.e., saving lives could annul other obligations). This support of territorial withdrawal suggests Shas's pragmatic approach to politics and to positions vis-à-vis the Israeli-Palestinian conflict. The movement's pragmatism is grounded in its initially indifferent attitude to Zionism and the Zionist political project, and its subsequent instrumental relations with state infrastructures. We qualified the preceding statement with the word "initially" to denote that both the state or the political landscape, as well as Shas itself, were transformed as a result of the utilitarian and symbiotic relations of mutual co-optation.

How could Shas, as a Jewish Israeli political party, be indifferent to Zionism? To respond to this query, we need to underscore that perhaps the most fervent opposition to the Zionist movement came from observant ultraorthodox (Haredi) Jews. This is precisely because the political secular movement of Zionism has cast itself in terms of human agency within historical time as opposed to divine agency and metaphysical (messianic) time in the process of redemption. In doing so, the movement has violated the traditional Jewish prohibitions against following false messiahs and idolatrous notions, such as redemption of the people through mass return to Zion (Ravitzky, 1996).

It is through this analytic lens that Zionism, however, exemplifies what Benedict Anderson described as one of the novel conditions that facilitated the emergence of the phenomenon of modern nationalism, that is, a radical shift in the conception of time from vertical (and messianic) to horizontal (and empty), a shift he took to be concurrent with the demise of religious empires (2006, 24). Zionism further exemplifies Anthony Smith's point about reinterpreting redemption as this-worldly, a helpful insight for explaining why national movements also carry normative conceptions about the types of social contract that ought to be implemented within the boundaries of the polity (2003).

Precisely those modern characteristics of Zionism profoundly contradicted the religious worldviews of observant Jews. Some sectors within the Haredi Jewish world have remained persistently anti-Zionist. A group by the name of Neturei Karta is a prominent example. Even if, as a result of the Holocaust, many affiliates of Neturei Karta reside within the geopolitical boundaries of Israel, they perceive their predicament to be "diasporic" nonetheless.

Shas, by contrast, is not anti-Zionist. However, as noted earlier in this chapter, its acceptance of the Israeli state is, many analysts suggest, merely instrumental and pragmatic. Therefore, the group is often seen as non-Zionist. This approach to the Israeli state may be attributed to Shas's incubation within the Haredi sectors and its subsequent assumption of traditional patterns of dependency on secular infrastructures. A lack of self-reliance of the prestate Jewish inhabitants of Jerusalem was a target for secular Zionists who wished to reinvent themselves as self-reliant.

As indicated earlier in this chapter, to dismiss Shas as merely engaging in a utilitarian relationship with the state would amount to caricaturing complex and dynamic processes of mutual transformation of both Shas and the broader Israeli sociopolitical fields. Scrutinizing Shas's activities, proclaimed agenda, and reflections by individual activists and leaders indicates that rather than rejecting Zionism, Shas endeavors to reimagine Zionism and especially integrate religion into this re-envisioning of an Israeli identity.

The integration of religion involves deconstructing Ashkenazi hegemony in religious matters as well as giving a voice to disenfranchised Mizrahim. While exhibiting an occasional degree of pragmatism on the front of the Israeli-Palestinian conflict (using tactics of political manipulations enabled by parliamentary politics that often depend on coalition formation with small parties), the leaders of Shas, for the most part, are inclined to portray the "Arab" as a mortal enemy who is normatively of a lesser quality. This translates into an inclination to lend support and reinforcement of ethnocentric and chauvinistic motifs within the Israeli ethos and provides a political expression for internalized Ashkenazi interpretations of Israeli identity. The false dichotomizing between "Arab" and "Jew" exposes the reliance of secular Zionism on Judaism (or a certain reading of Jewish sources) for its legitimization.

Israeli sociologist Yehouda Shenhav offers a fascinating analysis of how secular (and often atheist) Zionist emissaries sent to Iraq as well as other Islamic and Arab contexts in the prestate period construed the "Arab Jews" they sought to recruit into the Zionist movement. Shenhav identifies an intriguing and telling paradox in which the relative secularity of Arab Jews was downplayed. He writes: "The emissaries projected religiosity onto the Iraqi Jews, imputing religious feelings and sentiments to them in a way that reflected their own desire both to erase the difference between themselves and the Arab Jews at the national level and recreate it" (Shenhav, 2006, 104). What this statement suggests is precisely the process of homogenizing and universalizing Jewish history and identity, on one hand, and delineating internal differences, a process thoroughly reliant on the discourses of eurocentrism and orientalism. The prestate reports of Zionist emissaries to Arab and Islamic contexts highlight how the emissaries' self-characterization as "secular" was intricately bound to a particular political theology. "Why couldn't the emissaries accommodate the ostensible secularism among Arab Jews? Why did they project piety onto them?" Shenhav asks, "First, in order to erase their Arabness, as an act of de-Arabization. Here, religion is a signifier of their orientalist and colonialist perspective. Second, in order to define them as Zionists. Here religion is a signifier of ethnicity" (2006, 104–105). This discourse facilitated differentiating between Judaism qua ethnicity, nationality, and religion, essentializing each identity marker in the process and domesticating the "ethnic" and "religious" rifts as separated from discussions of the Israeli-Palestinian conflict.

That the enduring Ashkenazi political elite feels obliged to secure photo opportunities with Sephardic religious authorities, and that that elite grants them social, financial, and political gains, then, reflects the logic in which religious leaders become influential through an amplified cycle of political attempts to legitimize a national, political agenda. This observation concerning these patterns still does not explain *why* legitimacy is sought within the religious sectors.

Shenhav's reflection on the paradoxical pattern of concurrently differentiating yet conflating conceptions of Judaism as ethnicity, nationality, and religiosity provides a lens that helps account for why a movement like Shas has gained political momentum. In addition to its social justice ticket, on which it claims to represent the disadvantaged and disenfranchised Mizrahim, Shas also provides clues to the kind of discourses that enabled the construal of Israeli identity along exclusionary and

ethnocentric lines. As in other contexts, religion here contributes
to exclusionary conceptions of national identity through normative (yet highly selective) authorization of national narratives
and claims, and through the institutional mechanisms and networks of religious groups. Thus in the same manner in which religion can influence interpretations of identity in generating greater
belligerence and exclusivity, it can also swing the pendulum in
the other direction toward greater inclusivity, social justice, and
conflict transformation.

Despite the occasional pragmatic approach to the peace
process with the Palestinians, Shas—as well as other explicitly
religious political parties—is associated with ethnocentric interpretations of citizenship which are subsequently rendered as
"obstacles" to peace. Within this framework, liberal (mostly Ashkenazi) Israelis are portrayed as participants in liberal conceptions of the community, which is subsequently perceived as the
engine for peace. The underlying assumptions fall apart when
one studies how a group like Rabbis for Human Rights (RHR)
offers a critique, grounded explicitly in the tradition of Jewish
humanism, of Israeli expansionist policies in the Occupied Territories. RHR further connects questions of social justice pertaining
to gender discrimination, the status of Palestinian citizens of
Israel, foreign labor, Bedouin, and Mizrahim to its struggle for
the rights of Palestinians beyond the Green Line (the borders
demarcating Israel between 1948 and 1967) and in the refugee
camps (Omer, Chapter 5). Likewise, one of the greatest prophetic
critiques of nationalism as idolatry in the Israeli Jewish context
came from the Jewish scholar and public intellectual Yeshayahu
Leibowitz (1992).

The ambiguities and the paradoxes of secular Zionism,
therefore, demonstrate that analyses that view religion as necessarily associated with belligerence are overly simplistic. Not only
do such analyses gloss over the forms of structural and cultural
violence inflicted on Mizrahim in Israel, but they also overlook
the religious dimensions of secular Zionism. They overlook
how the political theology of secular Zionism becomes an
obstacle to justice and peace in the context of the Israeli-
Palestinian conflict (Omer, 2013). The commitment to a Jewish
democratic nation-state cannot be understood merely in demographic terms, especially not considering our discussion earlier
in the chapter of how essentially theological categories and
motifs such as "return" and the "ingathering of the exiles"

figure into Zionist mythology. We saw that the secular emissaries had to come to terms with Zionism's conceptual reliance on religion.

The "Gush"

Rather than presenting a polar opposite of secular nationalism or Zionism, the settlement movement, which often is the focus of discussions related to religious nationalism in Israel, amplifies the theological motifs inherent in Zionism. The phenomenon called religious Zionism is most closely associated with the Gush Emunim (literally, the Block of the Faithful) movement. Gush Emunim was established in 1974, in the aftermath of the Yom Kippur War. This movement provided the ideological backbone for a variety of organizations focused on the Greater Land of Israel through the policy of active settlement in the West Bank and the Gaza Strip. Adherents of this territorial maximalism refer to these territories by their biblical names, Judea and Samaria, thereby imposing biblical topography over geopolitical realities. In the 1980s, the movement morphed into the Yesha Council, Yesha being the acronym in Hebrew for Judea, Samaria, and Gaza.

The ideological tenets of Gush Emunim attempted to resolve the theological challenges posed by secular Zionism, namely the assumption of human agency as the engine of history. The emergence of Gush Emunim also signified the desire of religious youth to integrate meaningfully into the Israeli state and the Zionist dream, despite their realization that they could not subscribe to this dream as presented by the ruling ideology, with its secular and even antireligious tones. The youth wanted to locate the religious significance of the political project as well as resolve the theological contradictions and transgressions it presented. They found their answers in the teachings of Rav Abraham Isaac Kook (1865–1935), as interpreted by his son Zvi Yehuda Kook (1891–1982) in the context of his Torah learning center or Merkaz ha-Rav Yeshiva in Jerusalem.

Rav Kook (the father) was the first Ashkenazi chief rabbi of the British mandate for Palestine. In his teachings, he attempted to find a synthesis between religious conceptions of messianic history and secular Zionism. One of his intellectual influences was Hegel and his work on history. Rav Kook, accordingly, did not view the secular movement of Zionism as constituting a violation of the principles of Jewish messianic history. Rather, he rendered this movement as a part of or instrumental to the fulfillment of this history. Another critical influence on Kook's thought can be found in Kabbalistic teachings (Jewish mysticism) and the space they allow for human agency in the redemptive process of the world (*Tikkun Olam*, in Hebrew).

One of the problems that the elder Kook addressed was a sense of the fragmentation of the Jewish community as a result of various currents and processes associated with modernity. He was especially concerned with the profound rift between Zionism and its opponents from within the Jewish community. His undertaking, which provides explicit theological meanings to Zionism, was augmented by his calls to his coreligionists to cooperate with the Zionist impulse, sometimes despite Zionists' lack of awareness of the theological significance of their political project and despite their often self-proclaimed atheism. The Zionists were sacred despite themselves, while orthodox Jews' resistance to Zionism became a subject of critique. In their conservatism, Kook argued, they failed to read the signs of the time. In a signature essay, Kook writes to this effect, endorsing the work of the often iconoclastic Zionists as holy (without them necessarily being aware of it) and as part of the unfolding of a redemptive drama:

> These passionate souls reveal their strength so that no fence can hold them back; and the weaklings of the established order, who are guided by balance and propriety, are too terrified to tolerate them. Their mood is expressed in Isaiah (33:14): "Who among us can dwell with the devouring fire? Who among us can dwell with those who destroy the world?" But in truth there is no need to be terrified. Only sinners, those weak in spirit and hypocrites, are frightened and seized by terror. Truly heroic spirits know that this force is one of the phenomena needed for the perfection of the world, for strengthening the power of the nation, of man and of the world. Initially this force represents the realm of the chaotic, but in the end it will be taken from the wicked and turned over to the hands of the righteous who will show the truth about perfection and construction, in a

great resoluteness, inspired by clear perception and a
steady and undimmed sense of the practical. (1978,
257–258)

The younger Kook took the helm of Merkaz ha-Rav Yeshivah after
the death of his father. Kook (the son) is often called the popular-
izer of religious Zionism. However, he was significantly less
learned and versed in Jewish wisdom and in broader intellectual
traditions than his father, and his ideological construal of religious Zionism was significantly more ethnocentric than his
father's envisioning of the redemptive qualities of the Zionist
project.

A scholar of Gush Emunim and modern Jewish orthodoxy,
Gideon Aran of the Hebrew University, argues that it is not clear
whether the emergence of the Gush could be attributed to the
leadership of Rabbi Zvi Yehuda Kook or the desire of the Merkaz
ha-Rav Yeshivah's students to find consistency and harmony
between their religiosity and the Zionist project.

Aran studies the fundamental influence of a precursor youth
movement by the name of Gahelet (literally, "the Embers"). He
explains the emergence of both Gush Emunim and the antecedent
Gahelet as indicative of the radicalization of religious Zionism, an
upshot of an attempt to negotiate between modern society and
orthodoxy as well as between Judaism and Zionism. "Against
the background of the challenge of a secular modernity (in the
guise of Zionism) poised to conquer Judaism, and of the seeming
inability of the 'national religious' option to meet it, *Gahelet*
offered a new solution to the problem. It approached Judaism
and Zionism as a unity, and embarked on a course of dual radicalization: a more extreme Orthodoxy together with a more
extreme nationalism" (Aran, 1986, 137). Thus while the cataclys-
mic events of the wars of 1967 and 1973 are often identified as
the subtext for the emergence of the settlement movement (sud-
denly after millennia the Jews were reunited with the sacred sites
of their ancestral lands, the mythology goes), Aran's thesis suggests that these historical moments provide an insufficient
explanatory framework.

Aran, instead, locates the emergence of militant religious
Zionism in a broader historical context of modernity. Its emergence
"was a reaction to political secularism born within a defeated and

bewildered Orthodoxy" (Aran, 1986, 119). In many respects, it signaled a process of marginalization of the religious sectors born out of the structures and rhetoric of modern secular nationalism, a phenomenon observed in many other contexts as diverse as the United States, India, and Egypt.

Against the backdrop of the preceding extensive exploration of the case of religious nationalism in Israel, let us explore similar patterns as they pertain to the case of the United States. The intention here is not to provide an exhaustive account of religious nationalism in U.S. contexts, but rather to point to similar and dissimilar patterns than those observed in the preceding scrutiny of the Israeli case. This comparative angle can facilitate our attempt to think generally and conceptually about the phenomenon of religious nationalism.

A "New Israel": Puritan and Enlightenment Roots of Religious Nationalism in the United States

Despite the institutional separation of church and state, Protestant Christianity not only remains historically central, but also continues to affect both inclusivist and exclusivist interpretations of nationhood in the United States. On one hand, one can argue that the United States has an interpretation of nationalism that is rooted in modernist and Enlightenment conceptions of religion, individual autonomy, and freedom of conscience. On the other hand, forms of U.S. nationalism fairly consistently draw upon a variety of motifs that emerge from Puritan Christian traditions. This repertoire of nationalist concepts, symbols, and stories can be traced back to an early group (often mischaracterized as the original group) of European settlers of New England who believed themselves to be in a unique relationship to their God and that their journey to religious freedom was fulfillment of their destiny as the new Israel.

The Puritans who settled Massachusetts Bay based their civic and political practices upon several specifically Christian theological concepts. Some of the most central concepts were election, providence, vocation, and covenant. *Election* is an understanding that oneself or one's people have been specially chosen by God;

providence refers to the belief that, as God is the creator and sustainer of the world and history, God is also at work to accomplish what God wills to bring about within history, either directly or by working through human affairs; *vocation* (literally, "calling") is the sense that God has bestowed upon one a special purpose as an instrument by which God will accomplish God's purposes in history. These concepts were oriented by the biblical practice of *covenant*, a concept that the Puritans understood on a model drawn from the Old Testament scriptures as a contractual relationship, initiated by God, the terms of which were based upon the moral law instituted by God. The separatist Puritans understood their journey to the New World largely in terms of these theological concepts, and the biblical narratives from which these concepts came. They believed that the society they would establish would have a unique relationship with God and thus unique significance in world history. They interpreted their own flight from England in 1620 as a new version of the people of Israel's flight from slavery in Egypt, as narrated in the biblical book of Exodus.

In the story recounted in Exodus, God leads the Hebrews, God's chosen people, out of enslavement by the Egyptian Pharaoh, across the Red Sea and Sinai wilderness to the Promised Land of Canaan. The Puritans believed that, similarly, God was guiding them though the perilous journey across the Atlantic Ocean, to arrive in the wilderness of Cape Cod (Springs, 2012, 32). Quoting from Jesus's Sermon on the Mount (Matthew 5:14–16), John Winthrop, eventual governor of the Massachusetts Bay Colony, captured the Puritans' sense of providentially guided mission in lines that have come to be quoted throughout the 20th century to describe the United States' role in history:

> We shall find that the God of Israel is among us, when ten of us shall be able to resist a thousand of our enemies; when He shall make us a praise and glory that men shall say of succeeding plantations, "may the Lord make it like that of New England." For we must consider that we shall be as a city upon a hill. The eyes of all people are upon us. So that if we shall deal falsely with our God in this work we have undertaken, and so cause Him to withdraw His present help from us, we shall be made a story and a by-word through the world. (Winthrop, 149)

A similar account of national providential mission can be found in the writings of the two Kooks. Based on his Kabbalistic training, Kook the elder developed the connection between a Jewish national redemption and the redemption of humanity in a more nuanced manner than his son. The latter's teachings focused more on the ethnocentric redemption of Israel, without connecting it to a broader redemption of humanity. In any case, our account of Zionism earlier in this chapter illustrates that rather than occupying a polar opposite, the exclusivist interpretation of the nation born out of a conception of special divine destiny is rather located along a continuum with the implicit theology of secular Zionism and its historical, but nonetheless religious, imagination. Further, nationalisms have not only been about political self-determination, they have also entailed a particular normative interpretation of the "good society."

Of course, to tell of the Hebrew exodus from Egypt purely as a story of a people's liberation from bondage is to tell only half the story. That account hides what happened to all the people who were already living in the land that the Hebrews understood to be promised to them by their God. The biblical book of Deuteronomy (Chapter 20) continues that, having arrived in the Promised Land, God commanded the Hebrews to lay siege to the cities that they found there. They were instructed to wipe out the people who did not accept their terms for peace and to enslave those that did (Springs, 2012, 36).

In a similar way, the most influential versions of the Puritans' arrival in the New World obscure the fact that the allegedly uninhabited wilderness in which the Puritans arrived, and into which they quickly expanded, already had large numbers of indigenous peoples living in it. The Thanksgiving holiday in the United States recollects and re-enacts a mythic account of the "First Thanksgiving" in 1621 as one of friendly relations with the Wampanoag Indians of Massachusetts. And yet along with their vocation, or sense of having been called by God, to subdue and settle the wilderness of the new world, the Puritan settlers brought smallpox with them. Between 1633 and 1644, the indigenous population was devastated by smallpox outbreaks. The Puritans interpreted these developments as evidence of their role in God's providential mission. "[I]f God were not pleased with our inheriting these parts, why did he drive out the natives before us?" John Winthrop wrote in 1634. "And why dothe he still make roome for us, by deminishinge them as we increase?"

(1929–1944, 149). By 1675, the European settler population in New England had grown to 75,000. The Native American population in New England, by contrast, had diminished to 15,000 (Venables, 2004, 90). The decimation and displacement of the indigenous population occurred through a combination of epidemics brought by the European settlers, expansion of their settlements, and warfare against the Indians (Springs, 2012, 36–37).

Separation of Church and State

The Puritan settlers of Massachusetts Bay may have been seeking religious freedom, but they viewed God's law as the basis for both social morality and political governance. In fact, they looked to God's governance of Israel in the Old Testament for principles to inform their political system. They did not extend the principle of religious freedoms to dissidents. They viewed unorthodox beliefs and practices as challenges to the social order itself. They used the coercive powers of government to enforce orthodox belief and religious practice, expelling or executing any who were identified as dissidents.

Roger Williams was expelled from the Massachusetts Bay Colony because he was deemed too radical and unorthodox in his views and practices. He established a new colony in Rhode Island that identified itself as broadly tolerant of diverse religious beliefs. Williams based this view upon his belief that governments must avoid regulating personal conscience. When the church takes on political responsibilities, Williams argued, it corrupts its spiritual identity. For similar reasons, William Penn established a colony in Pennsylvania that provided space for a religious group that was deemed unorthodox, the Quakers. Quaker missionaries had been persecuted by Puritans in Massachusetts, and in some cases even put to death. In 1649, Lord Baltimore's colony of Maryland passed the Religious Act, which required religious tolerance for all Christians, so long as they adhered to the basic doctrine of the Trinity (Corrigan and Neal, 2010, 22–23).

Roger Williams's views emerged from his Christian worldview. And yet on certain points, those views were consistent with the Enlightenment philosophy of deism, another important basis of the religious heritage of U.S. national identity. Deism emphasized human reason over divine revelation. It claimed that human reason was capable of discerning certain basic moral truths as self-evident (plainly and uncontroversially true for any who would take the time to think reasonably about them), and that these truths had been inscribed in the basic operation of the natural order ("the Laws of Nature") by the divine being that had created it ("Nature's God"). The principles of deism influenced many civil and religious authorities across the new colonies as well as the Founding Fathers, who established the principles and ideals that would form the basis of the United States. Deist influences are perhaps most succinctly and famously evident in Thomas Jefferson's opening lines of the Declaration of Independence: "We hold these truths to be self evident, that all men are created equal and endowed by their Creator with certain unalienable Rights, that among these are Life, Liberty, and the pursuit of Happiness" (Jefferson, Declaration of Independence).

Of course, deism was not without exclusivist impulses. In fact, it helped set the stage for the religious/secular dichotomy, which in turn fuels the misconception that religious nationalism is intrinsically more fanatical and essentially less rational than secular nationalism. John Locke, a 17th-century philosopher whose writings about religion were sometimes associated with deism (though Locke was not himself a deist), argued that religion could be "good" in so far as it was constrained by the limits of reason, tolerant of opposing claims to truth, and domesticated (i.e., kept to its proper place the private sphere of personal belief and opinion). In writings such as *The Reasonableness of Christianity* (1695), Locke made the case that reasonably held religious beliefs stood in stark contrast to what he called the religious enthusiasts of his day. Such enthusiasts, he argued, refused to weigh and measure the reasonableness of what they took to be revelation from God. The result was socially dangerous. By contrast, a reasonable approach to religious belief would promote social stability and peace.

Heavily influenced by their readings of Locke, deists like Thomas Jefferson believed that the moral teachings of Christianity would provide moral instruction that could help the members of the polity become better citizens, as long as what they deemed to be archaic and superstitious content of that religion (e.g., biblical accounts of Jesus's miraculous acts) were removed, or at least downplayed in the public sphere. Jefferson believed that the supernatural claims of traditional religion could quickly become dangerous because they encouraged unreasonableness and invited superstition. Unconstrained, they were liable to generate social instability and harm the overall health of the polity. Jefferson thought the solution to this dilemma was not only to relegate such forms of religion to the private sphere, but to promote reasonable religion.

Jefferson thus took it upon himself to make available a "critically revised" edition of the Christian New Testament that could aid people generally in focusing upon what was morally edifying in Jesus's teachings (especially for civic purposes), while sidestepping the portions of the New Testament that tended toward what he considered destructive superstition. Jefferson thus sifted through the New Testament, cutting out all the references to miracles and supernatural occurrences. He aimed to exclude any dimension of Christian scripture, belief, and practice that could prove exclusivist, irrational, and intolerant, and thus socially and politically volatile. Jefferson's effort to make religion broadly encompassing enough to provide moral support for civil society and political life provide examples of how self-identified "inclusivist" perspectives on religion and national identity perpetrate their own forms of exclusivism (their own intolerance of intolerance). They do so against the backdrop of a secular/religion framework that views particular religions as tending or being inclined toward exclusiveness, irrationality, and volatility (from which the operations of the state must be protected) in ways that nonreligious ideologies (e.g., liberalism) allegedly are not.

It is crucial to note that the different legacies of Jefferson and Williams converged in their assertion that church and government should be kept separate. And yet each arrived at this conclusion from different directions. While Jefferson (like Locke before him) argued "that the church would corrupt the state," Williams feared that "the state would corrupt the church" (Marsden, 1990, 19). This dual legacy came to be inscribed in the First Amendment to the U.S. Constitution, which prohibits Congress from making laws that respect an established religion, thus protecting the state from the church. At the same time, the First Amendment prohibits Congress from passing laws that prohibit the free exercise of religion, thus protecting the church from the state (Marsden, 1990, 45).

The idea that the First Amendment sets up a rigid wall that separates church and state—and thus religion from politics—has come to be heralded by many as a defining feature of U.S. society. And yet this rigid understanding of the doctrine of separation of church and state, and the actual meaning and practical applications of the First Amendment, have been actually quite contested and far from thoroughly consistent across cases (Thiemann, 1996, 42–66). Marsden writes, "In fact, the best explanation of the Constitution's stance on religion is very simple. The Constitution stays away almost entirely from the subject of religion. The only thing it says is that 'no religious test shall ever be required' for public office." He continues:

> [T]he framers of the Constitution were political realists. They knew that getting the new document ratified was going to be a very close call. In the religiously divided tribal United States, nothing could kill the proposal quicker than to take a stand on religion. So the framers said as little as possible about the subject, not even invoking any pious language. (1990, 45–46)

The legacies of Roger Williams and Thomas Jefferson diverged in a particularly important respect: Williams objected to the Puritans' understanding of theirs as a civilizing mission of a new Israel. He rejected this view especially in so far as it was used to justify taking over lands from the Native Americans "as though they [the Puritans] were ancient Israelites taking over the Promised Land" (Marsden, 1990, 19). And yet the deism to which Jefferson and some other founders subscribed did not prohibit them from echoing the Puritan understanding of election and providential mission, nor a significant sense that the United States had a special role to play within history. Neither did their rationalist deism prohibit them from characterizing that role publicly. They drew on stories and symbols in Hebrew Scriptures that portrayed God's having chosen the children of Israel for a special providential mission.

Both Thomas Jefferson and Benjamin Franklin proposed that the Great Seal of the United States portray Moses leading the children of Israel across the Red Sea. Both proposals recalled the story depicted in the Hebrew Scriptures (Exodus, Chapter 14) in which God liberates the Hebrew people from slavery in Egypt. Both proposals were eventually passed over in the process by which a series of committees finally settled on a national seal. And yet the basic idea they sought to convey remained clearly expressed by the symbols chosen to represent the new nation. The concept of God's providential leading and watchful eye over the United States amid the dangers of history is represented by a single eye that sits atop the pyramid featured on the great seal. This image is known as the eye of providence. It appears today on the back of the U.S. $1 bill (Boyd et al., 1950, 494–495; Springs, 2012, 32–33).

The Puritan and Enlightenment legacies contribute greatly to the robust religious dimensions of U.S. nationalist sensibilities. The Puritan account, in particular, contributes to a widely taken for granted myth of origins that is broadly replicated in school textbooks. The enlightenment legacy contributes to the conception of providential mission of the United States in more broadly rationalist terms. When examined through lenses of discourse analysis, it becomes apparent that both are shot through with colonialist impulses, especially as they silence and suppress contradictory narratives and counterhistories (those of Native Americans and African slaves, among others), and justify and celebrate the dominant accounts of American national identity.

Moreover, in as far as the New World settlers are portrayed as a new embodiment of the legacy of the ancient Israelites (in a theological sense in the case of Puritanism; in a symbolic and mythical sense in the case of the deist founders), both participate in a version of what Gellner and Anderson identified as a "sleeping beauty" conception of the nation. That is, both accounts portray narratives of settlement and founding as recognition of, grasping hold of, and carrying forward an ancient and even primordial legacy that is chronicled in the Hebrew Scriptures—the legacy of a chosen people seeking and settling a promised land through divine guidance. As we will see in the remainder of this chapter, these elements contribute to a religious repertoire that resurfaces again and again throughout the 19th and 20th centuries, and permeates U.S. national self-perception. This repertoire affords a selectively retrieved and applied collection of myths, symbols, rituals, and doctrines that flourished and spread as means by which the origins, history, and significance of collective U.S. national identity are idealized and represented to the nation itself, and to the world, for the purpose of articulating and amplifying its significance in the present, as well as its destiny. These became especially powerful, we will see, in the increasingly rapid cultural and religious diversification of the U.S. population in the final decades of the 20th century, and even more so in the face of national emergency and perception of external pervasive threat in the first decades of the 21st century.

The Nation, the Land, and Manifest Destiny

In the wake of the American Revolution (1775–1783), the Second Great Awakening (ca. 1800–1865) brought a widespread series of countrywide revivals in which evangelical Christianity became largely enmeshed with the democratic ideals of the revolution. In fact, this period presents a unique manifestation of civil religion as a form of nationalism through "a happy marriage between evangelical Christianity and liberal democracy which in turn was presided over by a smiling Creator. Nineteenth century American Christians felt they could wholeheartedly give allegiance to the nation because it was God's chosen instrument to spread *both* Christianity and democracy" (Pierard and Linder, 1988, 57). The nation's "providential mission," in this sense, spread to the far reaches of national identity across the 19th century in the form of a doctrine that would come to be called Manifest Destiny.

Manifest Destiny justified America's westward expansion. In doing so, it not only demonstrated religion's enduring influence in imagining the nation, but also brought those imaginings into reality. Manifest Destiny emerged as a formal doctrine of national expansion in the mid-19th century. With the United States on the brink of war with Mexico in 1845, newspaper editor John O'Sullivan endorsed the annexation of Texas, explaining that it was "our manifest destiny to overspread the continent allotted by Providence for the free development of our yearly multiplying millions" (O'Sullivan, 1845, 5–10). The motivations for westward expansion were not exclusively religious. Expansion was also motivated by the increase in population, as well as the natural resources and wealth (often in the form of gold and precious metals) that these vast territories contained. When the United States emerged as the victor of the Mexican-American War (1846–1848), Mexico ceded nearly half its total land to the United States. The following year, gold was discovered in the newly acquired territory, initiating the gold rush westward.

And yet such national projects rarely—if ever—arise from a single motivation that can be easily untangled from other desires, incentives, and driving forces. Justifications for U.S. expansion were rhetorically and symbolically saturated by appeals to the God-given duty of this new nation to spread its unique mixture of Christianity and democracy as far as possible. As O'Sullivan explained in his column, applying the notion of "manifest destiny":

Texas has been absorbed in the Union in the inevitable fulfillment of the general law which is rolling our population westward; the connection of which with that ratio of growth of population which is destined within a hundred years to swell our numbers to the enormous population of two hundred and fifty millions (if not more), is too evident to leave us in doubt of the manifest design of Providence in regard to the occupation of this continent. . . . The Anglo-Saxon foot is already on [California's] borders. Already the advance guard of the irresistible army of Anglo-Saxon emigration has begun to pour down upon it, armed with the plough and the rifle, and marking its trail with schools and colleges, courts and representative halls, mills and meeting-houses. A population will soon be in actual occupation of California, over which it will be idle for Mexico to dream of dominion. They will necessarily become independent. All this without the agency of our government, without responsibility of our people—in the natural flow of events . . . (1845, 5–10)

This influential passage describes national expansion as occurring by way of an identifiable people occupying and settling the land, rather than only by military conquest or governmental declaration. And yet expansion was justified not merely by material necessity (acquiring the space and resources necessary for an expanding population), but also—and, arguably, primarily—by what was declared to be a "self-fulfilling" destiny. This sense of destiny is considered self-fulfilling in that each successful step in expansion was viewed as further evidence that such expansion was a preordained destiny. As a formal doctrine in national identity and policy, Manifest Destiny may have been novel in the 19th century. However, as we saw John Wintrhop interpret the destruction of the Native Americans as a sign of God's blessing upon Puritan efforts to settle the new world, powerful conceptions of providential mission and self-fulfilling destiny were as old as the arrival of European settlers in North America.

The divine mandate in Manifest Destiny continued to justify national expansion in the 19th century. In *Johnson v. MacIntosh* (1823), the U.S. Supreme Court ruled that by "right of discovery," European powers had acquired sovereignty of the land and were therefore justified in denying the occupancy rights of Native

Americans who had been living there. Through the Indian Removal Act of 1832, multiple Native American nations were forcibly expelled from the southeastern regions of the United States to present-day Oklahoma. Known as the Trail of Tears, these expulsions resulted in mass deaths (roughly one quarter of the Cherokee people perished, as did countless more from several other Native American nations). These cases represent the ruthlessness and genocide perpetrated against Native American populations under the doctrine of Manifest Destiny (Nunpa, 2009, 47–64).

When the Constitution was signed in 1787, the United States had reached as far as the Appalachian Mountains and covered 890,000 square miles. In the two centuries that followed, U.S. territory grew to include an additional 2.9 million square miles. The expansion of much of this territory—perhaps all of it—was either explicitly justified or subtly framed in some variation of Manifest Destiny, America's destined expansion "from sea to shining sea" (Moriarty, 2005).

"God's *Almost* Chosen People": Civil Religion, Nationalism, and the Civil War

In the context of the Civil War, Abraham Lincoln engaged with religion in ways that contrasted with the inclusivist views of religion during the early development of U.S. national identity. Thomas Jefferson had sought to keep irrational and enthusiastic tendencies of supernatural religion at the margins of public life (out of politics and statecraft). And while many of the founders had sought to avoid denominational specificity as a general rule, they nonetheless employed less specific religious language and symbolism (Providence, Creator, natural rights), much of which came to be identified as the substance of American civil religion (Bellah, 1992, 45). These terms served largely to bless and sanctify the nation as an object of allegedly secular—but, in actuality, powerfully religious—devotion.

Some scholars of civil religion seek to distinguish between it and religious nationalism, arguing that nationalism is a condition in which "individuals render their highest loyalty to their nationality, thus placing all other allegiances on a secondary level" (Pierard and Linder, 1988, 57). Civil religion, by contrast, functions *like* a religion in a much more commonplace way—providing the symbolic, ritual, mythical, and ethical "glue" for a society, namely, by generating moderate (as opposed to militant) forms of solidarity. And yet upon closer inspection, this distinction may not be so easy to maintain.

In the context of the Civil War, it was precisely the solidarity-generating "lowest common denominator" terms of civil religion that were vague enough to sustain and perpetuate diametrically opposed interpretations of the Civil War as divinely blessed and sanctioned from all sides. As Civil War historian George Rable argues, "The preachers and politicians, the churches and the editors, the Sunday school teachers and the families could all speak of a holy crusade against a heathenish enemy. They could interpret the course of the war to fit widely held notions about providence, they could view the outcome of battles as signs of divine favor or wrath, and they could expound on the war's larger purposes" (Rable, 2010, 159). Described in this way, the Civil War exemplifies how civil religion merges into, intermingles with, and presents a variation on religious nationalist themes.

In Rable's discussion of the Civil War context, religious nationalism did not require that the citizenry actually worship the nation as an idol, or perceive their nationality as the object of their highest loyalty. Rather, their civil religion manifested itself as religious nationalism simply by viewing their national causes and efforts as easily consistent with, and a natural extension of, their traditional religious commitments and practices—and thus as blessed by—their God (of which the God of civil religion was a reflection). Arguably, it was precisely because the deity of civil religion was an ever-present, benevolent, "smiling creator" that that conception of God could so easily be conscripted as an ally, defender, and source of blessing, for whichever national cause they happened to espouse. Such a God could easily be portrayed as judging and damning the causes of their opponent on the battlefields of the Civil War. This is a variety of religious nationalism. It is facilitated and fueled by the allegedly more benign and purportedly wholly distinct conception of civil religion.

In contrast to the inclusivist vagueness of American civil religion and its religious nationalist fruits, Lincoln invoked specific features of Jewish and Christian religious traditions in public, political life in order to portray the nation as accountable to a higher conception of justice. He grappled at length with the profound theological challenges that these traditions raised about the causes and conditions of the Civil War (Noll, 2006, 85–90). He deployed elements of these traditions in both prophetic and priestly capacities in public life as well as political contexts. On one hand, Lincoln used religion in a priestly function in his attempts to legitimate the Union (the nation) for which so many had died, and to heal and hold the nation together in the wake of the Civil War. On the other hand, Lincoln also used religion in a prophetic capacity, to criticize and correct the nation for its complicity in an institution as "peculiar"—as unjust and evil—as slavery.

The Tradition of American Jeremiad

Most famously, in his Second Inaugural Address, Lincoln described the horrors of the U.S. Civil War in terms of God's wrathful judgment visited on both North and South. The pivotal lines from Lincoln's address read:

> Both read the same Bible and pray to the same God, and each invokes His aid against the other. It may seem strange that any men should dare to ask a just God's assistance in wringing their bread from the sweat of other men's faces, but let us judge not, that we be not judged. The prayers of both could not be answered. That of neither has been answered fully. The Almighty has His own purposes. "Woe unto the world because of offenses; for it must needs be that offenses come, but woe to that man by whom the offense cometh" [Matthew 18:7]. If we shall suppose that American slavery is one of those offenses which, in the providence of God, must needs come, but which, having continued through His appointed time, He now wills to remove, and that He gives to both North and South this terrible war as the woe due to those by whom the offense came, shall we discern therein any departure from those divine attributes which the believers in a living God always ascribe to Him? Fondly do we hope, fervently do we pray, that this mighty scourge of war may speedily pass away. Yet, if God wills that it continue until all the wealth piled by the bondsman's two hundred and fifty years of unrequited toil shall be sunk, and until every drop of blood drawn with the lash shall be paid by another drawn with the sword, as was said three thousand years ago, so still

it must be said, "the judgments of the Lord are true and righteous altogether" [Psalm 19:9]. With malice toward none, with charity for all, with firmness in the right as God gives us to see the right, let us strive on to finish the work we are in, to bind up the nation's wounds, to care for him who shall have borne the battle and for his widow and his orphan, to do all which may achieve and cherish a just and lasting peace among ourselves and with all nations. (Lincoln, 1865)

Describing the nation as accountable to God, Lincoln noted that God would judge whether its laws, institutions, and actions were just or unjust, good or evil. He also believed that the unjust would suffer the consequences of God's wrath. Indeed Lincoln portrayed the nation—North *and* South—as experiencing judgment because it had gone astray. This prophetic criticism resonated powerfully in light of the widely held belief that "the nation existed not simply as an end in itself, but to serve some higher purpose" (Pierard and Linder, 1988, 97).

Lincoln's declarations echoed starkly the warnings delivered by the Puritan leader John Winthrop over 200 years earlier. Recall that Winthrop preached that God called the Puritans to become a new Israel in New England. This meant that they were to model Christian charity for the whole world to look upon and give glory to God. However, if the Puritans were unfaithful in their response to God's calling, they would incur God's judgment and wrath. In echoing the kind of prophetic reprimand that Winthrop had articulated, Lincoln participated in a rhetorical and literary tradition known as the jeremiad (White, 2002, 153–159).

The jeremiad is a form of address that laments and censures a set of status quo conditions and practices as inconsistent with, or contradictory to, what ought to be the case (either in contrast to a set of guiding ideals or a set of terms that have been contractually agreed upon in advance). This form of address takes its title from the name of the biblical prophet Jeremiah, whom the books of Jeremiah and Lamentations portray as lamenting and denouncing the sinfulness and idolatry of the people of Israel. Jeremiah is portrayed as keenly aware of God's role as ruler of the nations (Jeremiah 10:10, 25:15)—claiming that the providence of God is to the nations as a potter is to clay (Jeremiah 18:5–10)—and announcing that God's justice and righteousness stand in judgment over the wicked ways of God's people.

To understand and critically assess what emerged as a distinctively American tradition of the jeremiad, it is important to keep in mind two key elements of this form of address and its role in the Hebrew tradition of prophetic witness, lament, and criticism from which it came (Howard-Pitney, 2005, 1–14). First, while a jeremiad may take the form of a harsh denunciation of a people's wayward practices, it does not selectively apply the label of righteous to some and unrighteous to others. The measure of justice was understood to belong to God, and thus, it is applicable to all people. In fact, in the Hebrew tradition, time and again it is God's chosen people themselves that prophets such as Jeremiah, Amos, Isaiah, and Ezekial denounce, criticize, and call back to faithfulness because they have strayed from the righteousness of God.

Second, in the Hebrew prophetic tradition, the jeremiad typically either ends on, or makes room for, a note of hope and reaffirmation amidst seemingly despairing conditions (e.g., Jeremiah 30 and 31). In other words, while jeremiads may fiercely criticize present conditions and find all the people liable to be guilty of unrighteousness, this rhetorical form neither altogether demonizes nor pronounces blanket condemnation of the present. American variations of the jeremiad rhetorical practice sometimes appeal to a divinely inspired source of hope that the wayward people will respond to the prophet's call back to the pursuit of righteousness. At their best, however, participants in this tradition demonstrate some recognition that the voice of the prophet, and the very capacity of the prophet to speak, is evidence that evils of the present can be recognized and resisted (Stout, 2002, 248; Stout, 2004). So understood, prophetic criticism is, itself, a present glimmer of hope here and now that wayward conditions can be fought against and corrected. Rather than counseling despair, the speaker of a jeremiad stands within the present conditions. His or her denunciation of wrongs and unrighteousness in the present draws upon resources within that present in order to criticize it. In the cases of Lincoln, Frederick Douglas, David Walker, and Martin Luther King, Jr. to name a few exemplars, national narratives, myths, symbols, and explicitly professed national values provided substantial resources for resistance to, and criticism of, the nation itself. Representative instances in the American jeremiad tradition often end by calling America back to some more humbled sense of its providential mission, and to an enriched and expanded account of its orienting principles of justice.

Lincoln invoked biblical passages and deployed theological concepts in public, political contexts (i.e., God's purposes as distinct from the purposes of the nation, divine judgment of the nation, the mystery and sovereignty of God). And while Lincoln clearly drew upon a narrative of American exceptionalism, his version of that narrative was not glibly triumphalist nor a simple celebration of the Union's survival. In fact, it reflected a deeply tragic sensibility. In a speech before the New Jersey Senate in 1861, he claimed that Americans were God's "*almost* chosen people."

Heavily influenced by the jeremiads and prophetic activism by the black abolitionist Frederick Douglas, Lincoln grappled with the evils committed by the nation and the tragic conditions that resulted (Howard-Pitney, 2005, Chapter 2). In his hands, the usually vague terms of civil religion became theologically specific. Lincoln invoked specific passages from Old and New Testaments not only to declare that the nation was accountable for its evils, he also portrayed the nation in relation to God and, consequently, accountable to a higher order of justice and charity toward others. The complex elixir of civil religion and public religion that resulted also provided an encompassing—and potentially healing—unifying vision for the nation.

And yet at the same time, Lincoln also made clear that it was the nation-state that called for, and might in fact require, the "last full measure of devotion" from its citizens. Such sacrifices took the form of military conscription (i.e., the draft) and sacrifice of life and limb on the battlefield, and as necessary, taking the lives of others in defense of the nation and state. Lincoln portrayed these as sacrifices without which the nation might not survive. In other words, the nationalism of Lincoln's context was religious not merely because it recruited and deployed explicitly religious rhetorical modes and theological concepts as a form of civil religion in public life. It was religious also for the fact that the nation-state was portrayed as exerting its will with the absoluteness of a divinely sanctioned sovereign. Moreover, it was the nation-state that provided the frame within which those who sacrificed their lives on its behalf would live on. In other words, their sacrifice would be given meaning in the survival of the nation-state itself. The nation, Lincoln said, would recognize and sanctify the deaths of those whose blood "dedicated, consecrated, and hallowed" the battlefields of the war by (in the case of the Gettysburg Address) recognizing the battlefield at Gettysburg as a sanctified space. How would the nation do this? By keeping the dead alive in its collective memory. As Lincoln himself put it, the nation would resolve that "these dead shall not have died in vain—that this nation, under God, shall have a new birth of freedom—and that government of the people, by the people, for the people, shall not perish from the earth" (Lincoln, Gettysburg Address). American religious historian Harry Stout argues that, while dressed in the trappings of a seemingly benevolent civil religion, in fact, Lincoln's efforts to makes sense of, heal, and bless the Union's survival in the wake of catastrophic war mark the consolidation and emergence of a form of religious nationalism. Moreover, various versions of this religious nationalism would permeate much of the 20th- and 21st-century United States. "Visibly, most believed America (North and South) to be a "Christian nation." Invisibly, few could see that America was incarnating a millennial nationalism as the primal religious faith," Stout writes. "... They could not see a new religion, baptized and confirmed, imbuing a powerful unified nation-state with the power—and sanctity—of God" (Stout, 2006, 405).

At the same time, Lincoln's legacy brings the deep, and perhaps unresolvable, ambivalences of religious nationalism plainly into view. In the national mythological framework in which citizens sacrifice their lives so the nation can live on, Lincoln is an exemplary martyr who has been elevated to sainthood. Lincoln denounced slavery as a violation of human dignity and unequivocal evil (Bromwich, 2002). He refused to treat the abolition of slavery as a political issue that could be pragmatically settled on a state-by-state basis as his political opponent, Stephen Douglas, had claimed that it should. Lincoln legally freed the slaves by signing the Emancipation Proclamation (1862) and managed nonetheless successfully to hold the Union together. Ultimately, Lincoln's own life was sacrificed through his assassination by a Confederate sympathizer in the days following the end of the Civil War.

The Lincoln Memorial stands on the National Mall in Washington, D.C., as one of the most visited national monuments in American civil religion. On its north and south walls are inscribed the texts of Lincoln's Second Inaugural Address and his Gettysburg Address. Lincoln himself lives on—and his death is, in effect, redeemed—much in the way he described in the Gettysburg Address, that is, by being fixed and exalted in the memory of the nation. By his efforts, the United States did, in effect, undergo some degree of a "new birth of freedom" in so far as slavery was finally abolished, the Union was preserved, and "government of the people, for the people, and by the people [did] not perish from the earth" (Lincoln, Gettysburg Address).

Lincoln's case exemplifies how certain themes and features of religious nationalism can be deployed in ways that might hold the nation accountable to higher standards of justice. At the same time, it reflects what William Cavanaugh called "the migration of the holy" (as we discussed previously in Chapter 2) from centralized religious institutions of earlier eras to the modern nation-state as an absolute entity. The state is absolute in that it holds a monopoly upon the legitimate use of violence and coercive force within the boundaries of its sovereign territory, and can require its members to sacrifice their lives, and take the lives of others, for the sake of its continued existence. As a result, war can quickly become elevated to and—in effect—play a redemptive role for the nation-state. It can easily become romanticized and even glorified as the means to perpetuate the memory of those who laid down their lives as a sacrifice on behalf of the nation-state.

Some argue that in a world in which nation-states are standard entities, the forms of absolute power one finds in the modern state are unavoidable. And yet it is possible to draw distinctions between more and less perilous versions and uses of such power, and more and less absolute conceptions of the state. It is not necessarily the case, for instance, that state power must serve an imperialist agenda, nor that it engage in colonialist expansion, nor that it suppress and silence dissenting and countervisions of national identity and membership internal to the nation itself. It is possible that states participate in efforts to hold themselves accountable to higher authorities and standards of justice (e.g., treaties, conventions, international law, human rights, international criminal justice, principles of mutual recognition and reciprocal respect embodied in democratic practices, or ideally, some combination of all these).

At the same time, numerous religious groups throughout the history of the United States have opted out of the operations of state power, or have categorically resisted the claims of national identity, on the bases of their own theological commitments and traditions. Christian pacifist denominations, for example, largely due to their serious commitment to the teaching of Jesus in the Sermon on the Mount and their refusal to participate in idolatry, have rejected the absolute claims required by loyalty to the nation. Groups such as Quakers, Amish, Moravians, and Mennonites have conscientiously objected to the state's demand that they serve in war. In some cases, members of these groups have refused to pay state taxes that would fund warfare.

Nonetheless, for the vast majority of Americans, nationalism was and is a medium through which they not only reconcile their traditional religious and national identities, devotion, and obligations, but also through which they positively integrate these. Historically, "except for Pacifists," Marsden concludes, "almost all American religious groups saw their national loyalties not in conflict with their traditional religion but simply as an extension of their religion. Throughout the nation's history Americans overwhelmingly have insisted that loyalty to God and nation go hand in hand" (1990, 45).

The Cold War: A Judeo-Christian Nation versus a Godless Society

A key feature of national identity in the United States, the sense of providential mission, surged to the fore during the Cold War. The U.S. landscape changed radically in the early 20th century. Prevailingly Protestant Christian conceptions of American identity and civil religion were challenged by further European migrations, increased Catholic and Jewish populations, as well as scientific development, Darwinism, and Marxism. In particular, rapid industrialization and urbanization caused radical structural changes, which generated debates about how both American religion and American nationalism would respond to modernity. One response, the Social Gospel movement, applied Christian ethics to social problems such as poverty, poor labor conditions, inadequate schools, and racism; proponents of the movement believed that Christians were called to help the poor and needy as well as to work toward social justice and more equitable economic conditions. After the massive economic collapse in 1929 that led to the Great Depression, many proponents of the Social Gospel praised President Franklin D. Roosevelt's New Deal because it included programs to help the poor and unemployed.

On the eve of the United States' entry into World War II, Roosevelt appealed to America's providential mission to the world. "[T]here comes a time in the affairs of men," he stated in his 1939 State of the Union address, "when they must prepare to defend, not their homes alone, but the tenets of faith and humanity on which their churches, their governments and their very civilization are founded" (Roosevelt, 1939). This familiar rhetoric invoked a conception of the sanctity of the United States' Judeo-Christian values as a basis for war.

The Cold War era provided the context for an intensified and increasingly rigid reframing of American identity as uniquely embodying Judeo-Christian values. To emphasize the supposedly profound differences between the United States and the godless, communist Soviet Union, American political elites began to appeal to America's characteristic belief in God. Within this ethos, the values of democracy and freedom became intricately linked to America's foundation in Judeo-Christian origins, and its role as a guarantor of liberalism and democracy. In this social context, divisions between Protestants, Catholics, and Jews were significantly softened because all became assimilated into a representation of Judeo-Christian identity. Because communism was understood to be a false and nihilistic outlook, it was America's mission to counter the influence of communism and to ensure the spread of its own values across the globe. This theme was prominent in President Dwight D. Eisenhower's rhetoric. One slogan of his 1956 campaign was: "Faith in God and Country: that's Eisenhower—how about you?" (Hutcheson, 1988, 51).

Eisenhower's view of religion was roughly consistent with the predominantly mainline Protestant model of religious ecumenism (interdenominational pluralism) prevalent in that era. In his 1952 address to the Freedom Foundation, he famously remarked:

> ... [O]ur form of Government has no sense unless it is founded in a deeply felt religious faith, and I don't care what it is. With us of course it is the Jud[e]o-Christian concept but it must be a religion that all men are created equal. ... Even those among us who are, in my opinion, so silly as to doubt the existence of an Almighty, are still members of a religious civilization, because the founding Fathers said it was a religious concept they were trying to translate into the political world. (*New York Times*, December 23, 1952; Henry, 1981, 41)

The Cold War era, however, was not only marked by vaguely inclusivist "deeply felt religious faith and I don't care what it is" forms of ecumenism. There were also—as is inevitably the case—

countercurrents that articulated staunchly exclusivist visions of the society. The Baptist preacher Billy Graham described the war against communism as a holy war. Several leaders held this view of a sacred struggle, including General Douglas MacArthur, who linked religious fervor to patriotism, and Senator Joseph McCarthy, who depicted the Cold War with apocalyptic brushstrokes, proclaiming it a "final all-out battle between communistic atheism and Christianity" (Theiss-Morse, 2009, 63). Even Eisenhower cast the U.S.-Soviet conflict in terms of good versus evil, claiming: "What is our battle against Communism if it is not between anti-God and a belief in the Almighty? Communists know this. They have to eliminate God from their system. When God comes in, Communism has to go" (Manis, 2002, 64).

Eisenhower's Judeo-Christian ecumenism is largely responsible for setting the terms of the social and political conflicts over which set of values would constitute American national identity in the late 20th and early 21st centuries. These conflicts have occurred over the sense in which, and degree to which, the United States is and should continue to be conceived as a Christian or Judeo-Christian nation. Eisenhower fought to include the words "under God" in a line of the Pledge of Allegiance that had previously read "one nation, indivisible." The president was inspired to act, in part, by a campaign led by the Knights of Columbus, a Catholic men's organization. In 1954, Congress voted to amend the pledge to "... one nation, under God, indivisible ..." and Eisenhower signed the bill into law.

Two years later, with the influence of Eisenhower's administration behind it, the phrase "In God We Trust" was elected to be the official U.S. motto and promptly inscribed on all U.S. currency. Up to that point, the unofficial national motto *E pluribus unum* ("one from many") had no explicit religious association. From one perspective, these additions can be interpreted as acts of Cold War nationalism that intended to define itself in contrast to, and symbolically combat, the materialist atheism of Soviet Communism. At the same time, however, these changes reflected efforts to certify the identity of the nation as, at the most basic level, monotheistic and Judeo-Christian. While aiming to signify a broad monotheism that could encompass other religious identities in general, its Judeo-Christian orientation was considered to be essential and non-negotiable. U.S nationalism set forth clearly and distinctly (on each piece of its currency, and at each public school day's opening exercises) its divergence from identities that either affirmed no God or altogether rejected the existence of a God. When Eisenhower signed the alteration of the pledge into law, he declared:

> ... [F]rom this day forward, the millions of our school children will daily proclaim in every city and town, every village and rural school house, the dedication of our nation and our people to the Almighty. To anyone who loves America, nothing could be more inspiring than to contemplate this rededication of our youth, on each school morning, to our country's true meaning. ... In this way we are reaffirming the transcendence of religious faith in America's heritage and future; in this way we shall constantly strengthen those spiritual weapons which forever will be our country's most powerful resource, in peace or in war. (Eisenhower, 1954)

Of course, the mid-20th century liberal Protestant model of ecumenism was not without exclusivist tendencies of its own. As we will see later in the chapter, this vision of nationhood—as well as the symbol systems and repertoire of ritual practices that convey and maintain that vision—underwrote several of the most volatile legal and cultural conflicts over U.S. national identity in the first decades of the 21st century. Assessed through the lenses of discourse analysis, we will see that they infuse the religious dimensions of U.S. national identity with an orientalist orientation, and have fueled some of the most chauvinist and xenophobic episodes in the first decades of the 21st century.

The Ignoble Paradox of American Democracy: Race, Nation, and Religion

If the end of the of the Civil War brought a "new birth of freedom" in the freeing of African slaves in the United States, as President Lincoln had declared, this new birth was soon abandoned. The repeal of Reconstruction (1865–1877) in the southern United States witnessed the re-establishment of pervasive and degrading forms of segregation and discrimination toward people of color, especially blacks. The discriminatory laws and cultural practices that emerged were never limited to black people being made to ride at the back of buses, drink from "colored only" water fountains and use "colored only" restrooms (though they included these regulations). Nor did discrimination merely amount to "separate but equal" access to goods, services, and public and private institutions such as segregated schools (separate but equal laws were upheld by the U.S. Supreme Court's ruling in *Plessy v. Ferguson* [1896] and were not overturned until *Brown v. Board of Education of Topeka* [1954]). Nor did pervasive discrimination only manifest itself in widespread political disenfranchisement of black people through grandfather clauses, poll taxes, and literacy tests to vote. Blacks were also subject to persistent racially motivated violence. To consider but one example of such violence, the most conservative estimates state that between the end of Reconstruction and World War II, roughly 5,000 racially motivated lynchings occurred across the United States. About three out of every four persons lynched were black. Eighty percent of the total number of lynchings during this period occurred in the South. Of that number, 83 percent of the victims were black (3,245 total) (Berg, 2009, 92).

In the midst of such racism and discrimination, Martin Luther King, Jr., emerged as a black Baptist minister who dedicated himself to holding the American nation accountable to its own stated ideals of freedom, equality, and justice. As an activist and a leader of the civil rights movement (1955–1968), he did this by speaking directly from his own Christian commitments, drawing upon the prophetic dimensions of the Jewish religious tradition, and invoking the highest values of equality, freedom, and democracy expressed in the symbols and rituals of American civil religion. King's commitment to nonviolent social change was inspired by the social transformation achieved by the Indian politician and religious teacher Mahatma Gandhi, who helped to lead a nonviolent movement for Indian independence from British colonial rule (King, 1991).

On August 28, 1963, with the civil rights movement in full force, King stood on the steps of the Lincoln Memorial on the National Mall in Washington, D.C., and delivered his "I Have a Dream" speech. It was received by a crowd of some 250,000 marchers at the March on Washington for Jobs and Freedom, and by thousands more who viewed the proceedings on broadcast television. As with so many of King's addresses, this speech provided an exemplary instance of the American jeremiad tradition.

King opened his speech by acknowledging that he and his audience stood at a memorial space that was uniquely hallowed in the history of the American nation. He declared Abraham Lincoln's signing of the Emancipation Proclamation an act that served as a beacon of freedom, and illuminated the values inscribed in the Declaration of Independence and in the U.S. Constitution. King announced that he and his fellow marchers sought to carry forward Lincoln's legacy of rights, democracy, and freedom. King described his dream as "deeply rooted in the American dream that one day this nation will rise up and live out the true meaning of its creed—we hold these truths to be self-evident, that all men are created equal" (King, 1991, 219).

King, along with civil rights activist Rosa Parks (among others), stood beside President Lyndon Johnson as he finally signed the Voting Rights Act into law on August 6, 1965. A landmark victory for the civil rights movement, this legislation prohibited discriminatory voting practices that had fueled the disenfranchisement of blacks in the United States since the repeal of Reconstruction.

Until the end of his life, in ways that radically challenged the status quo conditions of his day, King continued to insist that the United States live up to its avowed ideals. He became an outspoken critic of the war in Vietnam and the imperialism by which the United States exerted its power around the world. He criticized economic exploitation and savage inequalities between rich and poor in the United States, and he called for a guaranteed annual income (King, 1992, 173–174). There is a vast discrepancy between the realities of King's prophetic criticism and the (frequent) glibness with which his legacy is exalted in the national memory. African American public intellectual and philosopher Cornel West has articulated this point with perhaps the greatest possible precision:

> King's thought remains a challenge to us principally in that he accented the anticolonial, anti-imperialist and antiracist consequences of taking seriously the American ideals of democracy, freedom and equality. He never forgot that America was born out of revolutionary revolt and subversive rebellion against British colonialism and imperialism and that although much of white America viewed the country as the promised land, black slaves saw it as Egypt, that just as Europe's poor

huddled masses were attracted to America, the largest
black mass movement (led by Marcus Garvey) was set
on leaving America! Through his prophetic Christian
lens, King saw just how far America had swerved away
from its own revolutionary past. In its support of
counterrevolution in Vietnam, Guatemala, Colombia,
Jamaica and South Africa—and today we can add Chile,
Nicaragua and South Korea—the United States betrayed
its own ideals. King acutely observed in 1968: "The
greatest irony and tragedy of all is that our nation, which
initiated so much of the revolutionary spirit of the
modern world, is now cast in the mold of being an arch
anti-revolutionary. We are engaged in a war that seems
to turn the clock of history back and perpetuate white
colonialism." King's universal and egalitarian religious
and moral commitments, as well as his historical consciousness, led him to *internationalize* the American
ideals of democracy, freedom and equality and thereby
measure not only domestic policies, but also U.S. foreign
policy by these ideals. (West, 1988, 11–12)

A vision of the American nation remained central to King's thinking
and activism even as he expanded and internationalized his effort
to hold the United States accountable to its own stated values.
Moreover, his vision of the nation remained religious in multiple
senses. It was interwoven with the symbols, rituals, myths, and
creeds in which American civil religion existed. It also brought the
commitments and understandings of organized religious traditions
to bear in order to enrich, challenge, and correct unjust and exclusivist laws, policies, cultural understandings, and tendencies in
the public life of U.S. society, and internationally.

The assassination of King on April 4, 1968, rendered him a
martyr in the struggle "to redeem the soul of America," and a
martyr who eventually would be elevated to the status of a saint
in the memory of the nation. Today, countless monuments have
been dedicated to his legacy, numerous streets bear his name in
cities and towns all across the United States, and his birthday
(January 15) was established as a federal holiday in 1983. In 2003,
a marker was engraved on the steps of the Lincoln Memorial to
commemorate the spot from which King delivered his "I Have a
Dream" speech in 1963. Positioned along the National Mall, the

Martin Luther King, Jr. National Memorial in Washington, D.C., was dedicated on October 16, 2011.

And yet, as is the case with so many who achieve sainthood in national memory and the nation's imagining of itself, King's legacy has come to be largely a romanticized reflection and affirmation of the nation as it would like to conceive of itself—that is, as a society that has, in fact, overcome its discrimination and bigotry toward people of color and has entered a "postracial" era. The reality, we will see in the remainder of this chapter, is otherwise.

Religious Nationalism and the Emergence of the Religious Right

Arguably, the "new birth of freedom" declared by Lincoln was not actually realized until the 1960s. The birth occurred through a series of tumultuous events—the assassination of President John F. Kennedy in 1963; the assassination of his brother, Senator Robert F. Kennedy, and Martin King in 1968; and countless race and antiwar riots that spanned the decade. In spite of the turbulence, this period is associated with the high tide of the progressive politics of the American left. Liberal interpretations of Christianity (e.g., the social gospel) provided a base and a consensus during the Democratic administrations of President John F. Kennedy and President Lyndon B. Johnson. At their best, liberal and ecumenical interpretations of religion and nation facilitated prophetic criticisms and significant social reforms (most notably, the civil rights and antiwar movements). Even so, these continued to be held together with a priestly endorsement of America's broadly providential mission in the world.

For many reasons, the 1970s saw a shift in U.S. conceptions of religion and nation away from liberal Protestant models of ecumenism. Hibbard accounts for this mainly in terms of the operations of political elites, arguing that Richard Nixon sought legitimacy by co-opting and deploying exclusivist interpretations of American society (Hibbard, 2010, 179). This invited people to mobilize "along cultural as opposed to class lines" and cultivate a popular base for the Republican Party that would vote on values rather than material economic considerations. This process later came into fruition during the presidencies of Ronald Reagan and George H. W. Bush and enabled long-term efforts to dissolve the social welfare programs associated with Johnson's domestic social programs, the Great Society.

Of course, agendas of political elites were far from the only factors that influenced tensions between the dual legacies of the religious heritage of U.S. society. During the 1960s and the 1970s, the United States underwent numerous cultural shifts and legal changes. Many of these changes were considered consistent with Protestant Christian understandings of the relationship between religious and national identities. Protestant liberalism embraced the idea that controversial religious views would best be limited to the private sphere and personal life. Strong religious claims about morality in politics were often portrayed as "legislating one's personal morality" and thus intolerantly forcing one's moral commitments upon the broader society. A society that was increasingly religiously and culturally diverse would need to keep particular ideas about morality a matter of personal choice. Its public life should be characterized by tolerant pluralism. From the opposite direction, civil authorities would need to remain neutral to any religious institutions and ideas.

Some of the most high profile changes that were perceived to mark the fragmentation of the inherited Judeo-Christian cultural consensus occurred by way of a series of U.S. Supreme Court decisions over the course of the 1960s and 1970s. The Court delivered landmark rulings that enforced the separation of church and state in the realm of public education. In *Engle v. Vitale* (1962), the Court ruled that prayer that was officially sponsored by a school (e.g., in daily opening or closing exercises, and later, at graduation ceremonies and athletic events) violated the First Amendment's Establishment Clause ("Congress shall make no law respecting an establishment of religion"). Then, the Court decided in *Abington Township v. Schempp* (1963) that school-sponsored Bible readings in public schools were also unconstitutional. The U.S. Supreme Court again invoked the Establishment Clause in *Epperson v. Arkansas* (1971) when it overturned state laws that prohibited public school teachers from teaching evolution since the laws were based on fundamentalist Christian beliefs of the biblical account of Creation.

Some regarded these events as necessary for society to adhere to its founding principles of religious freedom. Others claimed that these were necessitated by the realities of the increasing religious diversity of the U.S. population in the middle part of the 20th century. Still others believed these events were evidence of the disintegration of the Judeo-Christian religious character of the nation, represented the decay of its moral fabric, and reflected the rise of an aggressively antireligion secularism that sought to keep religious views out of public life and altogether marginalized.

Public opinion polls at the time suggested that these rulings were broadly unpopular. In his own intervention in the debates surrounding the history and character of American civil religion, distinguished American religious historian Martin Marty pointed to Gallup Poll reports indicating that 70 percent of a national sampling of U.S. citizens claimed deep opposition to the Court's ban on school-sponsored prayer and devotional Bible reading in public schools. And yet, Marty pointed out, little actual protest ensued, and even less effort was made to mobilize against these rulings. "Why did the people not protest?" Marty asked at the time of his writing in 1976. "Why, when they did protest, [was] there ... such a gap between their stated beliefs and their actions?" (193). The lapse between public opinion and action led Marty to question the efficacy of a substantial civil religion; he concluded that scholarly analysis may have invented the idea that civil religion held the nation together in any concrete and meaningful way. Marty, however, only needed to wait until the rise of the Religious Right in the 1980s.

As Marsden points out in his discussion of religion and American culture in the 1970s, the high profile Supreme Court rulings that limited the official role of religion in public life were further compounded by disillusionment due to the Nixon Watergate scandal (1972–1974), the 1973 Supreme Court decision that legalized abortion on demand (*Roe v. Wade*), and the emergence of the Equal Rights Amendment (debated from 1972 to 1979 and perceived by some as a threat to traditional conceptions of the family). Put together, these conditions compelled many religious conservatives in the United States to recognize that morality—and morality derived from Christian values, in particular—actually should play a central role in politics and in U.S. public life more broadly.

In the wake of bitter disappointment and even a sense of disenfranchisement resulting from the series of court decisions, legal statutes, and shifts in the cultural ethos of U.S. society mentioned previously, many conservative Christians in the United States hoped that President Jimmy Carter (1976–1980) might revive U.S. identity as a Judeo-Christian nation and counter what they perceived to be the wayward directions of U.S. civil society. Carter was an active member of a Southern Baptist church. During his presidential campaign, his self-identification as a "born-again" Christian sparked widespread interest in what it might mean to be an evangelical Christian who was active in political life (Pierard and Linder, 1988, 236–238). And yet religious conservatives were ultimately disappointed with Carter, who did not share the same vision for reasserting Christian values in the public sphere and in relation to national identity.

By the early 1980s, self-identification as a religious conservative had come to correlate strongly with support of "politically conservative" policies, political elites, and legislation. That identification also came to be associated with a sense of urgency to participate in—and actually alter—political processes (Wuthnow, 1989, 237–240). To mobilize the Religious Right, Baptist preacher and televangelist Jerry Falwell formed a political action movement and lobby group called the Moral Majority. Using direct mail campaigns, voter guides, and "checkbook activism," Falwell ultimately claimed responsibility for delivering two-thirds of the white evangelical Christian vote to Ronald Reagan in the 1980 presidential election. This movement took seriously the mythical and moral grounds of U.S. civil religion. The Moral Majority mobilized politically to culturally and legally reassert their understanding of the values that were associated with the origins of the United States as a Judeo-Christian nation. Its members viewed the break-up of the traditional model of the family (especially by way of rapidly increasing divorce rates), sexual libertinism, legalization of abortion, expansion of welfare and other social programs, and ban on school-sponsored prayer as indications that the nation was in moral decline, in part because it was neglecting its religious roots and the religious dimensions of its identity.

Falwell understood that the "exceptional" role of the United States in history was directly related to its Judeo-Christian identity. This identity was threatened by such cultural acids as multicultural relativism and secularism. In the following sermon directed to the U.S. public, Falwell made his case in terms reminiscent of John Winthrop's jeremiad to his fellow Puritans. And yet, arguably, Falwell departed from the American tradition of jeremiad in his willingness to ascribe righteousness to certain groups (namely, the "moral" Americans to whom he appealed) and to denounce others (e.g., liberals and socialists). Falwell declared:

> It is God Almighty who has made and preserved us as a nation, and the day that we forget that is the day that the United States will become a byword among the nations of the world. We will become nothing more than a memory in a history book, like the many great civilizations that have preceded us . . . I do not believe that God is finished with America. Yet America has more God-fearing citizens per capita than any other nation on earth. There are millions of Americans who love God, decency, and biblical morality. North America is the last logical base for world evangelization. While it is true that God could use any nation of means possible to spread the gospel to the world, it is also true that we have the church, the schools, the young people, the media, the money, and the means of spreading the Gospel worldwide in our lifetime. God loves all the world, not just America. However, I am convinced that our freedoms are essential to world evangelism in this latter part of the twentieth century. I am seeking to rally together the people of this country who still believe in decency, the home, the family, morality, the free-enterprise system, and all the great ideals that are the cornerstone of this nation . . . [B]ut when you ask the average person what can be done about revival in America, he will often reply, "I'm just one person. What can I do anyhow?" As long as the average moral American believes that, the political and social liberals in this society will be able to pass their socialistic legislation at will. We are late, but I do not believe that we are too late. It is time to put our lives on the line for this great nation of ours . . . I am convinced that God is calling millions of Americans in the so-often silent majority to join in the moral majority crusade to turn America around in our lifetime. (1980, 243–244, 265–266)

Falwell's call to action helped to set in motion a cultural, political, and social movement in the decades that followed. This movement articulated itself in the symbols and rites of civil religion, especially as those are deemed consistent with, or to reflect, the Judeo-Christian origins and identity of the nation. This movement saw the United States as uniquely called and equipped to spread democracy and Christianity around the world, if the American people would only turn from their wicked ways.

The Religious Right, as it came to be known, popularized an interpretation of American society and religion that aimed to recover, reinstate, and defend a deeply religious (indeed, largely Judeo-Christian) sense of national identity and national mission. Proponents of this interpretation believed that the Christian mission and identity had been jeopardized in the political and cultural shifts of the 1960s and 1970s as well as the subsequent diminishment of a recognizably Judeo-Christian default culture. Their response was not to condemn these as the effects of democracy upon the nation, but rather, to view democracy as the nation's true virtue and thus the channel by which the nation's wayward path (as they understood it) could be corrected. As a result, they organized and mobilized politically. They entered political life as avid participants in order to renew their vision of American national identity. In so doing, they rejected the assertion by many of their opponents that religiously vocal activism was intrinsically detrimental to the public life of a modern, pluralistic society, and that religious views and reasons ought to be contained in the private sphere (Wilcox and Larson, 2006, 1–25). The movement construed itself as a coalition of shared interests in an overarching vision of national morality and as such, ecumenical in its own right. While it fought against the disintegration of the traditional family model, homosexual rights, secularism, socialism, and liberalism, Jerry Falwell insisted that the Moral Majority widely encompassed "fundamentalists, evangelicals, Roman Catholics, conservative Jews, Mormons, and even persons of no religious belief who share our concerns about the issues we address" (Falwell, 1981, 17).

"One Nation under Vishnu": Pledging Allegiance to God and Country

Even as the Religious Right advocated for its vision of religious nationalism, the identity of the United States as a Judeo-Christian nation continued to be contested. In some cases, religious ties were held in place, and the symbolic and ritual substance of U.S. national identity was maintained through the force of law.

In *Elk Grove Unified School District v. Newdow* (2002), the phrase "under God" in the Pledge of Allegiance came under legal challenge in a federal appeals court. In the case, Michael Newdow, a self-identified atheist, filed a suit claiming that the daily recitation of the pledge at his daughter's public school infringed upon her constitutional right to not be compelled to participate in a religious ritual. Technically, recitation of the pledge was not compulsory because a 1943 Supreme Court ruling prohibits obligatory participation in the pledge. Nonetheless, Newdow argued, the Pledge of Allegiance is religious in character because it explicitly asserts that citizens of the United States are "one nation, under God"; because of its religious content, the pledge infringed upon her basic protection from religion. Even though she did not participate in reciting it, she was forced to "watch and listen as her state-employed teacher in her state-run school leads her classmates in a ritual proclaiming that there is a God, and that ours is 'one nation under God'" (Nieves, 2002).

The Ninth Circuit Appellate Court decided that the phrase "one nation, under God" did constitute the state's endorsement of a particular religious position and was therefore unconstitutional because it violated the Establishment Clause. In a key passage of the ruling, Judge Alfred T. Goodwin explained that asserting "under God" is no less prohibited than to say that "we are a nation 'under Jesus,' a nation 'under Vishnu,' a nation 'under Zeus,' or a nation 'under no god,' because none of those professions can be neutral with respect to religion" (Nieves, 2002). In the context of the Pledge of Allegiance, Goodwin added, the phrase "under God" does not simply acknowledge that some majority of Americans believe in a deity, nor is it simply descriptive of the religious and cultural heritage of the republic. In the ritualized recitation of the pledge, the phrase is an endorsement of a monotheistic belief. "[I]t impermissibly takes a position with respect to the purely religious question of the existence and identity of God" (Nieves, 2002).

To protest the Ninth Circuit Court of Appeals' ruling in *Elk Grove Unified School District v. Newdow*, dozens of congressional representatives convened on the front steps of the U.S. Capitol Building to recite together the Pledge of Allegiance and then sang "God Bless America." The Senate unanimously passed a resolution denouncing the court's decision. Such political theatre is rarely innocuous. In fact, when studied through lenses of symbolic systems and ritual practices, it has the capacity to mark a unifying, symbolic boundary; to ingrain a moment or event in political and social memory; and to establish a precedent that, in effect, reinforces the influence of popular perceptions and opinions. Indeed, the majority of Americans appeared to disagree with the court's decision to ban recitation of the Pledge of Allegiance in public schools. Conducted the same month as the Appellate Court's ruling, a Gallup poll indicated that 84 percent of respondents opposed the court's ruling, while 14 percent of respondents agreed with it (Lyons, 2004). Ultimately, the U.S. Supreme Court overturned the circuit court's ruling on the basis of a technicality (saying that the girl's father, as a noncustodial parent, did not have legal standing to file the complaint).

The "under God" phrase was challenged in court again in 2003. A Virginia man filed suit, claiming that the Pledge of Allegiance unconstitutionally exposed his children to a "civic religion" that challenged their religious tradition of Mennonite Christianity, which opposes oaths to any entity but God (Associated Press, 2005). The Fourth Circuit Appellate Court upheld the recitation of the pledge, claiming that it is a purely ceremonial and patriotic activity. The court conceded that the pledge is obviously an element of ritual and contains a reference to God but decided that these elements, when viewed as purely patriotic gestures, fail to constitute the features of a competitor religion.

Religious Diversity and National Identity in the Post-9/11 World

In the decade following the terrorist attacks of September 11, 2001, the United States has witnessed an upsurge of civic piety. In this context, national symbols, rites, and myths have been used to cultivate or manipulate popular sentiments and to mobilize animosity toward a common enemy. Motivated by fear and suspicious of threats to U.S. national security, Americans have demonstrated a willingness to concede to restrictions of civil liberties, perhaps most notably with the passage of the Patriot Act (2001). Moreover, some Americans have supported the use of extreme measures against suspected enemies of the state; these polices include the suspension of *habeas corpus* (a constitutional right that prevents unlawful and indefinite detention) and enhanced interrogation techniques (e.g., torture in the form of waterboarding, sleep deprivation, exposure to extreme temperatures, isolation, and religious and sexual humiliation) in the name of protecting "our way of life" (Danner, 2004). Arguably, elements of civil religion have been used to justify and perhaps to perpetuate a state of emergency in order to make it easier to portray the suspension of rights, legal protections, and international conventions (e.g., the Geneva Conventions) as necessary acts of patriotism.

In these uses of the elements of civil religion, Americans are called to suspend their personal and individual freedom in order to fulfill their patriotic duty and thus aid the nation in fulfilling its mission within history. Like Winthrop, Eisenhower, Reagan, and Falwell, among other political and religious leaders, many have claimed that the United States is uniquely called to a divine purpose—a sense of calling derived from the ethical monotheism (the belief that God instructs humanity through certain basic ethical principles) of U.S. civil religion. In his 2004 acceptance speech of the Republican Party's nomination for President, George W. Bush joined this list of elites in defending the U.S. invasion of Iraq:

> I believe that America is called to lead the cause of freedom in a new century. I believe that millions in the Middle East plead in silence for their liberty. I believe that given the chance, they will embrace the most honorable form of government ever devised by man. I believe all these things because freedom is not America's gift to the world; it is the Almighty God's gift to every man and woman in this world. (Bush, 2004)

To sustain this vision of providentially conferred national mission, and the patriotic duties it required, it was necessary to concretely identify an external enemy, which in turn affected how Americans viewed internal identities (i.e., the identities of groups within the United States). This had significant consequences for residents and citizens whose identities were perceived to relate to, or overlap with, the identity of the external threat. Anxiety about the "enemy within" is a predictable ingredient to maintaining a consolidated sense of "who we are" and is portrayed as a necessary part of defending against external threats.

For instance, in the weeks following the 9/11 terrorist attacks on the World Trade Center and Pentagon, President

George W. Bush juxtaposed "American values" and "the American way of life" with fanatical and militant factions of Islam. Bush quickly pointed out that one could be both a good Muslim and a good American; indeed, he maintained, extremist Islamic factions had hijacked a religion that is essentially peaceful. "The face of terror is not the true faith of Islam," he declared in the week following 9/11. "That's not what Islam is all about. Islam is peace" (Bush, 2001).

By identifying the essence of Islam as peace, Bush rhetorically aimed to expand the sacred canopy of American civil religion from the Judeo-Christian limits that had been ascribed to it for most of the 20th century. The expanded canopy appears to encompass the three "Abrahamic faiths" or "religions of the Book": Christianity, Judaism, and Islam. In this framework, these religions share the basic values understood to be essential to Western monotheism: a respect for the sanctity of human life created by God and a mutual respect between individual people, which is often associated with "the golden rule." By including Islam under the canopy of U.S. civil religion, Bush suggested that authentic Islam can function consistently with "the American way of life" and values articulated in its founding documents (the Declaration of Independence and U.S. Constitution). Authentic Islam should have no difficulty affirming the monotheistic values, rites, and symbols of American civil religion, as well as the conception of freedom they legitimate and forms of pluralism they accommodate. As such, fellow Americans should have no difficulty including peaceful Muslims under the canopy of American identity. And yet when one presses beyond the rhetoric of inclusion, one finds the trends in consolidated public opinion—and their potential implications for policy and law, and even hate crimes and violence—far more disturbing (Springs, 2012, 43–45).

In *America and the Challenges of Religious Diversity* (2005), sociologist Robert Wuthnow drew upon extensive survey data indicating that strong beliefs about the identity of the United States as a Christian nation correlated with strong views that religious minorities (and Muslims, in particular) ought to be monitored and have their freedom to assemble constrained. In fact, 78 percent of respondents agreed that the United States was founded on Christian principles, and slightly more than that (79 percent) agreed that the United States has been strong because of its faith in God. Fifty-five percent agreed that the democratic form of government in the United States is based on Christianity,

roughly 73 percent agreed that the United States is still principally a Christian society, and 63 percent agreed that U.S. public
schools should teach students the Ten Commandments. While
85 percent agreed that religious diversity has been good for
America, 23 percent of respondents endorsed policies to restrict
the basic rights of minority religious groups (Hindus, Buddhists,
and Muslims) to meet and worship altogether. About 38 percent
of Americans expressed support for initiatives that would make
it more difficult for Muslims to settle in the United States, and
47 percent and 57 percent (respectively) associated the words
"fanatical" and "close minded" with Islam. Sixty-six percent of
respondents favored the U.S. government "keeping a close watch
on all foreigners in the United States" (Wuthnow, 2005, Chapter 7,
Springs, 2012, 44). Gallup polls indicate that, as of 2010, similar
feelings of prejudice persisted at roughly the same rate, particularly toward Islam (Gallup, 2010). In fact, the Gallup World Religion
Survey reported that "United States citizens are more than twice as
likely to express prejudice against Muslims as they are against
Christians, Jews and Buddhists. Nearly two-thirds of those polled
said they have little or no knowledge of Islam, yet a majority have
an unfavorable opinion of the religion" (Tenenbaum, 2011).

Wuthnow identified conflicting—even contradictory—
perceptions of the religious dimensions of U.S. national identity.
While on one hand, Americans claimed to be proud of religious
diversity in the United States, and the value of religious tolerance
they believe to be associated with it, they also identify the United
States as, most basically, a Christian nation founded on Christian
principles (Wuthnow, 2005, 6–7). Moreover, they expressed considerable willingness to limit freedoms of assembly and religious
practice, especially for groups whose religious and cultural identities they perceive to diverge from the often nebulous, but nonetheless resilient, preconceptions of America as a broadly Christian
or Judeo-Christian nation (Wuthnow, 2007; Merino, 2010, 243–245).

In the current American context, the politically charged—and,
in many ways, legally vindicated—trappings of civil religion integrate and consolidate a shared national identity in two directions.
Internally, many uses of American civil religion have solidified the
sense that the meanings of these symbols are encompassingly
monotheistic and therefore generously accommodating to religious
pluralism. Legal sanction functions to authenticate the claim that
the United States is a broadly Judeo-Christian civilization. Secondly,
while such uses of civil religion appear to distinguish the elements

of the external threat that exist within the nation as a seemingly acceptable variation of the enemy (i.e., peaceful Islam), this group remains a *variation* of the enemy nonetheless. Thus, in the weeks following the September 11 attacks, one widely influential editorial column read:

> It may seem unfair that Muslims, especially those who are American citizens, are required to demonstrate that they have really chosen our side, but then, there are those terrorists who are aided and abetted by Muslims in this country, and there are those bodies that were buried, and some still buried, beneath the towers only a mile or so south of here, and there is a jihad declared and prosecuted by Muslims in the name of Islam, all adding up to yet another occasion for observing that life is unfair. ("In a Time of War," 2001, 16)

The suspicion and chauvinism that many perceive in this quotation—sometimes referred to as Islamophobia—surfaced in a particularly high profile way in the summer of 2010, in a series of developments that came to be known as the Ground Zero mosque controversy.

Islamophobia and the Ground Zero Mosque in American National Imagination

In the wake of the September 11 terrorist attacks, the former site of the World Trade Center Twin Towers in New York City came to be referred to as Ground Zero. It is the location in which al-Qaeda terrorists assaulted the United States literally (in a physical attack) and symbolically (in assaulting the values and prestige embodied by the Twin Towers). As a result, this space has been ascribed a form of sanctity—a unique and set-apart status in the nation's memory. In the eyes of many, sanctity is ascribed to this space because nearly 3,000 innocent Americans were killed there simply because they were Americans and because America was violently attacked by terrorists.

Plans to open a multifaith community center roughly three blocks from Ground Zero stirred controversy, in part because the project was initiated by a Muslim American businessperson and developer, and because the center would contain a Muslim prayer space. What began as a call to arms by a fringe, right-wing organization called Stop the Islamicization of America against the project was quickly picked up and amplified by national news media outlets and political elites such as former speaker of the House Newt Gingrich and former vice-presidential candidate and governor of Alaska Sarah Palin, among numerous other pundits, and political and cultural figures. At the height of the controversy, Gingrich declared, "America is experiencing an Islamist cultural-political offensive designed to undermine and destroy our civilization" (Nussbaum, 2012, 209–213).

On August 13, 2010, while attending an annual White House dinner marking the celebration of the Muslim holiday of Ramadan (a tradition sporadically observed by the White House dating as far back as Thomas Jefferson's presidency), President Obama responded to the controversy:

> The 9/11 attacks were a deeply traumatic event for our country. And the pain and the experience of suffering by those who lost loved ones is just unimaginable. So I understand the emotions that this issue engenders. And Ground Zero is, indeed, hallowed ground. But let me be clear. As a citizen, and as President, I believe that Muslims have the same right to practice their religion as everyone else in this country. And that includes the right to build a place of worship and a community center on private property in Lower Manhattan, in accordance with local laws and ordinances. This is America. And our commitment to religious freedom must be unshakeable. The principle that people of all faiths are welcome in this country and that they will not be treated differently by their government is essential to who we are. The writ of the Founders must endure. . . . And let us also remember who we're fighting against, and what we're fighting for. Our enemies respect no religious freedom. Al Qaeda's cause is not Islam—it's a gross distortion of Islam. These are not religious leaders—they're terrorists who murder innocent men and women and children. In fact, al Qaeda has killed more Muslims than people of any other religion—and that list of victims includes innocent Muslims who were killed on 9/11. (Editor, 2010)

In these remarks, President Obama held together both the hallowed status of Ground Zero and the commitment to religious freedom as essential to American national memory and identity. And yet one day later, he clarified that he had not commented (and would not comment) on whether it would be advisable, or wise, to build a Muslim prayer space near Ground Zero. In fact, a Cable News Network (CNN) public opinion poll conducted August 6 through 11, 2010, found that the majority of Americans opposed the placement of a multifaith community center (containing a Muslim prayer space) near Ground Zero in spite of America's tradition of religious pluralism and protection of religious freedom (68 percent of respondents opposed the plan to "build a mosque two blocks from the site in New York City where the World Trade Center used to stand") (CNN, 2010).

The high profile controversy surrounding the "Ground Zero mosque" obscured that across the United States (in Alabama, California, Connecticut, Florida, Georgia, Illinois, Kentucky, Maine, Maryland, Massachusetts, Michigan, Ohio, Tennessee, and Wisconsin) there were 36 concurrent cases of Muslim prayer spaces and mosques that were encountering varying degrees of public opposition, protest, and legal obstruction (Pew, 2011). In other words, the Ground Zero mosque controversy was not unique. If it appeared to be an isolated instance in which Muslim Americans were singled out as intrusive, and potentially dangerous, religious "others" in contrast to predominant conceptions of American national identity, it was not because other instances were not present in places throughout the contemporary United States. It was, rather, because those many other instances were less high profile.

Since the terrorist attacks of September 11, Muslim and Arab Americans have been subject to frequent profiling, suspicious treatment, detention, discrimination, and random acts of violence. Some compare this treatment with the U.S. suspicion, relocation, and internment of Japanese Americans into "war relocation camps" during World War II, more than half of whom were U.S. citizens (Elver, 2012; Goldman and Apuzzo, 2011; Goldman and Apuzzo, 2012). This treatment of Japanese Americans much more directly and visibly marginalized a group whose identity was perceived to overlap with that of the external enemy at the time. Members of that group were identified as a potential threat to the safety and well-being of the nation, and subjected to discrimination for the duration of the war.

While the analogy to discrimination against Japanese Americans is illuminating, others have added that the frequent suspicion and chauvinism encountered by Muslim Americans since 9/11 is more akin to the phenomenon of anti-Catholicism that pervaded U.S. society through the 19th and the early 20th centuries. As historians of American religion Scott Appleby and John McGreevey explained:

> In the 1840s and 1850s . . . anxieties about Catholicism in American society turned violent, resulting in mob attacks on priests and churches as well as the formation of a major political party, the American Party, dedicated to combating Catholic influence. This led to novel claims that the US Constitution imposed an absolute separation of church and state—claims that stem not from Thomas Jefferson and George Washington but from nineteenth-century politicians, ministers, and editors worried that adherents of a hierarchical Catholicism might destroy the hard-won achievements of American democracy. In 1875, a decade after accepting General Robert E. Lee's surrender at Appomattox, President Ulysses S. Grant publicly warned that Catholicism might prove as divisive in American society as the Confederacy. (2010, 48)

Throughout much of U.S. history, Catholic Christianity was portrayed as, or perceived to be, intrinsically at odds with democracy, as antimodern, and as an anti-American religion. Protestants such as John Locke had argued that Catholicism was politically destabilizing and socially dangerous. Catholics make unreliable citizens, Locke argued, because their unassailable allegiance to the Pope transcends any allegiance they have to secular authority (Locke, 1990 [1689]). These were default perceptions of Catholicism that had little or no basis in the actual content and character of practicing Catholic citizens and most Catholic institutions in the United States. And yet these perceptions fueled many violent episodes against American Catholics up until the third decade of the 20th century. In this way, the cultural waves of anti-Catholicism in the United States (sometimes called Protestant nativism) prefigure contemporary forms of Islamophobia (Casanova, 2009, 21–50). Islamophobia in the United States tends to conflate Arab ethnicity and Muslim religious identity (or what is perceived as Muslim identity, such as turbans and beards worn by many Sikh Americans). It is a case for which Max Weber's description of the persistently shifting elective affinities between ethnicity, nationality, and religion may present a helpful analytical lens.

Extremism is not unique to Islam. As we have seen throughout this book, even today, there are likewise violent activists and extremists whose nationalist efforts have been wrapped in Christian symbols, stories, and rituals, and who use these to justify and perpetuate their causes. In earlier chapters, we examined Jewish, Hindu, and Buddhist examples as well. Likewise, we examined violently extremist forms of secularism, atheism, and liberalism—all of which have interwoven (and do interweave) their religious (or religiously antireligious) claims into various national identities and visions.

And yet in so far as Muslim Americans and Arab Americans are targeted for chauvinism and suspicious treatment in the United States today because Islam is portrayed as, or perceived to be, intrinsically intolerant, uniquely inclined to violence, and incompatible with liberal democracy—regardless of the content and character of the actual people and institutions themselves—such treatment is shot through with all the chauvinistic and discriminatory marks of Islamophobia. Even when symptoms do not result in explicit hate crimes, such sensibilities nonetheless pervade the United States today.

As of 2012, Gallup surveys indicated that the only religious identification that U.S. voters reported being more opposed to voting for in a presidential election than a self-identified Muslim candidate (4 in 10 would refuse) is a self-identified Atheist (4.3 in 10 would refuse) (Jones, 2012). At the time of this writing, the month of Ramadan in 2012 witnessed an outbreak of violence against Muslim Americans and Arab Americans in the United States (7 mosques were attacked, and one cemetery was desecrated), the likes of which had not been seen since the months immediately following September 11, 2001, and the weeks following the Oklahoma City bombing in 1995, when many people initially supposed that Muslim terrorists were responsible for the attack (Amer and Basu, 2012).

Conclusion

In our discussion of the religious dimensions of American national identity, we demonstrate that religion functions in various ways in the contexts of national discourses. We have argued against approaches that assume religious and secular forms of nationalism are antithetical to one another because such lenses are deceptive. Such an approach tends to be misleading when one attempts to explore why certain policies and political frameworks are authorized; what the relationships are between civil religion, nationalism, and antecedent traditional religions; and how certain institutional and structural conditions enable changes in the ways religion relates to conceptions of national identity.

The question of religious nationalism, therefore, could never be adequately addressed simply in terms of structural separation—or lack thereof—between the state and religion. Rather, the powerful realities of religious nationalism (which form central currents coursing through the history and prehistory of the United States, as we have shown earlier in this chapter) must be situated within their historical contexts and thickly described. Assessment of religious nationalisms in the United States must remain critically attuned to all the ways that national identity relates to religion, ethnicity, and culture. In undertaking such an investigation, we have sought to demonstrate that even a case that appears to exemplify inclusivism and liberalism (i.e., the United States) has been, and still is, shot through with chauvinistic and xenophobic religious nationalist features and tendencies which must be critically examined and persistently fought against. At the same time, a case which appears to present an exemplar of religious nationalism (e.g., Israel) simultaneously manifests important resources and developments for criticizing, reimagining, and countering the tendencies toward exclusivism and injustice to which religious nationalist elements are prone.

We saw that sociocultural and political transformations are shaped by various processes—from tackling the challenges of modernity and secularity, to reimagining national identity in ways that are more consistent with particular interpretations of religious outlooks. U.S. political developments—such as the increased illiberality (i.e., narrowing) of an American identity as Judeo-Christian, the gradual dissolving of the liberal Protestantism into the cultural consensus of the 1950s and 1960s, the emergence of the Religious Right in the 1980s and 1990s, and the gradual legal reinforcement of civil religion in the United States—cannot simply be viewed as a reaction to the encroachment of "secular modernity." Understanding these developments requires, instead, careful study of the patterns and processes of social, political, and religious change over time. It requires careful assessment of strategic co-optation and manipulation of populist sentiments by political and religious elites. It requires examining the emergence of populist groups and social movements in response to specific historical developments and events. It requires critical attention to the ways that symbolic boundaries get conceptualized, embodied, and reinforced, and how they exert themselves socially and politically.

Since the nation's inception, the religious dimensions of American nationalism have always been present, but they have also evolved. The founders of the United States sought to establish new rights and freedoms for its citizens. Since the beginning of the "American experiment," the exclusivist impulses and the legacies of religious freedom and pluralism have been locked in conflict as its citizens and political leaders have attempted to shape the identity of the nation. Despite the institutional separation of religion and state, it would be a mistake to classify American nationalism as simply secular. As we saw, this institutional "separation of church and state" was instituted in large part for religious purposes: to shield religion from any attempt to impose political coercion on matters of personal conscience and belief.

In some cases, certain religious groups were marginalized and displaced as the result of attempts to clearly and distinctly separate church and state, religion and politics. Yet in response to efforts to keep the public sphere secular, many of those groups were motivated to affect broader sociopolitical transformations. They insisted that the religious dimensions—or basic religious character—were essential to the nation's identity. This provides yet another illustration of how questions of religion and modernity are intimately related to the emergence of explicitly religious interpretations of national identities.

Particularly since the rise of politically active religious conservatism in the 1980s, American religiosity has continued to flourish and exert itself in public and political matters through formal institutions of the state as well as through informal cultural practices that are nonetheless powerful and influential. Competing visions related to the religious dimensions of American nationality persist into the 21st century.

In the cases of both Israel and the United States, we have identified important links between the rise of religious radicalism and exclusivist national agendas. Moreover, we have explored the ways that religion is linked to national identities in order to subvert the broader political and social landscapes. These cases do not appear to demonstrate positive connections between religion and violent state practices. And yet we have also seen that there are many examples that support the potential for religion and the state to affect each other in positive ways. Time and again, religious organizations, theologians and religious leaders, and even political parties have articulated encompassingly self-critical, self-revising interpretations of the political community that are accountable to overarching conceptions of justice and peace. And religion, at times in a full range of prophetic and priestly voices, has stood against abuses of power, discrimination, injustice, atrocities, and the violation of human rights.

References

Almog, Shmuel and Lyael Maman. *Nationalism and Anti-Semitism in Modern Europe, 1815–1945* (Oxford: Pergamon Press, 1990).

Amer, Yasin and Moni Basu. "Attacks against U.S. Muslims Spike during Ramadan," *CNN*, August 18, 2012. http://religion.blogs.cnn.com/2012/08/18/attacks-against-u-s-muslims-spike-during-ramadan/ (accessed September 1, 2012).

Anderson, Benedict. *Imagined Communities: Reflections on the Origin and Spread of Nationalism* (London: Verso, 2006).

Appleby, Scott R. and John T McGreevy. "Catholics, Muslims, and the Mosque," *New York Review of Books* 57, no. 14 (September 30, 2010), p. 48.

Aran, Gideon. "From Religious Zionism to Zionist Religion: The Roots of Gush Emunim," *Studies in Contemporary Jewry* 2 (1986), pp. 117–143.

Associated Press. "Court Rejects Challenge to Pledge of Allegiance," *New York Times*, August 11, 2005.

Batnitzky, Leora. *How Judaism became a Religion* (Princeton, NJ: Princeton University Press, 2011).

Bellah, Robert. *The Broken Covenant: American Civil Religion in a Time of Trial* (Chicago: University of Chicago Press, 1992).

Berg, Manfred. *Popular Justice: A History of Lynching in America* (New York: Rowen and Littlefield, 2009).

Boyd, Julian P., Charles T. Cullen, John Catanzariti, Barbara B. Oberg, et al., eds. *The Papers of Thomas Jefferson, Vol. 1* (Princeton, NJ: Princeton University Press, 1950).

Bromwich, David. "Lincoln and Whitman as Representative Americans," *Yale Review* 90, no. 2 (April 2002), pp. 1–21.

Buber, Martin. *A Land of Two Peoples: Martin Buber on Jews and Arabs* (Chicago: University of Chicago Press, 2005 [1983]).

Bush, George W. "Remarks Accepting the Presidential Nomination at the Republican National Convention in New York City," September 2, 2004. Online by Gerhard Peters and John T. Woolley, *The American Presidency Project*. http://www.presidency.ucsb.edu/ws/?pid=72727 (accessed October 20, 2012).

Bush, George W. "Remarks at the Islamic Center of Washington," September 17, 2001. Online by Gerhard Peters and John T. Woolley, *The American Presidency Project*. http://www.presidency.ucsb.edu/ws/?pid=63740 (accessed October 20, 2012).

Capps, Walter. *The New Religious Right: Piety, Patriotism, and Politics* (Columbia: University of South Carolina Press, 1990).

Casanova, Jose. "Nativism and the Politics of Gender in Catholicism and Islam," in Hanna Herzog and Ann Braude, eds., *Gendering Religion and Politics: Untangling Modernities* (New York: Palgrave Macmillan, 2009).

Christison, Kathleen. *Perceptions of Palestine: Their Influence on U.S. Middle East Policy* (Berkeley: University of California Press, 1999).

Clark, Victoria. *Allies for Armageddon: The Rise of Christian Zionism* (New Haven, CT: Yale University Press, 2007).

CNN, "Opinion Research Poll, August 6–10, 2010," August 11, 2010. http://i2.cdn.turner.com/cnn/2010/images/08/11/rel11a.pdf (accessed August 29, 2012).

Corrigan, John and Lynn S. Neal. *Religious Intolerance in America: A Documentary History* (Chapel Hill: University of North Carolina Press, 2010).

Danner, Mark. *Torture and Truth: America, Abu Ghraib, and the War on Terror* (New York: New York Review of Books, 2004).

Dekel-Chen, Jonathan L. *Anti-Jewish Violence: Rethinking the Pogrom in East European History* (Bloomington: Indiana University Press, 2011).

Editor. "Obama's Remarks about Ground Zero Mosque: The Transcript," *Washington Post* (August 13, 2010), http://voices.washingtonpost.com/44/2010/08/obamas-remarks-about-ground-ze.html (accessed October 21, 2012).

Editors. "In a Time of War," *First Things* (December 2001), pp. 11–17.

Eisenhower, Dwight D. "Statement by the President upon Signing Bill to Include the Words "Under God" in the Pledge to the Flag," June 14, 1954. Online by Gerhard Peters and John T. Woolley, *The American Presidency Project*. http://www.presidency.ucsb.edu/ws/?pid=9920 (accessed October 21, 2012).

Elver, Hilal. "Racializing Islam before and after 9/11: From Melting Pot to Islamophobia," *Transnational Law & Contemporary Problems* 21, no. 1 (Spring 2012), pp. 157–174.

Falwell, Jerry. *Listen America!* (Garden City, NY: Doubleday, 1980).

Falwell, Jerry. "The Maligned Moral Majority," *Newsweek* 98 (September 21, 1981), p. 17.

Frykholm, Amy Johnson. *Rapture Culture: Left Behind in Evangelical America* (Oxford: Oxford University Press, 2004).

Gallup Wellbeing. "In U.S., Religious Prejudice Stronger against Muslims," January 21, 2010. http://www.gallup.com/poll/125312/religious-prejudice-stronger-against-muslims.aspx (accessed September 3, 2012).

Gellner, Ernest. *Nations and Nationalism* (Ithaca, NY: Cornell University Press, 1983).

Goldenberg, Suzanne. "Rioting as Sharon Visits Islam Holy Site," *Guardian* (September 28, 2000). http://www.guardian.co.uk/world/2000/sep/29/israel (accessed October 27, 2011).

Goldman, Adam and Matt Apuzzo. "NYPD: Muslim Spying Led to No Leads, Terror Cases," Associated Press, August 21, 2012. http://www.ap.org/Content/AP-In-The-News/2012/NYPD-Muslim-spying-led-to-no-leads-terror-cases (accessed September 2, 2012).

Goldman, Adam and Matt Apuzzo. "With CIA Help, NYPD Moves Covertly in Muslim Areas," Associated Press, August 23, 2011, http://www.ap.org/Content/AP-In-The-News/2011/With-CIA-help-NYPD-moves-covertly-in-Muslim-areas (accessed September 2, 2012).

Henry, Patrick. " 'And I Don't Care What It Is': The Tradition-History of a Civil Religion Proof-Text," *Journal of the American Academy of Religion* 49, no. 1 (1981), pp. 35–49.

Herzl, Theodore. Excerpts from Herzl's *The Jewish State*, Jewish Virtual Library. http://www.jewishvirtuallibrary.org/jsource/Zionism/herzlex.html (accessed October 20, 2012).

Hibbard, Scott W. *Religious Politics and Secular States: Egypt, India, and the United States* (Baltimore: Johns Hopkins University Press, 2010).

Hodgwon, Godfrey. *The Myth of American Exceptionalism* (New Haven, CT: Yale University Press, 2009).

Howard-Pitney, David. *African American Jeremiad: Appeals for Justice in America* (Philadelphia: Temple University Press, 2005).

Hutcheson, Richard. *God in the Whitehouse: How Religion Has Changed the Modern Presidency* (New York: MacMillan, 1988).

Jefferson, Thomas. "The Declaration of Independence." http://www
.ushistory.org/declaration/document/index.htm (accessed January 24,
2012).

Jones, Jeffrey M. "Atheists, Muslims See Most Bias as Presidential
Candidates," *Gallup* (June 21, 2012). http://www.gallup.com/poll/
155285/atheists-muslims-bias-presidential-candidates.aspx (accessed
August 14, 2012).

King, Martin Luther, Jr. "I Have a Dream," in *A Testament of Hope: the
Essential Writings and Speeches of Martin Luther King, Jr.* (New York:
Harper Collins, 1991, pp. 217–220).

King, Martin Luther, Jr. "My Trip to the Land of Gandhi," in *A Testament
of Hope: the Essential Writings and Speeches of Martin Luther King, Jr.* (New
York: Harper Collins, 1991, pp. 23–30).

King, Martin Luther, Jr. "Where Do We Go from Here?" in *I Have a Dream:
Writings and Speeches that Changed the World* (New York: HarperCollins,
1992, pp. 169–179).

Kook, Abraham Isaac. "Souls of Chaos," in Abraham Isaac Kook et al.,
eds., *Abraham Isaac Kook: The Lights of Penitence, Lights of Holiness, The
Moral Principles, Essays, Letters, and Poems* (Mahwah, NJ: Paulist Press,
1978).

Lehmann, David and Batia B. Siebzehnner. *Remaking Israeli Judaism: The
Challenge of Shas* (Oxford: Oxford University Press, 2007).

Leibowitz, Yeshayahu. *Judaism, Human Values, and the Jewish State*
(Cambridge, MA: Harvard University Press, 1992).

Lincoln, Abraham. "Address at the Dedication of the National Cemetery
at Gettysburg, Pennsylvania," November 19, 1863. Online by Gerhard
Peters and John T. Woolley, *The American Presidency Project*. http://www
.presidency.ucsb.edu/ws/?pid=73959 (accessed October 20, 2012).

Lincoln, Abraham. "Inaugural Address," March 4, 1865. Online by
Gerhard Peters and John T. Woolley, *The American Presidency Project*.
http://www.presidency.ucsb.edu/ws/?pid=25819 (accessed October 20,
2012).

Little, David. "Roger Williams and the Separation of Church and State,"
in James E. Wood, Jr., ed., *Religion and the State: Essays in Honor of Leo
Pfeffer* (Waco, TX: Baylor University Press, 1985).

Locke, John. *A Letter Concerning Toleration* (New York: Prometheus, 1990
[1689]).

Lyons, Linda. "The Gallup Brain: 'One Nation Under God,' " March 23,
2004. http://www.gallup.com/poll/11065/gallup-brain-one-nation
-under-god.aspx (accessed January 23, 2012).

Manis, Andrew. *Southern Civil Religions in Conflict: Civil Rights and the Culture Wars* (Macon, GA: Mercer University Press, 2002).

Marsden, George. *Religion and American Culture* (New York: Harcourt Brace Jovanovich, 1990).

Marty, Martin. *A Nation of Behavers* (Chicago: University of Chicago Press, 1976).

McAlister, Melani. *Epic Encounters: Culture, Media, and U.S. Interests in the Middle East since 1945* (Berkeley: University of California Press, 2001).

Merino, Stephen M. "Religious Diversity in a 'Christian Nation': The Effect of Theological Exclusivity and Interreligious Contract on the Acceptance of Religious Diversity." *Journal of the Scientific Study of Religion* 49, no. 2 (2010), pp. 231–246.

Merkley, Paul C. *The Politics of Christian Zionism, 1891–1948* (London: Frank Cass, 1998).

Meyer, Michael. *Jewish Identity in the Modern World* (Seattle: University of Washington Press, 1990).

Moriarty, J. T., ed. *Manifest Destiny: A Primary Source History of America's Territorial Expansion in the 19th Century* (New York: Rosen Publishing Group, 2005).

Nieves, Ellen. "Judges Ban Pledge of Allegiance from Schools," *New York Times*, June 27, 2002, http://www.nytimes.com/2002/06/27/us/judges-ban-pledge-of-allegiance-from-schools-citing-under-god.html?pagewanted=all&src=pm (accessed October 21, 2012).

Noll, Mark. *The Civil War as Theological Crisis* (Chapel Hill: University of North Carolina Press, 2006).

Nunpa, Chris Mato. "A Sweet-Smelling Sacrifice: Genocide, the Bible, and the Indigenous Peoples of the United States, Selected Examples," in Stephen Jacobs, ed., *Confronting Genocide: Judaism, Christianity, Islam* (Lanham, MD: Lexington Books, 2009, pp. 47–64).

Nussbaum, Martha. *The New Religious Intolerance* (Cambridge, MA: Harvard University Press, 2012).

Omer, Atalia. *When Peace Is Not Enough: How the Israeli Peace Camp Thinks about Religion, Nationalism, and Justice* (Chicago: University of Chicago Press, 2013).

O'Sullivan, John. "Annexation," *United States Magazine and Democratic Review* 17 (July 1845), pp. 5–10.

Pew Research Center. "Controversies over Mosques and Islamic Centers across the U.S.," Forum on Religion and Public Life (September 29, 2011). http://features.pewforum.org/muslim/controversies-over-mosque-and-islamic-centers-across-the-us.html (accessed August 14, 2012).

Pierard, Richard V. and Robert D. Linder. *Civil Religion and the Presidency* (Grand Rapids, MI: Zondervan, 1988).

Rable, George C. *God's Almost Chosen People: A Religious History of the Civil War* (Chapel Hill: University of North Carolina Press, 2010).

Ravitzky, Aviezer. *Messianism, Zionism, and Jewish Religious Radicalism* (Chicago: University of Chicago Press, 1996).

Roosevelt, Franklin D. "Annual Message to Congress.," January 4, 1939. Online by Gerhard Peters and John T. Woolley, *The American Presidency Project.* http://www.presidency.ucsb.edu/ws/?pid=15684 (accessed October 21, 2012).

Shenhav, Yehouda. *The Arab Jews: A Postcolonial Reading of Nationalism, Religion, and Ethnicity* (Palo Alto, CA: Stanford University Press, 2006).

Smith, Anthony. *Chosen Peoples: Sacred Sources of National Identity* (Oxford: Oxford University Press, 2003).

Spector, Stephen. *Evangelicals and Israel: The Story of American Christian Zionism* (Oxford: Oxford University Press, 2009).

Springs, Jason A. "Civil Religion," in Richard Hecht and Vincent Biondo, eds., *Religion and Culture: Contemporary Practices and Perspectives* (Minneapolis: Fortress Press, 2012).

Stolberg, Sheryl Gay. "Obama Strongly Backs Islam Center Near 9/11 Site," *New York Times* (August 13, 2010), http://www.nytimes.com/2010/08/14/us/politics/14obama.html?_r=0 (accessed October 21, 2012).

Stout, Harry. *Upon the Altar of the Nation: A Moral History of the Civil War* (New York: Penguin, 2006).

Stout, Jeffrey. *Democracy and Tradition* (Princeton, NJ: Princeton University Press, 2004).

Stout, Jeffrey. "Theses on Black Nationalism," in Eddie S. Glaude, Jr., ed., *Is It Nation Time?: Contemporary Essays on Black Power and Black Nationalism* (Chicago: University of Chicago Press, 2002), pp. 234–256.

Tenenbaum. "Muslims and Islam in the United States: Fact Sheet," Tenenbaum Center for Interreligious Understanding, 2011. https://www.tanenbaum.org/sites/default/files/P51%20Resources%20-%20Muslims%20and%20Islam%20in%20the%20US.pdf (accessed October 21, 2012).

Theiss-Morse, Elizabeth. *Who Counts as an American?: The Boundaries of National Identity* (Cambridge: Cambridge University Press, 2009).

Thiemann, Ronald. *Religion in Public life: A Dilemma for Democracy* (Washington, D.C.: Georgetown University Press, 1996).

Venables, Robert W. *American Indian History: Five Centuries of Conflict and Coexistence: Conquest of a Continent, 1492–1783* (Santa Fe, NM: Clear Light Publishing, 2004).

Weber, Max. "The Meaning of 'Ethical Neutrality' in Sociology and Economics," in E. A. Shils and H. A. Finch, eds. and translators, *The Methodology of the Social Sciences* (New York: Free Press, 1949 [1917]).

Weber, Max. "Objectivity in Social Science and Social Policy" in E. A. Shils and H. A. Finch, eds. and translators, *The Methodology of the Social Sciences* (New York: Free Press, 1949 [1904]).

West, Cornel. *Prophetic Fragments* (Grand Rapids, MI: Eerdmans, 1988).

White, Ronald C. *Lincoln's Greatest Speech: The Second Inaugural* (New York: Simon and Schuster, 2002).

Wilcox, Clyde and Carin Larson. *Onward Christian Soldiers? The Religious Right in American Politics* (Boulder, CO: Westview Press, 2006).

Winthrop, John. *Winthrop Papers*, 6 Vols. (Boston: Massachusetts Historical Society, 1929–1944), 4, p. 149.

Wuthnow, Robert. *America and the Challenge of Religious Diversity* (Princeton, NJ: Princeton University Press, 2005).

Wuthnow, Robert. "Religious Diversity in a 'Christian Nation': American Identity and American Democracy," in Thomas Banchoff, ed., *Democracy and the New Religious Pluralism* (Oxford: Oxford University Press, 2007, pp. 151–170).

Wuthnow, Robert. *The Restructuring of American Religion* (Princeton, NJ: Princeton University Press, 1989).

Yack, Bernard. *Nationalism and the Moral Psychology of Community* (Chicago, IL: University of Chicago Press, 2012).

4

Chronologies

This chapter reviews the chronologies of select cases of conflict zones defined by ethnoreligious national claims. Those cases were selected because they expose how various identity markers such as ethnicity, religion, nationality, and culture interrelate and even often conflate with one another both in our analysis of various conflicts as well as in the imaginations of individuals and groups caught in the dynamics of such conflicts. The cases also illuminate the complexities involved in rendering "religious" nationalism as a distinct form that is categorically different from "secular" nationalism. Religious nationalisms are not necessarily measured by an aspiration to institute a theocracy. Nor are they defined by the degree of religious observance of the individuals engaged in nationalistic struggles. In fact, most of the cases here suggest that sometimes, categorizing religion as a mere ethnic, cultural, and national identity marker overlooks the selective mode in which nationalisms, even in their secular varieties, draw upon religious motifs, symbols, and narratives. Another common theme informing many cases of nationalist struggles defined by ethnoreligious claims is the legacy of colonialism, even in the postcolonial period of independence. This chapter features the cases of Sri Lanka, Northern Ireland, Israel/Palestine, and the Muslim Brotherhood in Egypt, in order to illustrate how religion relates to the dynamics of national discourses.

Religious Nationalism and Conflict Zones

Sri Lanka

The Sri Lankan civil war was a conflict between the Sinhalese Buddhist majority and the Tamil Hindu minority. During colonial rule, the Tamils were given a disproportional amount of control in government, which angered many Sinhalese and caused the Sinhalese people to become "a majority population with a minority complex." Upon independence, the Sinhalese increasingly asserted their dominance, leading to the subjugation of the Tamil people who sought to gain independence from them. The justification for hegemonic conceptions of Sinhalese Buddhism in Sri Lanka emerged out of a selective reading of the chronicle of the Mahavamsa, a poem composed by Theravada Buddhist monks in the sixth century. The Mahavamsa, as read by Buddhist revivalists in the 19th century and later, singles out the destiny and sacred mission of the Sinhalese people to consolidate Buddhism and the monarchy. The island, the religion, and the political project—all are conflated within this mythological reading.

1948	Ceylon (the British colonial name for Sri Lanka, changed in 1972) gains independence from Great Britain. Although independence was gained, deep fractures exist due to the previous centuries of colonization. Although Tamils are only a small minority of the Sri Lankan population, they were overrepresented in colonial government, which gave them more governmental power than the Sinhalese majority, leading to resentment.
	After the country gained independence, steps are taken by Sinhalese to displace Tamils who held power and make legislation that benefitted the Sinhalese majority. In 1948, the Sinhalese nationalists introduce the Ceylon Citizenship Act legislation, denying citizenship to the majority of Hindu Tamils. Subsequent legislation declared Buddhism the official religion, further disenfranchising Tamils.
1956	Sinhala Only Act (Official Language Act) changes the official language from English to Sinhalese and sparks anti-Tamil riots.

1957	The Bandaranaike–Chelvanayakam Pact (B-C Pact) between Sri Lankan Prime Minister S. W. R. D. Bandaranaike and S. J. V. Chelvanayakam, the leader of the Tamil political party, agrees that Tamils will stop protests for language equality in exchange for designation of Tamil as a minority language and the establishment of regional councils to oversee education, agriculture, and Sinhalese colonization in Tamil areas. In response to continued protests by Buddhist monks, Bandaranaike dissolves the pact.
1960–1965	The government of Sirimavo Bandaranaike instates policies supporting Sinhalese superiority while disenfranchising the Tamil minority.
1965–1970	The United National Party, the main opposition party in Sri Lanka, leads a coalition government that uses the courts to reverse the Sinhala Only Act. The party's policies are more sympathetic to the Tamil people.
1970s	A rise in legislation that keeps qualified Tamils from government jobs and universities further marginalizes and subjugates the group. This correlates with the rise in militant Tamil groups.
April 5–23, 1971	The People's Liberation Front (Janatha Vimukthi Peramuna), a Sri Lanakan, Marxist political party, attempts a nationwide coup, but the Bandaranaika government prevents it.
1972	Ceylon becomes the Democratic Socialist Republic of Sri Lanka and is no longer a British dominion. A new constitution is adopted that disregards Tamils in favor of ethnocentrism (disregarding the Soulberry Constitution created by the British before independence, which made guarantees for minorities), focuses on Buddhism, and ignores other religions in Sri Lanka.
1972	TNT (Tamil New Tigers), a militant pro-secessionist Tamil group, forms.
January 1974	Police attack and kill 11 people at the Fourth International Tamil Conference in Jaffna, which leads to more calls for separatism.

1975	Alfred Duraiappah, the mayor of Jaffna (the unofficial Tamil capital), is assassinated by a Tamil extremist on his way to a Hindu temple. His assassin, Velupillai Prabhakaran, later forms the LTTE (Liberation Tigers of Tamil Eelam), the most ruthless Tamil militant group.
1976	LTTE, formerly known as the TNT, forms.
May 14, 1976	The Tamil United Liberation Front declares the right to Tamil statehood.
1978	The Prevention of Terrorism Act of 1978 is proposed. It would allow people suspected of terrorist or rebellious activities to be arrested and held for up to 18 months. The law is enacted temporarily in 1979 and made permanent in 1982. The law results in the capture and torture of many innocent Tamils without cause, subsequently radicalizing rebellious groups even more.
1981	A library in Jaffna containing rare manuscripts and historical documents is burned down.
July 13, 1983	Tamil Tigers (LTTE) kill 13 Sri Lankan soldiers, and Sinhalese residents violently retaliate against their Tamil neighbors. The result is a killing spree that goes on for a week, resulting in the massacre of 3,000 Tamils and the destruction of thousands of Tamil homes and businesses.
July 23, 1983 to July 29 1987	Eelam I, the first phase of the Sri Lankan civil war. In response to the riots in Sri Lanka, some Tamils leave the country, and others migrate north in hopes of creating a separate state. Overnight, small secessionist groups gain many members.
1984	LTTE commits the Kent Farms massacre, resulting in 33 Sinhalese civilian deaths, and the Dollar Farms massacre, resulting in 29 Sinhalese civilian deaths.
1985	LTTE commits the Anuradhapura massacre of civilians. This is one of the LTTE's largest massacres to date; LTTE members highjacked a bus in Anuradhapura, opened fire in a bus station, continued on to the Sri Maha Bodhi Shrine and opened fire, and then went on to the Wilpattu National Park. In total, 146 men and women are killed in the massacre.

May 26–31, 1987	The Sri Lankan government launches Operation Liberation, an offensive against the Tamil Tigers conducted by the Sri Lankan military.
July 1987	LTTE carries out its first suicide attack.
July 29, 1987	The Indo-Sri Lanka Peace Accord is signed, allowing Indian peacekeeping groups into northern Sri Lanka. The terms of the accord give the Tamil language official status, and more power is given to the provinces. Militant groups, including the LTTE, agree to hand over weapons to the Indian peacekeeping troops (though the LTTE later refuses to disarm). The accord ultimately led to a Sinhalese against Sinhalese civil war.
July 1987–March 1990	The LTTE wages war with the Indian peacekeeping forces.
1990	The idea of an ethnically homogenous Tamil state leads the LTTE to expel roughly 75,000 Muslim residents of northern Sri Lanka.
March 24, 1990	The Indian peacekeeping forces leave Sri Lanka.
1990–1995	Unprecedented violence—with massacres and abductions by the government and LTTE—marks Eelam II, the second phase of the Sri Lankan civil war.
May 1991	The LTTE, which is considered a pioneer in the use of suicide bombings, is the first group to ever use a female suicide bomber, in the murder of Rajiv Gandhi, the former Indian prime minister. Rajiv Gandhi had been instrumental in the Indian Peace Keeping Force (IPKF) intervention in the Sri Lankan civil war. In an interview of August 1990, Gandhi had asserted that he would send the IPKF to disarm the LTTE if it came back to power in Sri Lanka.
March 2, 1991	A car bomb set by a Tiger in Colombo kills deputy defense minister Ranjan Wijeratne.
May 1993	A Tamil Tiger (LTTE) suicide bomber kills Sri Lankan president Ranasinghe Premadasa.

1995–2002	Eelam III, the third phase of the Sri Lankan civil war, begins.
1994	President Chandrika Kumaratunga offers to allow the LTTE to rule the northeast for 10 years, during which time a more permanent solution would hopefully be found. There is debate about whether this offer was truly sincere because of the determination of Prabhakaran, the leader of the LTTE, to achieve independence militarily.
January 8, 1995	The LTTE and the government sign a truce agreement.
April 1995	The LTTE breaks the truce by blowing up two navy ships and killing 12 sailors.
December 6, 1995	The Sri Lankan flag is raised on the Tamil stronghold of Jaffna, marking the biggest victory since Eelam I was declared.
February 22, 2002	Peace accord between the Tamil Tigers and Sri Lankan government unite Tamils in the east and north. This leads to a short period of Tiger government in Tamil-dominated areas. With the Sri Lankan government allowing some autonomy in these areas, the LTTE hoped for full independence.
April 21, 2003	Peace talks break down.
March 2004	There is a split within the LTTE between the followers of northern commander Prabhakaran and eastern leader Colonel Karuna, reflecting the disparity among different Tamil groups. Eastern Tamils had long been treated as inferior to their northern counterparts.
July 26, 2006 to May 18, 2009	Eelam IV, the fourth phase of the Sri Lankan civil war, begins.
July 2006	Tigers block a reservoir that supplies water to farmers, leading Mahinda Rajapaksa, Sri Lankan president and commander and chief of the Sri Lankan armed forces, to split the north and east provinces, thus taking away hopes of a Tamil homeland.

January 3, 2008	The Sri Lankan government formally withdraws from the February 2002 cease-fire that existed only on paper for the past two years.
January 2009	Tigers let go of Kilinochchi, a stronghold up to that point, and begin to collapse.
May 16, 2009	General Sarath Fonseka declares victory over Tiger forces.

Northern Ireland

The Northern Ireland conflict mainly revolved around the rift between Unionists and Nationalists. The Unionists, mostly Protestant, opposed the Home Rule Act and wished to maintain a stronger connection to Great Britain and avoid being overshadowed by the Catholic majority and Nationalists. Predominantly Catholic, the Nationalists aspired to unite with the rest of Ireland. To understand the dynamics of this case, one must explore the legacy of British colonialism, enduring systemic patterns of discrimination based on ethnoreligious identity markers, and the role of religious leadership in both intensifying belligerence on occasions as well as constructively engaging in peacebuilding on others.

1912–1914	The Home Rule Act, which proposed that Ireland have its own parliament for domestic issues while still being connected to Great Britain, is passed. The Ulster Voluntary Forces form a militia group that opposes the act, and the Nationalist Irish Volunteers form a group that supports the act.
January 21, 1919	The Irish Republican Army (IRA) forms. It is a paramilitary group with the goal of ending British control of the northern region of Ireland. It will become one of the most important Republican groups in the Northern Ireland conflict.
1919–1921	The Anglo-Irish War occurs.

1920	The British Parliament passes the Government of Ireland Act, which partitions Ireland into North and South. Each part has autonomy and a parliament, though both will remain officially part of Great Britain.
1921	The Anglo-Irish Treaty ends the war in December 1921, formally partitioning Ireland into Northern Ireland and the Irish Free State.
1932	Protestant and Catholic poor unite as relief riots break out in response to the Unionist government's handling of the unemployment problem in Northern Ireland.
1935	Hopes of unity between Loyalists, predominately Protestant groups that wished to remain a part of England, and Republicans, predominately Catholic groups that wished to become independent, are shattered as militants from each group begin a campaign of shootings and bombings that leads to deeper divisions between the groups.
1937	New constitution in Dublin claims jurisdiction over the whole island of Ireland, despite the fact that Northern Ireland is separate.
1948	Irish Parliament passes the Irish Republic Act, declaring Ireland a republic and ending its status as a British dominion, and thus, subject to the British crown).
1949	The British Parliament responds to the Irish Republic Act by publishing the Ireland Act, which confirms that any change in the constitutional status of Northern Ireland cannot occur without the formal consent of the British Parliament.
December 1956	The IRA begins a border campaign named Operation Harvest in which it attacks infrastructure and security forces in Northern Ireland. This operation lasts until February 1962.
1960s	Civil rights campaigns emerge in an attempt to bring more attention to the plight of Catholic minorities in Northern Ireland.

1965	The Ulster Volunteer Force (UVA), a loyalist paramilitary group, is formed. Its first goal is to destabilize the government of Terence O'Neill's liberal regime in Northern Ireland.
1966	The UVA commits three murders and declares war on the IRA.
October 5, 1968	A march is organized in Derry to protest the bad conditions there related to housing, employment, and corrupt electoral practices.
August 1969	British troops are sent as peacekeepers to Northern Ireland. They will also serve as the military aid to civil powers there. Their deployment is named Operation Banner and is planned to be temporary, but the troops do not leave Northern Ireland until 2007. The British government also forces Northern Ireland to adopt various reforms.
December 1969	The IRA splits between those that support armed resistance and those who choose a political route. Out of this split form two groups, the official IRA and the Provisional IRA (the Provisional IRA also has an army).
January 1970	Sinn Fein is formed as a result of the split in the IRA. This new group represents the views of Republicans in Northern Ireland and supports the IRA.
1971	The Provisional IRA kills a soldier for the first time. Internment without a trial is used for the first time and continues until December 5, 1975. This leads Catholic communities to offer more support to the IRA.
September 1971	The Ulster Defense Association forms as a paramilitary Loyalist group.
January 30, 1972	A police shooting leaves 13 men dead at a riot in Derry. In response, Civil Rights Republicans and Nationalists speak out and the IRA receives increased support (this event is referred to as Bloody Sunday).
March 24, 1972	Unionists are angered upon hearing that law and order is transferred to British Parliament and direct rule is established.

July, 21 1972	Bloody Friday. Within 75 minutes, the IRA sets off 22 explosives in Belfast. In response, the British Army launches Operation Motorman to wrest control of the streets of Londonderry and Belfast from IRA control, leading to a boycott by Nationalists.
Summer 1972	The IRA calls a cease-fire and from then on, the group that was previously referred to as the Provisional IRA is called the IRA.
1973	Sunningdale conference establishes power sharing between Britain, Ireland, and Northern Ireland, and it is agreed that the constitutional status of Northern Ireland cannot be changed without the consent of the Protestant majority.
1975	A constitutional convention is held for different parties in Northern Ireland to discuss political arrangements for the future.
1982	Sinn Fein, a left-wing Irish political party, wins 10 percent of the votes for the Northern Irish Assembly, which is roughly one-third of the Catholic vote.
1984	The IRA bombs a conservative party conference and narrowly misses Prime Minister Margaret Thatcher.
November 15, 1985	An Anglo-Irish agreement is signed, giving Dublin the role of a consultant for Northern Ireland and restoring power sharing. This leads 100,000 Unionists to gather in Belfast to protest the agreement.
February 1989	Meetings are held in Germany between the predominantly Protestant Unionist and predominantly Catholic Nationalist parties, but the talks collapse because of disagreements over Dublin's now formalized role as a consultant in future settlements.
March 1991	Peter Brooke, Britain's secretary of state, announces a new "three-strand approach" that will consider the relationships of Ireland to Westminster, Northern Ireland to the Republic of Ireland, and Northern Ireland to the United Kingdom.
December 1993	The British and Irish governments publish the Downing Street Declaration, which reaffirms the

importance of consent from all parties involved in the conflict and calls on the IRA to renounce violent means.

October 1994 Representing the unionist paramilitary groups, the Ulster Volunteer Force and the Ulster Defense Association, the combined Loyalist Military Command declares a cease-fire.

January 1995 The Northern Ireland Office demands that decommissioning of the paramilitary groups occur before political talks can begin.

January 1996 George Mitchell is elected head of a commission to propose a way to end problems with decommissioning and talks. He suggests that decommissioning happen at the same time as talks.

September 1997 Sinn Fein agrees to George Mitchell's nonviolence principles and enters peace talks.

April 10, 1998 All parties (except for the Democratic Unionist Party, who walk out) sign the Good Friday Agreement between the British and Irish governments, and the eight political parties in Northern Ireland. The agreement determined that Northern Ireland would remain part of United Kingdom until a majority of its citizens there, and in Ireland, voted to unite with the Republic of Ireland. If that development occurred, both Britain and Ireland would be bound to recognize the result. In the meantime, both British and Irish national identities would be fully recognized and qualify for citizenship in Northern Ireland.

August 2001 The Ulster Volunteer Force and Ulster Defense Association call a halt to feuding, but this still leaves the position of the dissident Loyalist Volunteer Forces undecided.

January 2005 The IRA is accused of murdering a Catholic man, which leads to international condemnation of the group.

July 2005 The Provisional IRA calls a halt to campaigns and declares the war over.

May 3, 2007 UVF announces the end of its violent resistance.

May 2007	Ian Paisley, chief of the mainly Protestant Democratic Unionist Party, and Gerry Adams, leader of the predominantly Catholic group Sinn Fein, agree on a power-sharing which leads to the end of the stalemate of institutions.
November 2008	Local parties are able to agree upon a way to turn over policing and criminal justice functions to Stormont, the Northern Ireland Assembly (or Parliament of Northern Ireland).
February 2009	Shaun Woodward, the former British secretary of state, announces that policing and criminal justice powers will be given to Stormont in accordance with the St. Andrews Agreement.
March 2009	The Real IRA, an Irish republican paramilitary group that splintered from the Provisional IRA in 1997, shooting of two British soldiers preparing to leave for Afghanistan leads to a protest against violence that spans the different communities.
June 2009	The UVF and UDA announce that their weapons are beyond use, which signifies Loyalist decommissioning.

Israel/Palestine

Religious dimensions of the Israeli-Palestinian conflict are complex and cannot be understood outside of a careful analysis of how particular interpretations of Jewish history relate to the ideological claims of Israeli nationalism. Likewise, Palestinians—who are primarily Muslims but also include significant and influential Christian communities—attach religious significance to the land of Palestine. In the case of the Jews, the religious significance is grounded in the narration of Jewish history as a series of catastrophes dating back to the destructions of the Temples and the subsequent millennia of uprootedness in the diasporas. This story of uprootedness was finally reversed with the return of many Jews to the land of their ancestors in the aftermath of the Holocaust. Indeed, Zionism as a national movement had emerged already in the 19th century, but it was only the catastrophe of the Holocaust and the near destruction of European Jewry that facilitated the actual establishment of the modern Israeli nation-state in 1948. Zionism came in different shapes and forms, but the initial leadership and general tenor of Israeli society was thoroughly secular and, occasionally, even antireligious. Nonetheless, being a "Jewish state," Israel embraced Hebrew as its primary national language. Likewise, the Sabbath was recognized as the official day of rest, and the laws of Kashrut (Jewish dietary laws primarily derived form the Torah books of Leveiticus and Deuteronomy) were enforced in official contexts such as the Israeli Defense Forces (IDF) and governmental offices.

The reality of a prolonged occupation of the Palestinian territories and the Palestinian people contributed to significant transformations of Israeli national identity and to the intensification of Judaism or Jewish identity as claims authorizing the occupation. This is true even of the mainstream (mostly secular) commitment to the identity of Israel as Jewish and democratic. This commitment necessitates undemocratic acts to ensure a particular demographic arrangement that will enable Jewish majoritarianism. In addition, the settlement movement—born in the early 1970s—has affected a far-reaching transformation of Israeli society. The movement itself is considered radical, but it found a wide array of supporters from within the establishment. The settlement movement has been motivated by explicitly religious and theological reinterpretations of Zionism. Its commitment to settle the land, especially the sacred territories of the West Bank and the Gaza Strip, has turned its affiliates into vocal resisters of any kind of peace negotiations that might involve returning territories to the Palestinians.

In the case of Israel, the internal negotiation concerning the precise meaning and scope of the nation-state (territorial but also more subjective in terms of its inclusion of all the Jews in the entire world or only those who reside within its geopolitical borders) would bear upon how and what might be "negotiable" and "non-negotiable" from the point of view of Israeli interests. The Palestinian movement for liberation and self-determination is focused more on attaining these goals as well as redressing past injustices. It is less focused on how religion (Islam and Christianity) will relate to the process of state and nation formation. Clearly, there are Islamist movements within the Palestinian resistance that are very much concerned with the character of a future Palestine. Those movements (such as Hamas) are informed in their resistance to Israel and "the West" more broadly by Islamist principles. Israel, or rather the Zionist Entity, is perceived as an agent of the West that is also associated with the corruption of Islamic values as well as with the humiliation associated with colonialism, imperialism, the dissolution of the Islamic empires, and neoliberalism. Islamists frame their resistance in religious terms, but sometimes the relationships between a more localized movement for national liberation and a broader Islamist emancipation are thoroughly complex. Nationalism and its ethnic particularities are not easily reconciled with broader interpretations of the Islamic Umma (the Muslim world community), as the latter transcends such particularistic boundaries. It is important to note that within the Palestinian struggle for liberation, Islamists have often counteracted the corruption of the secularist leadership through the provision of social services on the Palestinian streets. It is therefore not surprising that Hamas has gained increasing support from a wide array of sectors within Palestinian communities.

1896	Theodore Herzl's *The Jewish State* is published.
1897	World Zionist Organization is founded in Basel, Switzerland.
November 2, 1917	British issue the Balfour Declaration, which is viewed by Jews and Arabs as promising a Jewish homeland in Palestine.
December 1917	British capture Palestine from the Ottoman Empire.
April 1918	A Zionist commission (Jewish supporters of the creation of a Jewish homeland) arrives in Palestine.
November 1918	The first Muslim-Christian associations are created in Jaffa in opposition to the creation of a Jewish homeland, and another soon forms in Jerusalem.
January 1919	The First Palestinian Congress meets and advocates incorporation into Greater Syria.
July 1919	Greater Syria Congress (including Palestinians, Trans Jordanians, Lebanese, and Syrians) meets in Damascus, supports the independence of greater Syria, and opposes Zionism. Ignoring calls for independence, Great Britain cedes control of Syria to the French.
August 28, 1919	At the request of U.S. president Woodrow Wilson, Henry King and Charles Crane gather information about general opinions in the Middle East related to

the creation of a Jewish state. The two men return with numbers showing that most are against it, but the report is ignored.

February–March 1920	Attacks upon Jewish settlements in Tel Hai and Metullah in Northern Palestine.
April 1920	Arab riots in Jerusalem and Hebron kills 46 Jewish people.
May 1921	Arabs riot in Jaffa against the Jewish population.
June 3, 1922	White Paper commissioned by Winston Churchill points out that the Balfour Declaration promises a Jewish homeland in Palestine and reserves East Palestine for Trans Jordanians.
July 1922	The League of Nations ratifies the mandate system.
March 25, 1923	Trans Jordanians declares independence under the rule of Emir Abdullah.
August 1929	Riots in Hebron and Jerusalem in response to the building of a wall to separate male and female worshipers.
1936–1939	Arabs revolt against Zionists' colonization of Palestine and British colonial rule.
1937–1938	Peel and Woodhead Commissions (also known as the Palestine Royal Commission and Palestine Partition Commission, respectively) recommend that Palestine be divided into a smaller Jewish area and a larger Arab area.
1939	In support of an Arab Palestine, a British White Paper recommends limiting British commitment to the establishment of a Jewish homeland in Palestine by restricting Jewish immigration to 75,000 and limits the amount of land Jewish people can buy in Palestine. In response, Jews form the Mossad and facilitate illegal immigration.
September 1939–August 1945	World War II and the Holocaust occur.

May 19, 1942	Establishment of the Biltmore Program, which would cede full control of immigration to Jewish people and aim for the creation of a Jewish Commonwealth. This surpassed the previous terms of the British mandate which affirmed the establishment of a Jewish national home in Palestine.
October 7, 1944	Arab leaders meet to discuss a way to avoid the implementation of the Biltmore Program.
May 1947	The Palestine issue is referred to the United Nations, causing that organization to create the UN Special Committee on Palestine (UNSCOP).
November 27, 1947	UNSCOP issues a resolution that suggests Palestine be divided into a Jewish state and an Arab state, with Jerusalem as an international domain. The Soviet Union and United States support this resolution, but all Arab countries and the Arab League reject it.
December 1947	The first phase of the 1948 Palestine war begins. Clashes between Jewish and Arab communities occur in response to the UNSCOP resolution. This war is also known (within the Palestinian context) as the Naqba or the catastrophe.
May 14– 15, 1948	The British mandate officially ends. The state of Israel is declared and is immediately recognized by the United States and Soviet Union. The second phase of the Israel War of Independence (Arab Israeli War) begins as the British leave Palestine and Egypt, Syria, Iraq, Lebanon, Jordan, and Saudi Arabia declare war on Israel. Egyptian, Syrian, and Jordanian forces invade Palestine.
February– June 1949	Israel signs separate Armistice Agreements with Egypt, Syria, Lebanon, and Jordan, officially ending the 1948 Arab Israeli War. These treaties give Israel 50 percent more land than the original UN resolution, creating over half a million Palestinian refugees.
May 1964	The Palestinian Liberation Organization (PLO) is formed.
September 13, 1964	An Arab summit in Alexandria, Egypt, clarifies the goal of liberating Palestine from Zionist colonialism.

September 18, 1965	Another Arab summit makes plans for combat with Israel.
June 5–10, 1967	Six Days War is waged. Following a period of tension, Israel attacks and destroys Egypt's air force on the ground and takes Sinai and Gaza from Egypt. Israel also takes the West Bank from Jordan and the Golan Heights from Syria. In November 1967, the United Nations calls for Israel to withdraw and establish peace.
March 21, 1968	In the Battle of Karameh, Jordanian and Palestinian forces partially defeat Israeli forces that are planning a raid on a Jordanian town.
June 1974	The Twelfth Palestine National Council states that the PLO will do whatever is necessary to liberate all Palestinian lands and establish an independent land. This declaration was eventually recognized as including diplomatic and nonviolent means by which to pursue liberation of Palestinian lands in whole or in part. This declaration, and the signing of the Oslo Accords, resulted in the Popular Front for the Liberation of Palestine (PFLP) splitting apart from the People's Liberation Organization (PLO).
December 1975	Gush Emunim (the settlement movement) enters the national Israeli discourse.
November 1975	UN General Assembly 3379 equates Zionism with racism (revoked in 1991 by UN General Assembly resolution 4686).
March 15, 1978	Israel invades Lebanon in response to a PLO hijacking of a bus on the main Tel Aviv–Haifa highway. A UN resolution on March 19 calls on Israel to withdraw, but all of the terms of the resolution are not achieved until 2000.
1977	Yitzhak Rabin's first government falls. The religious Zionist camp interprets the collapse as the result of Rabin's resistance to settlements in the Occupied Territories.
1977	Menachem Begin is elected prime minister. This watershed signals the emergence of the Likkud Party

1977 (cont.) to prominence and the dissolution of Labor dominance. The Likkud victory is enabled, in part, due to
its support from Mizrahi Israeli Jews who were systematically discriminated against by the Israeli state.
The Likkud is ideologically to the right in that it is
more reluctant to engage in territorial compromises.

March 26, Israeli prime minister Menachem Begin and Egyp-
1979 tian president Anwar El Sadat sign the Israel-Egypt
peace agreement following the Camp David Accords
of 1978 (convened by U.S. president Jimmy Carter).
This agreement necessitated relinquishing territories
occupied in the Sinai, which had been occupied in
the course of the Six Days War of 1967.

December The Yesha Council, and a later manifestation of the
1980 Gush Emunim settlement movement called Amana,
replaces Gush Emunim as the pivotal mechanism of
the settlement movement. This signals a transition
from a more spiritual rabbinic leadership to a more
political orientation in the settlement movement.

June 6, Israeli forces invade Lebanon to attack PLO forces.
1982 Despite a UN resolution to withdraw, they quickly
advance to Beirut.

August 22, The PLO evacuates Lebanon and heads to head-
1982 quarters in Tunis, Tunisia.

September With Israeli facilitation, Lebanese Christian Phalange
16–17, 1982 groups are allowed to enter Palestinian refugee
camps in Sabra and Shatilla, Beirut, Lebanon, and
800 to 3,500 Palestinians are massacred.

September Israel begins a partial withdraw from Lebanon.
3, 1983

June 1985 Israeli forces are ordered to withdraw from most of
Lebanese territory by Shimon Peres, head of the Israeli Unity Government.

December The first intifada occurs. A Palestinian youth attacks
8, 1985 an Israeli soldier, most likely because of an acci-
dent involving an Israeli vehicle that killed four Palestinians. The Israeli government responds with

many arrests. Rioting erupts, and the ensuing cycles of violence result in many Palestinian and Israeli deaths.

1987   Hamas is formed as a result of the first intifada. Israel and the United States view the group as a terrorist organization, but its supporters see it as a group that strives to protect Palestinians who are under occupation. It also has a clear Islamist agenda, calling for the establishment of an Islamic state in Palestine and further linking the liberation of Palestine with a broader Islamist agenda.

September   Oslo Declaration of Principles is made in which the
13, 1993   Israeli government and the PLO agree to recognize each other and discontinue the use of terrorism and other violence. As part of the agreement, the PLO removes pieces of its charter that mention the destruction of Israel, and Israel withdraws from a small area of territory, giving Palestinians sovereignty there. Israel also withdraws from a larger area, granting civil control to the Palestinians. Israel gives complete control to Palestinians in the West Bank and Gaza Strip (with the exception of areas of Jewish settlements).

October   Wye River Plantation talks lead to Israeli redeploy-
1998   ment and release of prisoners of war (POWs), and renews the Palestinian commitment to the Oslo Declaration despite earlier violations through media recruitment and illegal arms.

September   The second intifada begins as Palestinians protest
28, 2000   Ariel Sharon's visit to the Haram al Sharif (Temple Mount). Sharon is intimately associated with Israeli militarism and the settlement movement.

January   Israeli and Palestinian leaders meet for the Taba
21–27, 2001 Talks. The proposals made related to the refugee problem show that Palestinians still want a return of refugees from the war of 1948, while Israel refuses to accept a Right of Return for the Palestinians.

March 27–   The Fifth Arab League summit calls for a boycott
28, 2001   against Israel.

June 23, 2002	Israel begins building a Security Fence, or Separation Wall, that is used to prevent terrorist attacks. The fence takes several years to build. When it is finished, it isolates Palestinians in the West Bank and restricts movement.
July 9, 2004	The International Court of Justice rules that the separation wall violates international law and demands that it be torn down.
August 15–24, 2005	Israel begins to withdraw from Gaza and four other West Bank settlements. This event is often referred to as a unilateral disengagement.
January 25, 2006	Hamas wins electoral victory in Palestinian parliament.
June–November, 2006	Israel-Gaza conflict occurs.
February 8, 2007	Fatah and Hamas (secularist and Islamic forces within the Palestinian streets) agree to Mecca Accord. They agree to stop fighting each other in the Gaza Strip and to form a unity government.
June 2007	Unity government fails, and the Battle of Gaza between Hamas and Fatah erupts. Hamas wins control of Gaza, though its representatives are ousted from government positions in the West Bank.
November 27, 2007	President George W. Bush announces that Palestinian and Israel authorities have agreed to come to peace agreements by 2008.
June 19, 2008	Israel and Hamas begin a six-month truce.
December 27, 2008 to January 2, 2009	After aerial bombardment for seven days, Israeli forces invade Gaza to stop Palestinians militants that they claim were firing rockets into southern Israel. During the campaign, civilian and militant lives are taken, and Hamas continues to fire rockets into southern Israel.
January 21, 2009	Israeli forces withdraw from Gaza. The three-week invasion by Israeli forces leaves roughly 1,300 Palestinians dead.

June 4, 2009	In a speech that addressed the Muslim world, U.S. president Barack Obama confirms support of a two state solution and Palestine as a state.
June 14, 2009	For the first time, Israeli prime minister Benjamin Netanyahu supports a Palestinian state, but with stipulations such as it can possess no military power (which Palestinians leaders reject) and that it must recognize Israel as a Jewish state.
May 4, 2011	Fatah and Hamas, rival Palestinian factions, make a deal to become joint leaders in Palestinian government before the next election. This is seen as strengthening the drive for the creation of an independent state.
June 23, 2011	Documents are leaked of negotiations between Palestinian and Israeli leaders showing that Palestinian leaders are much more willing to make concessions than many had previously believed.
September 2011	Palestinian leadership goes to the United Nations to seek statehood for Arabs in Palestinian territories. November 2012 U.N. votes to recognize the Palestinian territories as a "nonmember observe state."

The Muslim Brotherhood in Egypt

1928	Hassan al-Banna forms the Muslim Brotherhood, which focuses on moral and social reform, with Islam as its core.
1936	The Muslim Brotherhood supports Palestine against the development of a Jewish state, beginning the Brotherhood's transition into a political entity.
1939–1945	The Muslim Brotherhood develops a secret entity within the group.
1940	The Muslim Brotherhood reveals that it has over 500 branches, each with its own mosque, center, and club. Militant training camps are also developed near Cairo and in southern Egypt.
1940s	The Brothers begin to share ideologies with nationalist leaders known as the Free Officers, a group of

1940s (cont.) separatist-minded army officers, thereby increasing membership through the recruitment of military officers in Egypt.

1942 Britain forces Egyptian king Faruq to appoint pro-British Wafd leader Nahas Pasha to the position of prime minister, which leads the Brotherhood to gain more support in reaction to the domination by Western forces.

1948 The Brotherhood begins subversive activities. It blames the Egyptian government for losses during the Arab-Israeli War. In December of this year, Prime Minister Nahas Pasha bans the Brotherhood and declares martial law. Soon following this declaration, he is assassinated by a member of the Brotherhood.

1949 Hasan al-Banna, the founder of the Brotherhood, is assassinated.

1950 Martial law and the ban against the Brotherhood are lifted, and the Brotherhood is allowed to operate as a religious body.

1952 The Brotherhood returns as a political power in the wake of anti-British riots. Gamal Abdul Nasser and the Free Officers' Movement lead a coup. By the following year, Egypt is declared a republic.

1954 Nasser becomes president, and British forces finally complete their withdrawal (which was begun in 1936).

October 23, 1954 Abdul Munim Abdul Rauf attempts to assassinate President Nasser and fails. Following this incident, he and five other Brothers are assassinated; 4,000 Brotherhood activists are arrested; and thousands of Brothers go into self-imposed exile.

October 1956 Egypt is invaded by Britain, France, and Israel as a result of Nasser's decision to nationalize the Suez Canal.

1964 Nasser releases Muslim Brotherhood members from jail. Nasser makes this move with the goal of using them to combat communists, who are also released.

1966	One thousand Brothers are arrested, and the top leaders of the organization are killed.
1967	The Brotherhood enters a period of quiet after the Six Days War ends in severe defeat. Some attribute the defeat to a lack of a belief in God. The perception of Israel as a Jewish state reinforces this perception as well as the imperative to engage in processes of Islamicization of Egyptian society.
1970	Anwar Sadat accedes to the presidency after Nasser's death and releases all members of the Brotherhood from prison.
1973	Yom Kippur (or October) War begins. Egypt and Syria collaborated in this war against Israel. The war began on the Jewish holiday Yom Kippur.
1976	Sadat fears the Brotherhood's popularity but allows them to participate in parliamentary elections. Six Brothers are elected as a part of the socialist party, nine are elected on the independent ticket, and some militant activists leave the organization to form radical groups.
September 1978	Camp David Accords for peace with Israel are signed between Sadat and Israeli prime minister Menachem Begin.
1979	A peace treaty between Egypt and Israel is signed.
October 1981	Sadat is assassinated by militant jihadi activists and Hosni Mubarak assumes the presidency.
1984	The Brotherhood cooperates with the Neo-Wafd party in elections, resulting in the election of some Brothers to the parliament.
1987	The Brotherhood combines with the Socialist Labor Party and the Liberal Socialist Party to form the Labor Islamic Alliance, which wins 60 seats in parliament. Thirty-seven of these newly elected representatives are Brothers.
1990	The Brothers boycott elections to protest government control of elections.

1997	Fifty-eight tourists are killed near Luxor by gunmen allegedly associated with the Egyptian radical group al-Jama'ah al'Islamiyah.
2005	The Brothers are prevented from running for parliament as a political party, but 80 members gain seats in parliament on an independent ticket. These members form the largest opposition group. President Mubarak is re-elected for a fifth consecutive term.
August 2006	Egypt expresses support of the guerilla warfare of the Lebanese group Hezbolla against Israel.
November 2006	Repression of the Muslim Brotherhood (primarily through arrests) is intensified.
April 2008	About 800 members of the Brotherhood, including 25 key activists, are arrested in the course of a month. As a result, the organization boycotts municipal elections.
January 2011	Riots begin in Cairo, and the National Democratic Party's headquarters burns down. The Muslim Brotherhood is originally blamed for the riots, but they insist it is a popular uprising.
February 2011	The Muslim Brotherhood demands that Mubarak's regime be taken down and that a national unity government be formed. Western forces fear that if the Muslim Brotherhood takes control in Egypt, it will enact Sharia (Islamic law). Although this is not assured, if the Brotherhood does take control in Egypt, it is believed that Islam will gain a bigger role in society.
February 2011	President Mubarak steps down. The military takes over as a transitional regime.
April– August 2011	Disappointed by the slow progress toward democracy, protests continue in Tahrir Square, the main square of Cairo, with Islamist voices stepping to the foreground.
September 2011	Clashes between Coptic Christians (the minority Christian population of Egypt) and the military result in the killing of 24 people.

November 2011	Violent clashes in Tahrir Square between security forces and protesters who suspect that the military's aspiration is to hold on to power rather than relinquish it to a democratic process result in great unrest, many deaths, and the resignation of the temporary prime minister, Essam Sharaf. The first phase of three-tier parliamentary elections results in a strong showing by the Muslim Brotherhood as well as other Islamist political parties.
June 25, 2012	Muslim Brotherhood candidate Mohamed Morsi is elected president of Egypt.

5

Biographical Sketches

This chapter provides selective biographical sketches of thinkers, political figures, and religious leaders who performed key roles in conflicts involving the framing of national claims in terms of religious and ethnic entitlements and/or theological imperatives. Some of the sketches illustrate active and explicit uses of religious and theological agenda. Others, however, are more implicit and sublimated, reflecting broader contexts where national, cultural, ethnic, and religious facets of one's identity are conflated.

Sri Lanka

Velupillai Prabhakaran (1954–2009)

Prabhakaran was born in 1954 into a middle class family in Jaffna and a Tamil society that was struggling against Sinhalese discrimination. He began to envision a separate Tamil state and in July 1975, he committed the first political assassination in the north, killing the progovernment mayor of Jaffna, Alfred Duraiappah. A year later, he founded the Liberation Tigers of Tamil Eelam (LTTE), a militant group determined to achieve independence. In dedication to his goal of an independent Tamil state, he told his followers to shoot him if he ever gave up on the goal of independence. In 1983, the LTTE began to engage in suicide bombings and recruit child soldiers. Prabhakaran is seen as a central reason for the successes and failures of the LTTE; his refusal to compromise on his goals is associated with the refusal of the LTTE to seek a political solution. His charismatic leadership led to a fanaticism within the LTTE that borders on worship of Prabhakaran. The vision of Eelam became unrealistic after a part of the LTTE broke away under the leadership of Colonel Karuna. On May 17, 2009, the LTTE was forced to admit defeat, and Prabhakaran's body was displayed on May 19, forcing some members of the LTTE, who had previously refused to believe that Prabhakaran had died, to admit that their leader was gone.

Sirimavo Bandaranaike (1916–2000)

Bandaranaike was born in 1916. Bandaranaike was educated at Catholic schools and volunteered to help the rural poor. In 1960, she was elected prime minister of Sri Lanka, the first woman in the world to serve as prime minister. After her husband Solomon, who was prime minister also, was assassinated by a Buddhist monk in 1950, she became leader of his party and won election in a sweeping victory. She was prime minister for two terms (1960–1965 and 1970–1977). Although she inherited a government that was already beginning to take the rights of the Tamil people, Bandaranaike's policies further contributed to the usurpation of Tamil rights. She instituted policies that continued Sinhalese domination such as requiring civil servants to learn Sinhalese and stationing Sinhalese civil servants in Tamil areas, and she instituted the 1972 constitution, which ignored minority concerns. She nationalized all industries, including shutting down teahouses run by Tamils and decreasing the number of seats in parliament that Tamils could win. She engaged in a systematic Sinhalezation of the social, political, and cultural spheres. Power was eventually taken from her by Junius Jayawardene; she was expelled from parliament and deprived of her civil rights for six years because of her abuse of power while in office. Although her political prominence did end, her daughter, Chandrika Kumaratunga, became president later in 1994. Her family ruled Sri Lanka for a combined 21 years.

Vinayagamoorthi Muralitharan (also known as Colonel Karuna) (1966–)

Muralitharan is a Tamil from the east and the leader of the LTTE in the Eastern Province of Sri Lanka. He led a revolt against LTTE leadership in March 2004. He used the oppressive taxes placed on the eastern Tamil areas to justify his split from the LTTE and the creation of Tamil People's Liberation Tigers. Many eastern Tamils, who had long felt that they had been seen as and treated as less than northern Tamils, celebrated his defection. His departure from the LTTE is seen as one cause for the LTTE's goal of independence becoming unrealistic. Tamil forces were split between the proindependence forces led by Prabhakaran and the progovernment forces led by Karuna. He began to help the Sri Lankan military and in July 2007, he helped the Sri Lanka government "liberate" the Eastern Province from LTTE control. By 2007, there was a split within his group; while he was imprisoned in the United Kingdom for entering under false pretenses, a dissident group led by Sivanesathurai Chandrakanthan gained the government's support. Karuna returned and was made a noncabinet minister for national integration, with the government hoping he could lead an effort to develop the Eastern Province. He was elected to parliament in October 2008, which supported the government's initiative to support anti-LTTE Tamil forces.

Chandrika Kumaratunga (1945–)

Kumaratunga was born on June 24, 1945, to Solomon and Sirimavo Bandaranaike, both of whom served as prime minister of Sri Lanka. She was educated in a convent school in Colombo and was at the University of Paris for five years. Her father was assassinated when she was 14, and her husband was gunned down in 1989. Her family background gave her the appearance of a perfect fit for the presidency when she was elected to the office in 1994. Although she was more educated then her mother, who was criticized for her lack of education, she struggled to move out of her mother's shadow. As president, she promised to attempt to extend the hand of friendship to Tamils, but six months into her presidency, she gave up on this strategy. In 2000, she was almost killed by a Tamil Tiger suicide bomber; she was blinded in one eye in the process. In December 2001, Ranil Wickramasinghe, her political opponent, was made prime minister. Their differences caused them to have a difficult relationship, and she believed that he made too many concessions to the LTTE. In November 2003, she took control of parliament while he was out of the country. On August 12, 2005, she issued an indefinite state of emergency after the assassination of the foreign minister, Lakshman Kadirgamar. After the Supreme Court ordered her to step down from office on August 25, 2006, because a third term would be unconstitutional, she was succeeded by Mahinda Rajapaksa. Although there were some problems with her administration, she sought a constitution that would resolve many of the Tamil people's grievances.

Mahinda Rajapaksa (1945–)

Rajapaksa was born on November 18, 1945, in Hambantota. His father served in parliament from 1947 to 1965. He was a human rights lawyer and in 1970, he became the youngest person elected to parliament. He was labor minister under President Chandrika Kumaratunga and was elected prime minister in 2004. He followed Chandrika Kumaratunga to the presidency in November 2005. He appointed his brother, who was a former military officer, to head of the defense ministry. Rajapaksa has been accused of using terrorist and extraconstitutional tactics to stop the LTTE. During his presidency, journalism criticizing the military was discouraged, and many foreign journalists were expelled from the country. Despite receiving international criticism for his violent strategies against the LTTE, he still used a final violent push to defeat the LTTE, which resulted in the deaths of 300,000 people. To some, he is seen as the savior of Sri Lanka, but to others, his violent tactics have tainted his victorious end to the long civil war. On January 26, 2010, he was elected president once again, although he is not as popular in the northern and eastern areas of Sri Lanka, which are heavily populated by Tamils who fear the policies that he may adopt in the future. Following his election, his opponent Sarath Fonseka was court-martialed and in September 2010, parliament ended limits on presidential terms, opening the door for him to serve a third term.

Israel/Palestine

Mahmoud Abbas (1935–)

Born in Safed in 1935, which was at the time under a British mandate, Abbas studied law in Egypt and later obtained his doctorate in Moscow. During the 1950s, he was exiled to Qatar. While there, he recruited Palestinians, some of whom later became crucial members of the Palestinian Liberation Organization (PLO). He was one of the founding members of the Palestinian political faction Fatah. Although he was not always one of the most publicized members of the PLO, he was able to build an important network of connections with Arab leaders and intelligence services that were important to the PLO in later years. In the 1970s, he was able to gain an important role in security, and in 1980s, he gained a role in the PLO related to national and international relations. He was one of the initiators of talks with the Jewish left-wing and pacifist movement in the 1970s. Abbas became the Palestinian Authority's prime minister in May 2003, but he resigned three months later over a power struggle. He succeeded Yasser Arafat in leadership and has been president of the Palestinian Authority since 2005. Abbas has struggled with the militant group Hamas throughout his career. Hamas forces have kept him from gaining control of the Gaza Strip, and the ongoing fights between Hamas and Israeli forces have left him on the sidelines. He has suffered criticism for not stopping Hamas activities, but so far his efforts to do so have not been successful. After he assumed leadership, many believed that he would be able to create a change in Israeli-Palestinian relations, but conflicts between Hamas and Israeli forces have prevented him from promoting change. Abbas has stated his commitment to the peaceful establishment of a Palestinian state. In September 2011, Abbas went to the United Nations to request that Palestine be recognized as a state. This was an important step in the peaceful movement toward statehood that he promised, but the Israeli government refused to support Palestine's request despite its past endorsement of a Palestinian state.

Yasser Arafat (1929–2004)

Arafat was born August 24, 1929, in Cairo. After his mother died when he was five, he was sent to live with his uncle in Jerusalem, which was then the capital of British Mandate Palestine. He later moved back to Cairo, and before he was 17, he was smuggling arms to Palestine for the fight against the British and Jews. At 19, he left the University of Faud I to fight in the Israeli War of Independence (Arab-Israeli War). After Arab forces lost the fight and the state of Israel was established, he applied for a visa to study at the University of Texas but later returned to the University of Faud I. After receiving his degree in 1956, he eventually resettled in Kuwait and was employed by the department of public works while being involved in politics in his spare time. In 1959, he established Al-Fatah, a secular political party, along with some friends. Al-Fatah's goals included taking back Palestinian lands and establishing an independent state. In 1964, he left Kuwait to devote all his efforts to the revolutionary cause by organizing Fatah raids in Israel from Jordan. Arafat was also an important member of the Palestinian Liberation Organization, which united different groups working toward taking back Palestinian land, and in 1969, he became a chairman of the executive committee of the PLO. The king of Jordan eventually expelled the PLO from Jordan due to concerns over its attacks on Israel. Arafat then moved the PLO to Lebanon but was soon expelled by Israeli forces. This caused problems for the PLO, but the intifada protest movement brought attention to the Palestinian plight. In 1988, he changed the policy of the PLO by stating that it would not use terrorist means, but instead would respect the rights of all groups in the Middle East. He was able to start peace talks with Israel, which lead to the Oslo Accords in 1993, which allowed for more peaceful relations. Despite the peace agreements, violence continued, and on July 11 to 14, 2000, a talk was negotiated by former U.S. president George W. Bush in hopes of reconciliation. Arafat refused the terms of agreement because they required ending the fight to regain Palestinian lands. This refusal led to a decline in his popularity. On February 28, 2002, Israeli forces entered Palestinian territory and kept him isolated in his headquarters in Rammallah. His popularity slowly decreased for the next two years, until he died on November 11, 2004.

Salam Fayyed (1952–)

Fayyed was born in 1952 in the West Bank town of Tulkarm, and he received a PhD in economics from the University of Texas. He worked at the World Bank in Washington, D.C., from 1987 until 1995 and then served as representative for Palestine at the International Monetary Fund until 2001. Fayyed also served as finance minister from 2002 until 2005. After the Palestinian unity government formed in 2007, he lobbied with U.S. officials to continue aid to the Palestinian Authority. In 2007, he was appointed to the position of prime minister. He is considered by many to be liberal and is respected by many international organizations. Fayyed supports a system in which neither violence nor negotiation is used to build Palestine; instead, he believes that it is through good government, good opportunity, and building institutions that the Palestinian government will be best served. This view has caused some problems with Israelis who see him as hostile and Palestinians who see him as too complacent with the Palestinian predicament. Fayyed believes that in case peace talks break down within the Israeli government, it is important to have a strong Palestinian government to maintain Palestinian society. In August 2009, he set a deadline for Palestine to become a state in two years. Fayyed's beliefs have even created the term "fayyedism," a concept that focuses on a new legitimacy for a Palestinian state through creating a competent and strong government that shows the ability to govern. Fayyed is seen as pro-Western, and he supports a democratic and secular Palestinian state.

Mahmoud Al-Zahar (1945–)

Al-Zahar was born in Gaza in 1945. He spent many of his formative years in Cairo and attended Ain Shams University in Cairo, where he studied medicine. He graduated in 1971 and spent another five years at Ain Shams to gain specialization in general surgery. After this, he returned to the place of his birth to teach medicine at the Islamic University of Gaza. In 1987, he helped Sheikh Ahmed Yassin form Hamas, which began in response to fears of members of the Palestinian Muslim Brotherhood that they were losing followers to militant Islamist groups. He continued to be a leader within the group even after Yassin was arrested, and in 1990, he became an official representative of Hamas to the PLO. He was deported to South Lebanon along with 400 Islamist activists in 1990. The deportation helped garner more worldwide support for Hamas. A year later, he was able to return to Gaza, but once there, he clashed with Palestinian authorities and was arrested several times. After the intifada in September 2000, Hamas grew in popularity as the military wing Izzedine al-Qassam Brigades killed Israeli officers through suicide bombing. Israeli forces began targeting Hamas, and on September 11, 2004, his house was bombed. Although he survived, his son and a bodyguard did not. Within the following week, Yassin and another leader of Hamas were also killed. Al-Zahar was an important part of involving Hamas in the political process, and in February 2005, an informal truce was made with Israel. Although many have demanded that Hamas give up violence, Al-Zahar refuses because he believes it is within the rights of Hamas to resist. However, he has suggested the possibility of peace talks with Israel.

Ahmed Qurei (also known as Abu Ala) (1937–)

Born in Abu Dis (a Palestinian town adjacent to Jerusalem) in 1937, Qurei joined the Fatah wing of the PLO in 1960, but did not gain a significant role until he took over economics and production operations in Lebanon in the 1970s. He went to Tunis when the PLO was expelled from Lebanon and as PLO leaders died or were assassinated, he was able to move up in the ranks until he was elected to the position of central member in the Fatah committee. He negotiated an aid plan at a World Bank conference, which is considered one of his biggest achievements. After this, he became important in politics, and he was involved in peace talks such as the Oslo Accords in 1993, which gave Palestinians more authority by creating the National Palestine Authority. Qurei hopes to establish a secular Palestinian land. In January 1996, he was elected to the Palestinian Legislative Council in Jerusalem. He became prime minister in 2003 after Mahmoud Abbas resigned. Qurei does not support the policies of Hamas and hopes to defeat them politically.

Israel

David Ben-Gurion (David Green) (1886–1973)

Ben-Gurion was born in 1886 in the Polish town of Plonsk that was then dominated by Russia. He received a traditional Jewish education, but czarist rules that restricted the number of Eastern European students prevented him from attending high school; much of his education was self-taught. In 1906, he immigrated to Palestine and in 1911, he enrolled in law school in Istanbul. He was expelled from law school when World War I broke out because of his support of Zionism. In 1918, he returned to Palestine and became a major leader in the Jewish Workers Movement. In 1920, he became one of the cofounders of the General Federation of Labor and remained its general secretary for the next 15 years. In the 1930s, he led a struggle that gave the Jewish labor movement control of the World Zionist Organization and then guided Jewish efforts to settle in Palestine. After he gained leadership of the Jewish community in Palestine, he struggled against the British government that had mandated control of Palestine. In 1947, he accepted the League of Nations suggestion to partition Palestine between Jewish people and Palestinians. After the British withdrew from Palestine, he declared a Jewish state and led the fight against Arab forces from neighboring countries. He served as prime minister and minister of defense in the 1950s. He led state-building efforts. The "Status Quo Agreement" signed with the religious party Agudath Yisrael on the eve of the vote at the United Nations that recognized the Jewish state in 1947 has had far-reaching influences on the patterns of synagogue-state relations.

Ariel Sharon (1926–)

Sharon was born in 1928 in Kfar Malal in Palestine while it was under British Mandate. He fought during the War of Independence in 1948 and distinguished himself for his fighting in Jerusalem and elsewhere. He was appointed to be a Central Command and North Central Command officer in 1951 and 1952. He entered Hebrew University but was recalled in 1953 to lead the 101, a special commando unit that was later responsible for the raid on Qibieh that caused the deaths of 69 civilians in Jordan. He studied at Camberley Staff College in Great Britain and later in Tel Aviv for a law degree. He became chief of the Northern Command in 1964, head of the army's Training Department in 1966, and commander of the armored division during the Six Days War. In 1973, he was elected to the Knesset (Israeli parliament), but resigned a year later to become security adviser to prime minister Yitzhak Rabin, and in 1977, he was elected to the Knesset again. He joined and helped organize the Likkud political party. He was appointed minister of agriculture in Menachem Begin's government and assisted in the Camp David Accords. He was appointed to be defense minister in 1981 but resigned in 1983 after he was found to be indirectly responsible for the massacre of Palestinian people during the 1982 Lebanon War. Sharon did not support the Oslo Accords and tried to undermine them in different ways. On February 6, 2001, he was elected prime minister and developed a hardline attitude against terrorism. His government went to greater lengths to prevent terrorist attacks and was able to decrease the number of successful terrorist attacks to only 10 percent. In December 2003, he took a completely unexpected route and began supporting the removal of Israeli forces from Palestinian territory. This caused dissent among his supporters and led him to leave his political party and form the Kadima Party. But on January 4, 2006, he suffered a stroke that took him out of politics, a change that left the Israeli government distraught. Despite his orchestration of the "unilateral withdrawal" from the Gaza Strip in 2005, Sharon maintains a legacy of patron saint of the settlement movement. The settlement project, within Sharon's ideological and geopolitical outlook, served to reinforce and secure the borders of the Israeli state. He facilitated the construction and consolidation of the settlements in his various capacities as minister of security, building and construction, and of course during his tenure as a prime minister. Though he was a secular Zionist, his particular brand of Zionist ideology cohered with and enabled the (often devoutly religious) settlement agenda.

Benjamin Netanyahu (1949–)

Netanyahu was born in 1949 in Tel Aviv. He moved to the United States with his family and completed his education there. He returned to Israel and from 1967 to 1973, he served in the military, distinguishing himself in the army and becoming a commando captain. He returned to the United States to attend Harvard and the Massachusetts Institute of Technology (MIT) for further education and then attained a job in Washington, D.C., at the Israeli embassy. He gained notoriety in this position as well as support for Israel. He became the UN ambassador from Israel in 1984. In 1988, he returned to Israel, became involved in domestic politics, and entered the Knesset. In 1996, he became prime minister. He promised that he would not relinquish land in hopes of peace with Israel; however, in 1997, he ceded 80 percent of Hebron to Palestinian Authority control and in 1998, he signed the Wye River Memorandum, which provided a path toward withdrawal from the West Bank. In 1999, he was defeated by Ehud Barack for the position of prime minister. From 2002 through 2003, he served as foreign minister. He served as finance minister from February 2003 until August 2005, when he resigned over the withdrawal of Israeli forces from Gaza. In December 2005, he was able to gain leadership of the Likkud party. In March 2009, he became prime minister of Israel for a second time. Netanyahu has said that he supports the idea of peace negotiations with Palestine but has not supported the Palestinian request for UN recognition of statehood and its recognition by the majority of UN member states in November 2012. In addition, he refuses to use the Palestinian borders agreed upon in 1967. Netanyahu provides an example of a secular political leader whose ideological upbringing within the corridors of territorial maximalist Zionism enabled him to form coalitions with explicitly religious proponents of the settlement movement. Like other Israeli politicians, he also had to cater to the religious agenda of groups such as Shas.

Avraham Isaac Hacohen Kook (1865–1935)

Kook was born in 1865 in Latvia. He immigrated to Palestine in 1904 and became a rabbi in Jaffa. He identified with the Zionist movement and unlike other rabbis, he joined the political movement. He was forced to remain in London during World War I and influenced the Balfour Declaration. Kook believed that establishing a physical presence in Palestine constituted the beginning of divine redemption for Jews. Kook linked the particular redemption of the Jewish people with a broader and global redemptive narrative of humanity. He was centrally influenced by Jewish mysticism (Kabbalah), which facilitated a dialectic interpretation of history, with its acceptance of the possibility that sometimes redemptive avenues (rendered as "lights" within the mystical imagination) are hidden within vessels that may be unaware of their instrumental position in the linear redemptive history. The secular Zionists were rendered such vessels within the religious Zionist framework of Avraham Kook. The Kabbalistic outlook also facilitated a space for human agency in the process of redemption (in Hebrew, *Tikkun Olam*; the restoration of the world). This is a departure from orthodox and conventional injunctions against human hastening of the messianic age, injunctions that informed the strong Jewish religious opposition to the movement of political Zionism in the 19th and early 20th centuries. Kook was elected as the first chief rabbi in Palestine under the British mandate in 1921. He formed a type of religious Zionism and was able to face cultural and social revolutions more radically than other rabbis at the time. In 1924, he established a yeshiva, a Jewish educational institution, called Merkaz ha-Rav. The future graduates of Merkaz ha-Rav became leaders of the settlement movement in the West Bank and Gaza, and more broadly in the struggle for Greater Israel. He was popular among religious and nonreligious Jews and accepted both groups as long as they identified themselves as Jews. The fact that he was open to new ideas allowed him to appeal to many. He died in 1935, but his ideas are still influential.

Zvi Yehuda Kook (1891–1982)

Kook was born in 1891 as the son of Avraham Kook and was deeply involved in Zionist efforts from a young age. In 1921, he was sent abroad to encourage religious Jews to immigrate to Palestine. From 1929 to 1933, he was dedicated to helping yeshiva students leave Russia and immigrate to Palestine. After his father's death in 1935, he became head of Merkaz ha-Rav yeshiva and spent much of his time studying his father's writings and spreading his mission. He believed that the land that Israel claimed after the Six Days War should remain in Israeli possession. He believed that the land of Israel was given to the Jewish people by God. He later became a spiritual leader of settlers in Judea, Samaria, and the Gaza Strip. Until his final days, he continued to teach his students that settlement of Israel would lead to redemption. He and his followers interpreted the events of 1967 as indications of the unfolding of a messianic drama. They perceived themselves to be tracing the footsteps of the Messiah. Kook's ideological outlook rendered even secular Israelis and the secular instruments (such as the military) of the Israeli state as holy because they were deemed dialectically necessary for his messianic theology.

Yigal Amir (1970–)

Born in 1970, Amir is a Jewish fundamentalist. He was a student at Bar-Ilan University in Tel Aviv, and he was involved in protests against the Oslo Peace Accords. Amir felt that the accords threatened the stability of Israel and violated religious injunction to settle the land. On November 4, 1995, he shot and mortally wounded Israeli prime minister Yitzhak Rabin because he disagreed with Rabin's signing of the Oslo accords. He was sentenced to life in prison, and most of the right wing condemned his actions despite the fact that they also disagreed with Rabin's policies. Amir has never repented for murdering the prime minister, claiming that he acted in accordance with the Torah, Jewish law. He remains in prison today.

Rabbi Meir Kahane (1932–1990)

Kahane was born in New York in 1932. His belief in Zionism began at an early age as a member of the Betar Zionist Youth Movement. In 1968, he founded the Jewish Defense League (JDL) to defend against rising anti-Semitism in the United States. As leader of the JDL, he fought against prosecution of Jews in the Soviet Union, discrimination of Jews in Arab countries, and attempts of Christian missionaries to convert Jews. He advocated for more violent tactics to be used against Palestinians and other threats to Israel and Jewish people. He moved to Israel in 1971 and in 1980, he formed the political party Kach in Israel. In 1984, he was elected to be a member of the Knesset. He promoted legislation that would transfer hostile Arabs out of Israel, revoke citizenship of non-Jews, and prohibit Gentile-Jew marriage. In 1988, the Knesset passed the Anti-Racist Act, which disqualified him and the Kach party from being elected to the Knesset due to their racist ideologies. In 1990, he was assassinated by an Egyptian militant in New York City. After his death, his influence continued to live on. The Kach party and an offshoot of that party were later identified as terrorist organizations by the Israeli government. However, the influence of the Kach's ideology has endured in certain sectors of Israeli society and is thought to be behind various manifestations of Jewish militias and underground organizations that engage in hostile activities against Palestinians as well as dangerous and religiously explosive plots such as blowing up the Dome of the Rock (an act that was seen as hastening the coming of the messianic moment).

Yosef Burg (1909–1999)

Burg was born in Germany in 1909. From 1946 to 1949, he helped Holocaust survivors in Paris. In 1956, he became a founding member of the National Religious Party in Israel. The group was the only party that believed Israel should be ruled by both secular and religious laws; although Israel was established as a homeland for Jewish people, there was a divide between those who felt the country should be ruled by conservative Jewish values and those who felt that more secular rules should be put in place. Burg was sometimes called a bridge between the two groups. The party gradually became more right wing, and Burg was criticized for not doing more to keep the party moderate. He was a member of the Knesset from 1949 to 1988 and held different ministerial positions. From 1977 to 1986, he led the National Religious Party, but his moderate ideologies led to fewer seats in the Knesset. He was known to solve many problems between religious and nonreligious Jews.

Baruch Goldstein (1956–1994)

Goldstein was born in Brooklyn, New York, and was greatly set apart from his peers at a young age due to his orthodox values. He supported the Jewish Defense League and was a follower of Rabbi Meir Kahane. After receiving his medical degree, he immigrated to Israel in 1983. He was known for his extremist views against Arabs and was even known to view Arabs in the same vein as Nazis. On February 25, 1994, Baruch walked into Ibrahimi Mosque in Hebron and killed 29 Palestinian worshipers with a rifle and bomb before he was killed. His actions raised much controversy; initially, riots erupted in Israel from anger over the death of victims, which led to the deaths of 12 more Palestinians. His actions also led to controversy because some Israelis have honored his death, which has offended Palestinians who view him as a terrorist. Israel's government recognized his acts as a horrible crime, but some still honor him.

Ovadia Yosef (1920–)

Born in 1920 in Iraq, Yosef is highly revered in the Sephardic religious community in Israel and holds a distinguished authority among religious leaders. In the 1980s, he supported peace with Egypt on the basis of the religious principle of *pikuach nefesh* (the imperative to save life can trump other obligations). In 2001, following the second intifada, he began to favor right-wing politics; in 2005, he condemned the Israeli withdrawal from Gaza and claimed that Ariel Sharon, who was then prime minister, was tormenting the people of Israel with the plan. He also sparked controversy when he claimed—during a sermon in 2001—that all Arabs should be exterminated. As the spiritual leader of the Shas party, he has exerted a tremendous influence on Israeli parliamentary politics.

Daniella Weiss (1945–)

Born into a conservative family, Weiss has been involved with the settlement movement since the 1970s. She believes the land gained from the Six Days War of 1967 was liberated, not occupied, and that Jews are entitled to the land. In response to international conventions that outlaw settling of this land, she has underscored the religious and historical connections of the Jewish people to Eretz Yisrael (the Land of Israel). Her vision of a Jewish land is expansionist, encompassing the Jordan River and the Sinai Peninsula. Weiss believes that Arabs who do not recognize the prerogatives of the Israeli government should leave and those that respect the sovereignty of Israeli government can receive a passport after taking a test to prove their loyalty to the Israeli government.

Northern Ireland

Gerry Adams (1948–)

Born on October 6, 1948, into a family that had long supported Northern Ireland's independence from Britain and reunification with the Republic of Ireland, Adams quickly became involved in Roman Catholic civil rights protests. By 1970, he was suspected of being one of the important leaders of the Irish Republican Army (IRA) and in 1972, he was considered to be important enough to be released from jail to participate in a delegation that met with the British government in London to discuss a peace deal. The talks failed, and he was then claimed to become the top strategist of the IRA. He was imprisoned again between 1973 and 1976, and in 1978. He was charged, but never convicted, of being affiliated with the IRA. Adams has never admitted to being affiliated with the IRA because such an affiliation is illegal in Northern Ireland. As early as 1979, he adopted the view that violent attacks alone would not accomplish reunification, and that a political battle must be waged also. In 1983, he was elected head of the political party Sinn Fein and also gained a position in Parliament, which he rejected because it required him to pledge loyalty to the British queen. He later did away with this Sinn Fein tradition of rejecting seats in Parliament, which caused a split in the group in 1986. He was re-elected in 1987, lost his seat in 1992, and regained it in 1997. During the 1990s, he made a series of trips to the United States to raise funds and raise awareness of the Sinn Fein cause. In 1998, he supported the Belfast Agreement, which allowed a power-sharing government. In 2001, he left the Northern Ireland Assembly and ran for a position in the lower House of Ireland in 2011. Since taking leadership of the IRA and Sinn Fein, he has never faced a serious challenge to his leadership, and has remained a pivotal republican leader in the war and peace process for over 18 years.

Brian Faulkner (1921–1977)

Born February 18, 1921, Faulkner entered politics in 1949 and became the youngest person to be elected to the Northern Ireland Parliament. He became the minister of home affairs in 1959. He was made minister of commerce in 1963, but tensions with Terrance O'Neill, the fourth prime minister of Northern Ireland and leader of the Ulster Unionist Party, caused him to quit the position in response to reforms O'Neill introduced in 1969. Later the same year, O'Neill resigned and Faulkner returned as minister of development. In 1971, the replacement for O'Neill resigned and Faulkner became prime minister. During the same year of his appointment, there was an increase in paramilitary activity, which led him to introduce the increased practice of internment, arrest and imprisonment of political activists often without trial. Unfortunately, instead of curtailing paramilitary activity, this led to more alienation and did not diminish paramilitary activity. In 1972, the British government suspended the Northern Ireland Parliament and replaced it with a policy of Direct Rule. Faulkner responded by joining militant unionist activists but later entered negotiations and agreed to a power-sharing system. A new government was set up in January 1974 with Faulkner as chief executive, but he had already alienated unionists because of the agreement to power sharing and even more so because of the Sunningdale Agreement he signed, which allowed cross-border relations. This all led to a loyalist strike in May 1974 and the end of his political career. He officially announced that he was quitting politics in 1977.

Tony Blair (1953–)

Born May 6, 1953, in Scotland, Blair studied law at Oxford and by 1976, he was a qualified barrister. He worked in law until he was elected to Parliament in 1983 as a member of the

Labor Party. He quickly moved up in the party and by 1994, he was head of the party. He started to modernize its policies to garner more support for the party. In 1997, he was elected prime minister of England. He adopted a hands-off neutral position toward the Northern Ireland situation and supported the view that no peace talks should occur without decommissioning of weapons on both sides of the conflict. He set September 25, 1997, as the date for talks to occur and by July 1997, the IRA had re-established a cease-fire, the Republican party Sinn Fein had agreed to participate, and the Ulster Unionist Party agreed to attend, all of which allowed peace to successfully begin. As the deadline for the peace talks to end in April 1998 began to approach, Blair joined the peace talks and was able to help secure the Good Friday Agreement. Blair also helped gain the support of Unionists during the referendum campaign to approve the Good Friday Agreement. Implementing the Good Friday Agreement has proven to be difficult, and many called upon Blair to implement a new solution.

Ian Paisley (1926–)

Paisley was born on April 6, 1926, to a Baptist family in Lurgan, in Northern Ireland. In 1946, he was ordained as a Baptist minister and soon established the Crossgar Congregation of the Free Presbyterian Church of Ulster. He gained public notice through his religious activities, especially his condemnation of other Protestant churches that were in unity with Catholic churches. He also targeted fellow Unionist groups that he claimed were too accommodating to Irish Nationalist demands and weakening the connection between Northern Ireland and Britain. In response to civil rights protests, he organized the Ulster Constitution Defense Committee and the Ulster Protestant Volunteers. In 1968, he was able to challenge the prime minister-ship of Terrance O'Neill and in 1970, he gained a seat in Parliament. Although he originally represented the Protestant Unionist party that he established, he later joined with other Unionist groups to form the Democratic Unionist Party in September 1971. He took leadership of the party in 1973. After the Northern Ireland Parliament was suspended in 1972, he supported efforts to restore governmental powers. In 1974, he led the Ulster Workers Council in a strike that led to the collapse of the power-sharing government. He also fought against the Ulster Unionist Party, which he believed accepted too many concessions. In 1985, his DUP (Ulster Democratic Party) did work with the UUP (Ulster Unionist Party) to protest the Anglo-Irish Accords, but by the time they were suspended in 1990, relations between the groups had gotten worse. At the last minute, the DUP backed out of the peace talks that led to the Good Friday Agreement; since then, he has rallied against the terms of the agreement. He remained leader of the DUP until he resigned in 2008.

David Trimble (1944–)

Trimble was born October 15, 1944, in Bangor, in Northern Ireland. He attended Queen's University and received certification as qualified barrister in 1969. He became involved in politics in the 1970s as his faith in the Unionist government faded. When power was taken in 1972 by the British government, he joined the Vangaurd Unionist Progressive Party (VUPP). He helped ensure that the workers strike of May 1974 against the Sunningdale Agreement was successful. He was a member of the constitutional convention of 1975 that was set up to decide on a new government of Northern Ireland. In 1978, the VUPP fell apart, but he was able to quickly establish himself in the UUP. By 1990, he was elected to Parliament as a member of the UUP and soon became an important member as well as part of the UUP delegation. He was skeptical about peace talks in the early 1990s, but in 1997, he entered the peace talks and signed the Good Friday Agreement despite some opposition in his own party. He received the Nobel Peace Prize for his efforts. He was a member of the Northern Ireland Assembly in 1998 and helped decide the new government that would rule Northern Ireland in accordance with the Good Friday Agreement. Disagreements within his political party over the Good Friday Agreement led him to resign in January 2004 and join the DUP.

John Hume (1937–)

Hume was born in Derry, Northern Ireland, on January 18, 1937. After receiving his BA from St. Patrick's College, he became a teacher. He gained notice within his community by being involved in the local credit union and the campaign to have a university built in his hometown. He was frustrated by the Northern Ireland Parliament's failure to address the need for economic, social, and political reform in the minority community. He became a member of the Derry Citizens Action Committee after the civil march there on October 5, 1968, and was committed to peaceful protests. He was able to gain a seat in Parliament during the February 1969 election, and was one of the cofounders of the Social Democrat and Labour Party (SDLP), which aimed at being a new, vibrant opposition to Unionists. As a leader in the SDLP, he was part of the negotiations that led to the Sinningdale Agreement, an attempt to establish power sharing between a Northern Ireland executive, and a Council of Ireland. After loyalist strikes in 1974 aimed at bringing down the Sunningdale Agreement, he began using another strategy that involved gaining the support of leaders in other countries. The strategy led him to become a member of the European Parliament and a member of the Northern Ireland Parliament. In 1988, he arranged talks between himself and Gerry Adams (the leader of the Republican Party and the leader of Sinn Fein), thus attempting to overcome some of the obstacles that the Anglo-Irish Agreement faced. In 1998, he was awarded the Nobel Peace Prize for his efforts, which helped pave the way toward the peace process in the 1990s. He was elected to the Northern Ireland Assembly in 1998 but resigned in 2000 and stepped down as leader of the SDLP in 2001.

Nationalism in Islamic Contexts and Debates

Muhhamad Abduh (1849–1905)

Abduh was encouraged by Amal al-Din al-Afghani, a controversial 19th-century Muslim activist who worked for a pan-Islamic unity, to study theology, politics, and philosophy. Like other Egyptian intellectuals, he disliked British rule. In 1877, Abduh graduated and gained a teaching position but later lost it because of his connection with al-Afghani. Abduh then became chief editor of the *Official Egyptian Gazette*, which he used to spread anticolonial propaganda. He was exiled from Egypt and later joined Afghani in Paris, where they collaborated to write the anticolonial newspaper *al-Urwah al-Wuthqa* ("The Indissoluble Link"). Abduh and Afghani supported a new interpretation of the Quran that could be adapted for modern times, but they diverged because

Abduh believed that internal changes were more important than protesting British rule. In 1888, he returned to Egypt, where his willingness to cooperate with British authorities led him to attain the position of judge and later mufti (supreme Muslim authority). He also created the political journal (*al-Manar)* in which he spread his belief that the Quran should serve as a reference for morality but should be adapted to fit the concerns of modern society.

Hassan Al-Banna (1906–1949)

Al-Banna was a member of the Society for Moral Behavior at the young age of 12. After attending school in Cairo, Al-Banna moved to Ismailia in Egypt, a city located on the west bank of the Suez Canal (and an area with great foreign influence due to military and economic interests) to teach. He was greatly influenced by the scenes he saw there. Al-Banna believed that Western culture was secularizing society; thus he created the Muslim Brotherhood in 1928 with the goal of revitalizing Islam. Al-Banna and the Muslim Brotherhood aimed to create a state ruled by Sharia (Islamic law). By 1940, the group had over 1 million followers, and its ideas had spread through the Arab world. Al-Banna supported working with the government, but many members of the group began to see the government as working against nationalist goals, and some members were responsible for several political assassinations. Al-Banna created a paramilitary wing called the Special Apparatus that fought against British rule using bombings and assassinations. Although he denounced the assassination of Prime Minister Mahmoud al-Nuqrashi, he was killed by unknown men believed to be associated with the Egyptian government.

Ruhollah Khumeini (1900–1989)

Born in central Iran, Khumeini became a religious scholar and by the 1920s was named an ayatollah (leading Shi'ite scholar). In 1963, he was arrested for protesting the close attachments to the West that the ruling regime of Reza Shah Pahlevi in Iran had, leading him to be seen as a national hero. Also in 1963, Khumeini gave speeches, the most famous of which was the 15th Khordad speech against U.S. interference in Iran and the Pahlevi regime. Khumeini was later arrested and exiled in hopes of stopping the riots that occurred in response to the 15th Khordad, but his arrest did not stop protests against the Pahlevi, and his 15th Khordad speech is seen as an important connection to the end of the Pahlevi regime. Khumeini continued to support efforts against the Pahlevi regime while in exile. Khumeini's 15th Khordad speech and his exile are seen as important to his development of the wilayat al-faqi (guardianship of the jurists). According to this theory, there is a divinely legitimate leader who has the same governmental powers as the Prophet. In 1979, the shah was overthrown. Khumeini returned to Iran and became a political and religious leader. He also declared Islamic law in Iran.

Mawlana Mawdudi (Syed Abul Ala Mawdudi) (1902–1979)

In the 1920s, Mawdudi was only a journalist, but after studying Western literature and politics, he developed an Islamist worldview that later became important in South Asia and in Iran. He envisioned an Islamic state that would be a theo-democracy in which officials were elected but took advice from clerical officials. Most laws would be based on Sharia (Islamic law). He believed that through jihad, Muslims must free themselves from all non-Muslim influences. In 1941, he formed the Jamaat-e-Islami (JI), which was constituted by a network of organizations that included student and union groups. Mawdudi led the group until 1972. By the 1920s, his teachings were influential in Egypt, Palestine, and elsewhere, and Hassan Al-Banna—one of the founders of the Muslim Brotherhood—was a faithful pupil of his. Mawdudi was most influential in Pakistan. After Pakistan gained independence in 1947, the JI campaign for Islamization of society was successful, with the rapid Islamization of laws in the 1970s. During the 1970s, the JI was also able to infiltrate Pakistan's military and intelligence agencies with its Islamist views. Mawdudi died in September of 1979.

Hosni Mubarak (1928–)

Mubarak came to power in 1981 after the assassination of Anwar Sadat, the president of Egypt, on October 6, 1981. Mubarak continued the policy of peaceful relations with Israel, which gave him support from the West, and he cracked down on Islamic militants. Mubarak blocked most outlets for opposition and negotiation, causing increased membership of oppositional Islamist groups. Throughout his presidency, he kept the country under emergency rule, which in some ways was necessary to fight Islamic opposition; however, it also allowed imprisonment for supposedly challenging the status quo. Mubarak's oppression of the Muslim Brotherhood led the group to become an underground organization. Mubarak was able to maintain regional security, keep peaceful relations with Israel, have a good connection with the West, and hold back Islamic militants. Part of the reason Mubarak was able to maintain power for so long was his ability to form connections with Western allies that supported him; however, this also put him in direct conflict with the Muslim Brotherhood, which was against Western influence. Mubarak imprisoned and tortured many members of the Muslim Brotherhood. He lost power due to popular protests in spring of 2011. Later in the year, he stood trial for abuse of power and complacency in the killing of protestors.

Gamal Abdel Nasser (1918–1970)

Nasser was a member of the Free Officers, a secret group that opposed British rule and King Faruq, and in 1952, he instigated a successful coup. The group quickly began implementing radical measures by abolishing the monarchy in Egypt. Nasser assumed primary leadership of the group in 1954 and negotiated the British leaving Egypt after being there for 72 years. In 1956, Nasser was officially elected president of Egypt. The Muslim Brotherhood originally supported the Free Officers but later turned against Nasser because of his secular agenda. The group even attempted to assassinate him, leading Nasser to adopt restrictive policies against the Brotherhood. The constitution that was adopted under Nasser's rule offered some protection for citizens but still allowed Egypt to become a police state and enabled the minister of the interior to arrest people at his discretion. Nasser declared Islam the official religion of Egypt but maintained a goal of a secular state, which led to clashes with some Islamists who claimed that Nasser's commitment to Islam was merely nominal. Although Nasser was able to emerge as a world leader and become a hero in the Arab world, he did not have good relations with the West. Nasser was a pan-Arabist and envisioned a united Arab world. To this end, he helped form the United Arab Republic in 1958 (which joined Syria and Egypt), but Syria withdrew in 1961 and Egypt stopped being known as the United Arab Republic in 1971. After Israel occupied the Sinai Peninsula up to the Suez Canal in response to Egyptian forces blocking the Gulf of Aqaba in 1967,

Nasser took responsibility for it and stepped down from his position but was called back by a vote by the people. He died in 1970.

Sayyid Qutb (1906–1966)

Qutb attended the secular secondary college in Cairo, Dar al-'Ulum and later worked for the Egyptian ministry of education. In 1948, he was sent to the United States to study education and was fundamentally changed by what he saw there. He was shocked by the prejudice he saw exhibited toward Arabs and the amount of freedom given to American women. This led him to become further committed to Islam. When he returned to Egypt in 1951, Qutb joined the Muslim Brotherhood. At that point, the Brotherhood was moving from gradual political methods to using violence to accomplish its goals, and Qutb joined in this transition. In 1954, he was arrested along with other members of the Brotherhood after an attempted assassination of President Nasser, and released in 1964. He was rearrested in 1965, for allegedly planning to overthrow the state, and hanged in 1966. Qutb's most important contribution was the writing he did while he was in prison. He wrote a commentary of Quran. He spoke against the Westernized leaders of the Nasser and Saudi regimes that did not follow Sharia and were, thus, condemning all of their people to be Jahili Arabs (Arabs ignorant of God). Qutb believed that the Nasser regime should be overthrown and looked to the era of the Mameluke Sultans of Egypt as an example by which to justify jihad against those that did not correctly practice Islam. Qutb is seen by some as one of the most influential writers of the latter half of the 20th century, and he is believed to be Osama bin Laden's inspiration.

Anwar Sadat (1918–1981)

Sadat was an ally of Gamal Nasser before the Free Officers took over the government of Egypt, and he gained the position of minister of public relations and trusted lieutenant in the postrevolutionary era. Sadat took over after Nasser's death and proved to be a capable leader. Sadat adopted policies on Islamists that were not as harsh as Nasser's; he believed that Islam could be a uniting force in Egypt and even used some groups like al-Gama'a al-Islameya, a militant Islamist group, against leftist opponents. He offered a peace deal with Israel in return for the Suez Canal, and after the Israeli government continued to reject it, he plotted a military attack that pushed Israeli forces back into the desert past Sinai. Although it did not last long, it changed the dynamics between Israel and Egypt. Sadat was finally able to talk to the Israeli government by agreeing to do so in the Knesset. This bold move led to the Camp David Accords in 1978 and a peace treaty in 1979. Sadat faced opposition in Egypt for his relationship with the West as well as the peace treaty. In 1981, he was assassinated by an Islamist who denounced the peace treaty with Israel.

6

Data and Documents

Nationalism as Civil Religion: The Case of the United States

Even secular varieties of nationalism include myths of origin, stories of heroic sacrifices, demands to commit the utmost sacrifice for the unifying good of the "nation," sacred spaces (museums of national history, memorials, battlefields), sacred times (national and religious holidays that are observed by the state), and other ritualistic moments and spaces. The designation "civil religion" refers to a collection of practices, symbols, rituals, and myths (many elements of which are appropriated from organized religious traditions) that embody, perpetuate, and convey the significance of an overarching conception of national identity to mark out symbolic boundaries (Who we are as a nation or as a society? Who will be included? Who is excluded? What are the requirements for membership?). The ritualistic aspects of a civil religion often provide the means by which a society legitimates itself, illuminates and amplifies its significance in history, and reproduces itself through processes of socialization. But these practices and processes always contain the possibility for facilitating creative modes of challenging, rethinking, and transforming "who we are."

An American Civil Religion: Central Motifs and Moments of Contestation

John Winthrop Comparing the mission to settle a new society to the establishment of a "City upon a Hill" excerpted from the sermon "A Model of Christian Charity," by Governor John Winthrop (1630 on board the Arbella)

This 17th-century text is often quoted to explicate an engrained sense of American prestige and special providential mission. A self-perception of possessing a special kind of chosen-ness is a common theme in national mythologies. In this particular instance, it reflects the Puritan tradition that renders the American experiment as an exemplary one, "The New Israel."

Thus stands the cause between God and us. We are entered into covenant with Him for this work. We have taken out a commission. The Lord hath given us leave to draw our own articles. We have professed to enterprise these and those accounts, upon these and those ends. We have hereupon besought Him of favor and blessing. Now if the Lord shall please to hear us, and bring us in peace to the place we desire, then hath He ratified this covenant and sealed our commission, and will expect a strict performance of the articles contained in it; but if we shall neglect the observation of these articles which are the ends we have propounded, and, dissembling with our God, shall fall to embrace this present world and prosecute our carnal intentions, seeking great things for ourselves and our posterity, the Lord will surely break out in wrath against us, and be revenged of such a people, and make us know the price of the breach of such a covenant.

Now the only way to avoid this shipwreck, and to provide for our posterity, is to follow the counsel of Micah, to do justly, to love mercy, to walk humbly with our God. For this end, we must be knit together, in this work, as one man. We must entertain each other in brotherly affection. We must be willing to abridge ourselves of our superfluities, for the supply of others' necessities. We must uphold a familiar commerce together in all meekness, gentleness, patience and liberality. We must delight in each other; make others' conditions our own; rejoice together, mourn together, labor and suffer together, always having before our eyes our commission and community in the work, as members of the same body. So shall we keep the unity of the spirit in the bond of peace. The Lord will be our God, and delight to dwell among us, as His own people, and will command a blessing upon us in all our ways, so that we shall see much more of His wisdom, power, goodness and truth, than formerly we have been acquainted with. We shall find that the God of Israel is among us, when ten of us shall be able to resist a thousand of our enemies; when He shall make us a praise and glory that men shall say of succeeding plantations, "may the Lord make it like that of New England." For we must consider that we shall be as a city upon a hill. The eyes of all people are upon us. So that if we shall deal falsely with our God in this work we have undertaken, and so cause Him to withdraw His present help from us, we shall be made a story and a by-word through the world. We shall open the mouths of enemies to speak evil of the ways of God, and all professors for God's sake. We shall shame the faces of many of God's worthy servants, and cause their prayers to be turned into curses upon us till we be consumed out of the good land whither we are going.

And to shut this discourse with that exhortation of Moses, that faithful servant of the Lord, in his last farewell to Israel, Deut. 30. "Beloved, there is now set before us life and death, good and evil," in that we are commanded this day to love the Lord our God, and to love one another, to walk in his ways and to keep his Commandments and his ordinance and his laws, and the articles of our Covenant with Him, that we may live and be multiplied, and that the Lord our God may bless us in the land whither we go to possess it. But if our hearts shall turn away, so that we will not obey, but shall be seduced, and worship other Gods, our pleasure and profits, and serve them; it is propounded unto us this day, we shall surely perish out of the good land whither we pass over this vast sea to possess it.

> Therefore let us choose life,
>
> that we and our seed may live,
>
> by obeying His voice and cleaving to Him,
>
> for He is our life and our prosperity.

Source: The Religious Freedom Page, University of Virginia, Governor John Winthrop's A Model of Christian Charity (1630 on board the Arbella). http://religiousfreedom.lib.virginia.edu/sacred/charity.html (accessed November 11, 2012).

Roger Williams (1864)

The following selection from Roger Williams illuminates another central motif of an American ethos. Like Winthrop's notion of "city upon a hill," Williams's commitment to an absolute freedom of conscience is grounded in his religious convictions. The principles of religious freedom and of the freedom of conscience more broadly have become central tenets of an American self-perception. Williams was excommunicated from the Massachusetts Bay Colony as a result of his convictions. Subsequently, he founded the colony of Rhode Island.

First, That the blood of so many hundred thousand soules of Protestants and Papists, split in the Wars of present and former Ages, for their respective Consciences, is not required nor accepted by *Jesus Christ* the *Prince of Peace*. Secondly, Pregnant Scriptures and Arguments are throughout the Worke proposed against the Doctrine of Persecution for the cause of Conscience.

Secondly. Pregnant scriptures and arguments are throughout the work proposed against the doctrine of persecution for cause of conscience.

Thirdly. Satisfactory answers are given to scriptures and objections produced by Mr. Calvin, Beza, Mr. Cotton, and the ministers of the New English churches, and others former and later, tending to prove the doctrine of persecution for cause of conscience.

Fourthly. The doctrine of persecution for cause of conscience, is proved guilty of all the blood of the souls crying for vengeance under the altar.

Fifthly. All civil states, with their officers of justice, in their respective constitutions and administrations, are proved essentially civil, and therefore not judges, governors, or defenders of the spiritual, or Christian, state and worship.

Sixthly. It is the will and command of God that, since the coming of his Son the Lord Jesus, a permission of the most Paganish, Jewish, Turkish, or anti-christian consciences and worships be granted to all men in all nations and countries: and they are only to be fought against with that sword which is only, in soul matters, able to conquer: to wit, the sword of God's Spirit, the word of God.

Seventhly. The state of the land of Israel, the kings and people thereof, in peace and war, is proved figurative and ceremonial, and no pattern nor precedent for any kingdom or civil state in the world to follow.

Eighthly. God requireth not an uniformity of religion to be enacted and enforced in any civil state; which enforced uniformity, sooner or later, is the greatest occasion of civil war, ravishing of conscience, persecution of Christ Jesus in his servants, and of the hypocrisy and destruction of millions of souls.

Ninthly. In holding an enforced uniformity of religion in a civil state, we must necessarily disclaim our desires and hopes of the Jews' conversion to Christ.

Tenthly. An enforced uniformity of religion throughout a nation or civil state, confounds the civil and religious, denies the principles of Christianity and civility, and that Jesus Christ is come in the flesh.

Eleventhly. The permission of other consciences and worships than a state professeth, only can, according to God, procure a firm and lasting peace; good assurance being taken, according to the wisdom of the civil state, for uniformity of civil obedience from all sorts.

Twelfthly. Lastly, true civility and Christianity may both flourish in a state or kingdom, notwithstanding the permission of divers and contrary consciences, either of Jew or Gentile.

Source: Williams, Roger. *The Bloudy Tenet of Persecution, for Cause of Conscience, Discussed, in A Conference between Truth and Peace*. In Perry Miller, ed., *The Complete Writings of Roger Williams* (New York: Russell and Russell, 1963).

The First Amendment to the Constitution (1791)
This definitional amendment to the Constitution embodies the principles of the United States. The principle of nonestablishment does not mean, however, a lack of religiosity. The contrary is the case since Americans are thoroughly religious. The principle of religious freedom of course undergirds the American ethos. This, however, does not entail the cultural disestablishment of Christianity (and later of a Judeo-Christian construct) as a prominent feature of an American civil religion.

Amendment 1—Freedom of Religion, Press, Expression. Ratified December 15, 1791.

Congress shall make no law respecting an establishment of religion, or prohibiting the free exercise thereof; or abridging the freedom of speech, or of the press; or the right of the people peaceably to assemble, and to petition the Government for a redress of grievances.

Source: U.S. Constitution Online. The United States Constitution. http://www.usconstitution.net/const.html#Am1 (accessed August 16, 2012).

The Pledge of Allegiance

The Pledge of Allegiance was originally composed in 1892 by Francis Bellamy (1855–1931). The original text included a declaration of loyalty to the flag and the indivisibility of the republic. It did not include reference to God. Only in 1954 and in response to the perceived communist threat, did Congress add "under God," with the encouragement of President Eisenhower. The inclusion of these words intended, in part, to draw a clear distinction between an American identity and the militant atheism associated with communism. The Pledge was recited by students in public schools and in 2002 was legally challenged by a parent who felt that the inclusion of "under God" violated their atheistic belief. The contestation of the wording of the Pledge reached the U.S. Court of Appeals for the Ninth Circuit that ruled the phrase unconstitutional because it endorsed religion (monotheism). This ruling was overturned by the Supreme Court on the basis of a technicality, namely, that the father filing the suit was ruled a noncustodial parent (Elk Grove Unified School District v. Newdow, 2004). *The text reproduced here is what was ratified in 1956.*

I pledge allegiance to the Flag of the United States of America, and to the Republic for which it stands, one nation under God, indivisible, with liberty and justice for all.

Source: Historic Documents. http://www.ushistory.org/documents/pledge.htm (accessed January 4, 2012).

The Battle Hymn of the Republic

These lyrics were composed in 1861 during the U.S. Civil War. The song serves both as a broadly patriotic song and appears as a hymn in numerous Christian denominational hymnbooks. The lyrics allude to numerous biblical passages to God's wrath and judgment of the wicked and unjust. It was played on September 14, 2001, in Washington, D.C.'s National Cathedral during memorial services for the victims of September 11, 2001. The lyrics also appear in various of Martin Luther King, Jr.'s speeches and sermons, most famously his 1965 speech at the Alabama state capital building, "How Long, Not Long," and his final sermon in 1968, just prior to his assassination, entitled "I Have Been to the Mountain Top." The use by King illustrates how deeply engrained this hymn is in the American political and religious culture.

Mine eyes have seen the glory of the coming of the Lord;

He is trampling out the vintage where the grapes of

Wrath are stored;

He hath loosed the fateful lightning of His terrible

Swift sword;

His truth is marching on.

CHORUS

Glory, glory! Hallelujah!

Glory, glory! Hallelujah!

Glory, glory! Hallelujah!

His truth is marching on. ...

He has sounded forth the trumpet that shall never call retreat;

He is sifting out the hearts of men before His judgment-seat:

Oh, be swift, my soul, to answer Him! be jubilant, my feet!

Our God is marching on.

CHORUS. ...

In the beauty of the lilies, Christ was born across the

Sea,

With a glory in His bosom that transfigures you and me;

As He died to make men holy, let us die to make men free,

While God is marching on.

CHORUS

Source: More Lyrics. http://www.lyricsmode.com/lyrics/i/independence_day/#share (accessed January 3, 2011).

Official Speeches

Official speeches of presidents and other political and religious leaders often provide important clues as to the visions of the society those leaders aspire to reinforce and/or capitalize on. It is no surprise that often those official speeches draw selectively on the religious imagination and motifs that might resonate powerfully with constituents. In the U.S. context, the occasions of presidential speeches, such as on the day of inauguration, constitute part and parcel of a civil religion. Presidents make references to core U.S. values as well as sense of national destiny and providential mission.

George Washington: Farewell Address, September 19, 1796

The following excerpts provide an early outline of a U.S. civil religion. President Washington talks about patriotism as an intense love and commitment to the land and to the principles of liberty U.S. independence represents. He also alludes to broadly shared cultural and religious backgrounds of all Americans and to critical distinctions between religion and morality as well as their ramifications to the U.S. commitment to the principle of religious freedom.

For this you have every inducement of sympathy and interest. Citizens, by birth or choice, of a common country, that country has a right to concentrate your affections. The name of American, which belongs to you in your national capacity, must always exalt the just pride of patriotism . . . with slight shades of difference, you have the same religion, manners, habits, and political principles. You have in a common cause fought and triumphed together; the independence and liberty you possess are the work of joint counsels, and joint efforts of common dangers, sufferings, and successes.

Of all the dispositions and habits which lead to political prosperity, religion and morality are indispensable supports. In vain would that man claim the tribute of patriotism, who should labor to subvert these great pillars of human happiness, these firmest props of the duties of men and citizens, The mere politician, equally with the pious man, ought to respect and to cherish them. A volume could not trace all their connections with private and public felicity. Let it simply be asked: Where is the security for property, for reputation, for life, if the sense of religious obligation desert the oaths which are the instruments of investigation in courts of justice? And let us with caution indulge the supposition that morality can be maintained without religion. Whatever may be conceded to the influence of refined education on minds of peculiar structure, reason and experience both forbid us to expect that national morality can prevail in exclusion of religious principles.

Source: Washington, George. "The Farewell Address," *The Papers of George Washington*, http://gwpapers.virginia.edu/documents/ farewell/transcript.html (accessed August 16, 2012).

Woodrow Wilson: Address to a Joint Session of Congress Requesting a Declaration of War against Germany, April 2, 1917

The following excerpt illustrates the motif of sacrifice, one integral to the national imagination. President Wilson frames the need for U.S. involvement in World War I in terms of an inevitable commitment to and pride in defending U.S. values around the world. He ends the speech by invoking God, suggesting that U.S. military engagements represent the unfolding of a U.S. providential responsibility.

But the right is more precious than peace, and we shall fight for the things which we have always carried nearest our hearts—for democracy, for the right of those who submit to authority to have a voice in their own Governments, for the rights and liberties of small nations, for a universal dominion of right by such a concert of free peoples as shall bring peace and safety to all nations ... To such a task we can dedicate our lives and our fortunes, every thing that we are and everything that we have, with the pride of those who know that the day has come when America is privileged to spend her blood and her might for the principles that gave her birth and happiness and the peace which she has treasured. God helping her, she can do no other.

Source: Wilson, Woodrow. "Address to a Joint Session of Congress Requesting a Declaration of War against Germany," April 2, 1917. Online by Gerhard Peters and John T. Woolley, *The American Presidency Project*. http://www.presidency.ucsb.edu/ws/?pid =65366 (accessed August 16, 2012).

Franklin D. Roosevelt: Annual Message to Congress, January 4, 1939

Storms from abroad directly challenge three institutions indispensable to Americans, now as always. The first is religion. It is the source of the other two—democracy and international good faith.

Source: Roosevelt, Franklin D. "Annual Message to Congress," January 4, 1939. Online by Gerhard Peters and John T. Woolley, *The American Presidency Project*. http://www.presidency.ucsb.edu/ws/?pid=15684 (accessed August 16, 2012).

The following excerpts provide further illustration of linking American foreign policy with a sense of a providential mission.

Franklin Roosevelt, Campaign Address, Cleveland, Ohio, November 2, 1940

We look at the country in which we live. It is a great country, built by generations of peaceable, friendly men and women who had in their hearts faith that the good life can be attained by those who will work for it.

Ours is the foreign policy of an Administration which has undying faith in the strength of our democracy today, full confidence in the vitality of our democracy in the future, and a consistent record in the cause of peace.

For you can build ships and tanks and planes and guns galore; but they will not be enough. You must place behind them an invincible faith in the institutions which they have been built to defend.

I see an America devoted to our freedom—unified by tolerance and by religious faith—a people consecrated to peace, a people confident in strength because their body and their spirit are secure and unafraid.

Source: Roosevelt, Franklin D. "Campaign Address at Cleveland, Ohio," November 2, 1940. Online by Gerhard Peters and John T. Woolley, *The American Presidency Project*. http://www.presidency.ucsb.edu/ws/?pid=15893 (accessed August 16, 2012).

Harry Truman, Inaugural Address, January 20, 1949

The American people stand firm in the faith which has inspired this Nation from the beginning.

To that end we will devote our strength, our resources, and our firmness of resolve. With God's help, the future of mankind will be assured in a world of justice, harmony, and peace.

Source: Truman, Harry S. "Inaugural Address," January 20, 1949. Online by Gerhard Peters and John T. Woolley, *The American Presidency Project*. http://www.presidency.ucsb.edu/ws/?pid=13282 (accessed August 16, 2012).

John F. Kennedy: Radio and Television Report to the American People on Civil Rights, June 11, 1963

U.S. civil religion or nationalism is of course a contested construct. As a result of the civil rights movement, President Kennedy—in the following excerpts—reflected on what it means to truly live up to the definitional U.S. principles of equality.

Today we are committed to a worldwide struggle to promote and protect the rights of all who wish to be free. And when Americans are sent to Vietnam or West Berlin, we do not ask for whites only. It was founded on the principle that all men are created equal, and that the rights of every man are diminished when the rights of one man are threatened.

One hundred years of delay have passed since President Lincoln freed the slaves, yet their heirs, their grandsons, are not fully free. They are not yet freed from the bonds of injustice. They are not yet freed from social and economic oppression. And this Nation, for all its hopes and all its boasts, will not be fully free until all its citizens are free.

Now the time has come for this Nation to fulfill its promise. The events in Birmingham and elsewhere have so increased the cries for equality that no city or State or legislative body can prudently choose to ignore them.

Source: Kennedy, John F. "Radio and Television Report to the American People on Civil Rights," June 11, 1963. Online by Gerhard Peters and John T. Woolley, *The American Presidency Project*. http://www.presidency.ucsb.edu/ws/?pid=9271 (accessed August 16, 2012).

Richard Nixon: First Inaugural Address, January 20, 1969

The following passage features excerpts from the first inaugural address of Richard Nixon that exemplify the providential global role that Nixon believed the United States held. Nixon was president during the Vietnam War and faced an American population that was torn over the subject of their involvement in the foreign war.

What kind of nation we will be, what kind of world we will live in, whether we shape the future in the image of our hopes, is ours to determine by our actions and our choices.

The greatest honor history can bestow is the title of peacemaker. This honor now beckons America—the chance to help lead the world at last out of the valley of turmoil, and onto that high ground of peace that man has dreamed of since the dawn of civilization.

This is our summons to greatness.

When we listen to "the better angels of our nature," we find that they celebrate the simple things, the basic things—such as goodness, decency, love, kindness.

We cannot learn from one another until we stop shouting at one another—until we speak quietly enough so that our words can be heard as well as our voices.

The American dream does not come to those who fall asleep.

Our greatest need now is to reach beyond government, and to enlist the legions of the concerned and the committed.

What has to be done, has to be done by government and people together or it will not be done at all. The lesson of past agony is that without the people we can do nothing; with the people we can do everything.

To match the magnitude of our tasks, we need the energies of our people—enlisted not only in grand enterprises, but more importantly in those small, splendid efforts that make headlines in the neighborhood newspaper instead of the national journal.

With these, we can build a great cathedral of the spirit—each of us raising it one stone at a time, as he reaches out to his neighbor, helping, caring, doing.

I do not offer a life of uninspiring ease. I do not call for a life of grim sacrifice. I ask you to join in a high adventure—one as rich as humanity itself, and as exciting as the times we live in.

Until he has been part of a cause larger than himself, no man is truly whole.

No man can be fully free while his neighbor is not. To go forward at all is to go forward together.

With those who are willing to join, let us cooperate to reduce the burden of arms, to strengthen the structure of peace, to lift up the poor and the hungry.

But to all those who would be tempted by weakness, let us leave no doubt that we will be as strong as we need to be for as long as we need to be.

I know that peace does not come through wishing for it—that there is no substitute for days and even years of patient and prolonged diplomacy.

I have taken an oath today in the presence of God and my countrymen to uphold and defend the Constitution of the United States. To that oath I now add this sacred commitment: I shall consecrate my office, my energies, and all the wisdom I can summon, to the cause of peace among nations.

Let this message be heard by strong and weak alike:

The peace we seek to win is not victory over any other people, but the peace that comes "with healing in its wings"; with compassion for those who have suffered; with understanding for those who have opposed us; with the opportunity for all the peoples of this earth to choose their own destiny.

We have endured a long night of the American spirit. But as our eyes catch the dimness of the first rays of dawn, let us not curse the remaining dark. Let us gather the light.

Our destiny offers, not the cup of despair, but the chalice of opportunity. So let us seize it, not in fear, but in gladness—and, "riders on the earth together," let us go forward, firm in our faith, steadfast in our purpose, cautious of the dangers; but sustained by our confidence in the will of God and the promise of man.

Source: Nixon, Richard. "Inaugural Address," January 20, 1969. Online by Gerhard Peters and John T. Woolley, *The American Presidency Project*. http://www.presidency.ucsb.edu/ws/?pid=1941 (accessed August 16, 2012).

George W. Bush: Address to the Nation on the Terrorist Attacks, September 11, 2001

These acts of mass murder were intended to frighten our nation into chaos and retreat. But they have failed. Our country is strong. A great people has been moved to defend a great nation. Terrorist attacks can shake the foundations of our biggest buildings, but they cannot touch the foundation of America. These acts shatter steel, but they cannot dent the steel of American resolve.

This is a day when all Americans from every walk of life unite in our resolve for justice and peace. America has stood down enemies before, and we will do so this time. None of us will ever forget this day. Yet, we go forward to defend freedom and all that is good and just in our world.

Source: Bush, George W. "Address to the Nation on the Terrorist Attacks," September 11, 2001. Online by Gerhard Peters and John T. Woolley, *The American Presidency Project*. http://www.presidency.ucsb.edu/ws/?pid=58057 (accessed August 16, 2011).

George W. Bush: Excerpts from His Remarks at the National Day of Prayer and Remembrance, the National Cathedral, Washington, D.C. (2001)

The speech was made only a few days after the terrorist attacks of September 11, 2001, and it was an attempt to unify and console the American population during a mournful period.

We mourn with those who have suffered great and disastrous loss. All our hearts have been seared by the sudden and sense-less taking of innocent lives. We pray for healing and for the strength to serve and encourage one another in hope and faith.

Scripture says: "Blessed are those who mourn for they shall be comforted." I call on every American family and the family of America to observe a National Day of Prayer and Remembrance, honoring the memory of the thousands of victims of these brutal attacks and comforting those who lost loved ones. We will persevere through this national tragedy and personal loss. In time, we will find healing and recovery; and, in the face of all this evil, we remain strong and united, "one Nation under God."

Now, therefore I, George W. Bush, President of the United States of America, by virtue of the authority vested in me by the Constitution and laws of the United States, do hereby proclaim Friday, September 14, 2001, as a National Day of Prayer and Remembrance for the Victims of the Terrorist Attacks on September 11, 2001. I ask that the people of the United States and places of worship mark this National Day of Prayer and Remembrance with noontime memorial services, the ringing of bells at that hour, and evening candlelight remembrance vigils.

Source: Bush, George W. "National Day of Prayer and Remembrance for the Victims of the Terrorist Attacks on September 13, 2001," White House, George W. Bush, http://georgewbush -whitehouse.archives.gov/news/releases/2001/09/20010913-7. html (accessed December 22, 2011).

George W. Bush: Address before a Joint Session of the Congress on the U.S. Response to the Terrorist Attacks of September 11, September 20, 2001

The following excerpts are taken from President George W. Bush's speech to Congress and the U.S. population just days after the tragedy of September 11, 2001. The speech tries to draw distinctions between

Muslim terrorists who pervert Islam and the many Muslim Americans who practice their religion peacefully. Further, the speech underscores that the values of democracy, including the respect of religious freedom, are what define America in juxtaposition to the terrorist networks that attacked its soil. Interestingly, the speech suggests that the Islamist networks constitute a threat to governments and regimes across the Middle East and North Africa. By 2011, many of those autocratic and dictatorial regimes will fall as a result of popular revolutions that also include Islamist voices.

I also want to speak tonight directly to Muslims throughout the world. We respect your faith. It's practiced freely by many millions of Americans, and by millions more in countries that America counts as friends ... The terrorists are traitors to their own faith, trying, in effect, to hijack Islam itself.

Americans are asking, why do they hate us? They hate what we see right here in this chamber—a democratically elected government. Their leaders are self-appointed. They hate our freedoms—our freedom of religion, our freedom of speech, our freedom to vote and assemble and disagree with each other.

They want to overthrow existing governments in many Muslim countries, such as Egypt, Saudi Arabia, and Jordan. They want to drive Israel out of the Middle East. They want to drive Christians and Jews out of vast regions of Asia and Africa.

... [F]ellow citizens, we'll meet violence with patient justice—assured of the rightness of our cause, and confident of the victories to come. In all that lies before us, may God grant us wisdom, and may He watch over the United States of America.

Source: Bush, George W. "Address before a Joint Session of the Congress on the United States Response to the Terrorist Attacks of September 11," September 20, 2001. Online by Gerhard Peters and John T. Woolley, *The American Presidency Project*. http://www.presidency.ucsb.edu/ws/?pid=64731 (accessed August 16, 2012).

Barack Obama: Inaugural Address, January 20, 2009

The following excerpts from President Obama's inaugural speech in January 2009 illustrate the common rhetorical motifs of national sacrifice, references to the legacy and meanings of the Constitution and American values, as well as an attempt to broaden the definition of U.S. society to include Muslims and nonbelievers. This is an important departure from a U.S. civil religion that presumes a belief in God as the norm. The speech also makes references to the greatness and superiority of the United States, another motif common in national rhetoric.

The words have been spoken during rising tides of prosperity and the still waters of peace. Yet, every so often the oath is taken amidst gathering clouds and raging storms. At these moments, America has carried on not simply because of the skill or vision of those in high office, but because We the People have remained faithful to the ideals of our forebears, and true to our founding documents.

We remain a young nation, but in the words of Scripture, the time has come to set aside childish things. The time has come to reaffirm our enduring spirit; to choose our better history; to carry forward that precious gift, that noble idea, passed on from generation to generation: the God-given promise that all are equal, all are free, and all deserve a chance to pursue their full measure of happiness.

In reaffirming the greatness of our nation, we understand that greatness is never a given. It must be earned. Our journey has never been one of shortcuts or settling for less. It has not been the path for the faint-hearted, for those who prefer leisure over work, or seek only the pleasures of riches and fame ... For us, they packed up their worldly possessions and traveled across oceans in search of a new life. For us, they toiled in sweatshops and settled the West, endured the lash of the whip and plowed the hard earth. For us, they fought and died in places Concord and Gettysburg; Normandy and Khe Sanh.

They saw America as bigger than the sum of our individual ambitions; greater than all the differences of birth or wealth or faction.

We are a nation of Christians and Muslims, Jews and Hindus, and nonbelievers. We are shaped by every language and culture, drawn from every end of this earth. And because we have tested the bitter swill of civil war and segregation and emerged from that dark chapter stronger and more united, we cannot help but believe that the old hatreds shall someday pass; that the lines of tribes shall soon dissolve; that as the world grows smaller, our common humanity shall reveal itself; and that America must play its role in ushering in a new era of peace.

To the Muslim world, we seek a new way forward, based on mutual interest and mutual respect.

Source: Obama, Barack. "Inaugural Address," January 20, 2009. Online by Gerhard Peters and John T. Woolley, *The American Presidency Project*. http://www.presidency.ucsb.edu/ws/ ?pid=44 (accessed August 16, 2012).

Religion and the Authorization of Force and Empire

George W. Bush, Address to the Nation from Atlanta on Homeland Security, November 8, 2001

In the following excerpts, President Bush invokes a strong image of Americans as champions against terror in order to unite Americans in support of the war effort. The first speech was delivered shortly after declaring the "War on Terror," and it shows the belief that the war was truly one to maintain justice and spread U.S. values. The second speech occurred a few years later, and it tries to bring back the idea of the role of Americans as protectors of peace throughout the world.

We meet tonight after two of the most difficult and most inspiring months in our nation's history. We have endured the shock of watching so many innocent lives ended in acts of unimaginable horror. We have endured the sadness of so many funerals. We have faced unprecedented bioterrorist attack delivered in our mail.

. . .

We are a different country than we were on September the 10th, sadder and less innocent, stronger and more united and in the face of ongoing threats, determined and courageous. Our nation faces a threat to our freedoms and the stakes could not be higher. We are the target of enemies who boast they want to kill, kill all Americans, kill all Jews and kill all Christians. We've seen that type of hate before. And the only possible response is to confront it and to defeat it.

. . .

Above all, we will live in a spirit of courage and optimism. Our nation was born in that spirit, as immigrants yearning for freedom courageously risked their lives in search of greater opportunity. That spirit of optimism and courage still beckons people across the world who want to come here. And that spirit of optimism and courage must guide those of us fortunate enough to live here.

. . .

We will never forget all we have lost and all we are fighting for. Ours is the cause of freedom. We've defeated freedom's enemies before. And we will defeat them again. We cannot know every turn this battle will take. Yet we know our cause is just and our ultimate victory is assured. We will no doubt face new challenges, but we have our marching orders. My fellow Americans, let's roll.

Source: George W. Bush. "Address to the Nation from Atlanta on Homeland Security," November 8, 2001. Online by Gerhard Peters and John T. Woolley, *The American Presidency Project*. http://www.presidency.ucsb.edu/ws/?pid=62836 (accessed August 16, 2012).

George W. Bush, President Discusses War on Terror at National Endowment for Democracy

Recently our country observed the fourth anniversary of a great evil, and looked back on a great turning point in our history. We still remember a proud city covered in smoke and ashes, a fire across the Potomac, and passengers who spent their final moments on Earth fighting the enemy. We still remember the men who rejoiced in every death, and Americans in uniform rising to duty. And we remember the calling that came to us on that day, and continues to this hour: We will confront this mortal danger to all humanity. We will not tire, or rest, until the war on terror is won.

Some call this evil Islamic radicalism; others, militant Jihadism; still others, Islamo-fascism. Whatever it's called, this ideology is very different from the religion of Islam. This form of radicalism exploits Islam to serve a violent, political vision: the establishment, by terrorism and subversion and insurgency, of a totalitarian empire that denies all political and religious freedom. These extremists distort the idea of jihad into a call for terrorist murder against Christians and Jews and Hindus—and also against Muslims from other traditions, who they regard as heretics.

Defeating the militant network is difficult, because it thrives, like a parasite, on the suffering and frustration of others. The radicals exploit local conflicts to build a culture of victimization, in which someone else is always to blame and violence is always the solution. They exploit resentful and disillusioned young men and women, recruiting them through radical mosques as the pawns of terror. And they exploit modern technology to multiply their destructive power. Instead of attending faraway training camps, recruits can now access online training libraries to learn how to build a roadside bomb, or fire a rocket-propelled grenade—and this further spreads the threat of violence, even within peaceful democratic societies.

The murderous ideology of the Islamic radicals is the great challenge of our new century. Yet, in many ways, this fight resembles the struggle against communism in the last century. Like the ideology of communism, Islamic radicalism is elitist, led by a self-appointed vanguard that presumes to speak for the Muslim masses. Bin Laden says his own role is to tell Muslims, quote, "what is good for them and what is not." And what this man who grew up in wealth and privilege considers good for poor Muslims is that they become killers and suicide bombers. He assures them that his—that this is the road to paradise—though he never offers to go along for the ride.

We didn't ask for this global struggle, but we're answering history's call with confidence, and a comprehensive strategy. Defeating a broad and adaptive network requires patience, constant pressure, and strong partners in Europe, the Middle East, North Africa, Asia and beyond. Working with these partners, we're disrupting militant conspiracies, destroying their ability to make war, and working to give millions in a troubled region of the world a hopeful alternative to resentment and violence

We don't know the course of our own struggle—the course our own struggle will take—or the sacrifices that might lie ahead. We do know, however, that the defense of freedom is worth our sacrifice. We do know the love of freedom is the mightiest force of history. And we do know the cause of freedom will once again prevail.

Source: George W. Bush. "President Discusses War on Terror at National Endowment for Democracy," White House, George Bush, November 5, 2005. http://georgewbush-whitehouse .archives.gov/news/releases/2005/10/20051006-3.html (accessed December 21, 2011).

Jean Bethke Elshtain

The following passage illustrates how an influential ethicist working within the tradition of just war theory came to justify the U.S. invasion of Iraq in 2003. Elshtain, a professor of ethics at the University of Chicago Divinity

School, lent her learned support to the Bush administration. In many ways, the language of just war came to dominate the public and political debates surrounding the onset of the invasion.

The first criterion may be the most controversial of all, namely, whether there was a preeminent threat. During the run-up to the Iraq War—a war openly declared by legitimate authority and meeting, therefore, criterion number two—I argued that there were sufficient grounds to embark on a justified war. I would argue the same had I to do it all over again. In my arguments, I reminded those debating the war that St. Thomas Aquinas, among others, insisted that preventing the innocent from certain harm could well be a justified *casus belli*—the innocent being those without the means to defend themselves. All civilians are in this category. Force to spare the innocent is an obligation of Christian *caritas*, or neighbor regard. One does not have to be a theologian to agree that there was something horrifically ugly about the world dithering as Rwandan Hutus slaughtered Rwandan Tutsis by the hundreds of thousands and no state or group of states or international body did anything to stop it. What is the point of bold commitments to universal human rights—the most fundamental of which is a right to life itself—if such rights can be violated systematically and the so-called international community, rather than enforcing those rights, wrings its hands and express regrets?

These are the sorts of questions that just war thinkers put to themselves. Although the Bush administration stressed the dangers of weapons of mass destruction (WMD), both their outright possession and their likely development, as the preeminent justification for a war against the regime of Saddam Hussein, the administration cited other reasons that were more akin to the classic just war insistence that crimes against the innocent should be punished.

Source: Jean Bethke Elshtain. *Just War against Terror: The Burden of American Power in a Violent World* (New York: Basic Books, 2004), pp. 185–186.

Contesting the Meanings of American National Identity

Walter Rausenbush (1861–1918)
A Christian theologian and a Baptist minister, Rausenbush was influential within the social gospel movement in the United States.

Propelled by Christian ethics, this movement sought to eradicate social ills, focusing the Christian background of the United States on reforming social conditions and institutions. This focus denotes a departure from a preoccupation with the relevance of religion as it relates to individual perfection and conversion. This movement believed that the Second Coming can occur only after society is repaired through the exercise of human agency. This social and theological movement represents an inclusivist interpretation of U.S. national identity. The following selections represent Rausenbush's attempt to articulate a theology based on the social gospel and one that would be applicable to the urgency and demands of the time (the early years of the 20th century). Many analysts argue that principles behind the social gospel movement resurged in the era of the civil rights movement.

The Great War has dwarfed and submerged all other issues, including our social problems. But in fact the war is the most acute and tremendous social problem of all. All whose Christianity has been ditched by the catastrophe are demanding a Christianizing of international relations. The demand for disarmament and permanent peace for the rights of the small nations against the imperialistic and colonizing powers, for freedom of the seas and of trade routes . . . The social problem and the war problem are fundamentally one problem, and the social gospel faces both. After the War the social gospel will "come back" with pent-up energy and clearer knowledge. . . .

The social gospel is the old message of salvation, but enlarged and intensified. The individualistic gospel has taught us to see the sinfulness of every human heart and has inspired us with faith in the willingness and power of God to save every soul that comes to him. But it has not given us an adequate understanding of the sinfulness of the social order and its share in the sins of all individuals within it. It has not evoked faith in the will and power of God to redeem the permanent institutions of human society from their inherited guilt of oppression and extortion. Both our sense of sin and our faith in salvation have fallen short of the realities under its teaching. The social gospel seeks to bring men under repentance for their collective sins and to create a more sensitive and more modern conscience. It calls on us for the faith of the old prophets who believed in the salvation of nations.

Source: Walter Rausenbush. *A Theology for the Social Gospel* (New York: MacMillan Company, 1917), pp. 4–6.

Jim Wallis (1948–), "Dangerous Religion: George W. Bush's Theology of Empire"

The following selections from the writings of evangelical Christian activist Jim Wallis provide cotemporary examples of the application of a Christian lens, with a focus on social justice and transformation through prophetic criticism, in interpreting American social, political, and economic realities and in debating what kind of society will be most consistent with Christian social teachings. Wallis, an American evangelical Christian, is often called to offer spiritual advice in the corridors of power in Washington, D.C.

To this aggressive extension of American power in the world, President George W. Bush adds God—and that changes the picture dramatically. It's one thing for a nation to assert its raw dominance in the world; it's quite another to suggest, as this president does, that the success of American military and foreign policy is connected to a religiously inspired "mission," and even that his presidency may be a divine appointment for a time such as this. . . .

Bush seems to make this mistake over and over again—confusing nation, church, and God. The resulting theology is more American civil religion than Christian faith.

Since Sept. 11, President Bush has turned the White House "bully pulpit" into a pulpit indeed, replete with "calls" and "missions" and "charges to keep" regarding America's role in the world. George Bush is convinced that we are engaged in a moral battle between good and evil, and that those who are not with us are on the wrong side in that divine confrontation.

But who is "we," and does no evil reside with "us"? The problem of evil is a classic one in Christian theology. Indeed, anyone who cannot see the real face of evil in the terrorist attacks of Sept. 11, 2001, is suffering from a bad case of postmodern relativism. To fail to speak of evil in the world today is to engage in bad theology. But to speak of "they" being evil and "we" being good, to say that evil is all out there and that in the warfare between good and evil others are either with us or against us—that is also bad theology. Unfortunately, it has become the Bush theology. . . .

The real theological problem in America today is no longer the Religious Right but the nationalist religion of the Bush administration—one that confuses the identity of the nation with the church, and God's purposes with the mission of American empire.

In our own American history, religion has been lifted up for public life in two very different ways. One invokes the name of

God and faith in order to hold us accountable to God's intentions—to call us to justice, compassion, humility, repentance, and reconciliation. Abraham Lincoln, Thomas Jefferson, and Martin King perhaps best exemplify that way. Lincoln regularly used the language of scripture, but in a way that called both sides in the Civil War to contrition and repentance. Jefferson said famously, "I tremble for my country when I reflect that God is just."

The other way invokes God's blessing on our activities, agendas, and purposes. Many presidents and political leaders have used the language of religion like this, and George W. Bush is falling prey to that same temptation.

Christians should always live uneasily with empire, which constantly threatens to become idolatrous and substitute secular purposes for God's. As we reflect on our response to the American empire and what it stands for, a reflection on the early church and empire is instructive.

In the meantime, American Christians will have to make some difficult choices. Will we stand in solidarity with the worldwide church, the international body of Christ—or with our own American government? It's not a surprise to note that the global church does not generally support the foreign policy goals of the Bush administration whether in Iraq, the Middle East, or the wider "war on terrorism." Only from inside some of our U.S. churches does one find religious voices consonant with the visions of American empire.

Source: Jim Wallis. "Dangerous Religions," *Sojourner's Magazine* (September–October 2003).

Religion and Exclusionary Interpretations of American National Identity

The following selections provide examples of expressions of exclusivist and chauvinistic interpretations of American identity. Some reflect xenophobic expressions born out of a reactionary reaffirmation of a Judeo-Christian identity. Others are born out of particular convictions concerning cultural, social, and personal values. These issues came to the fore in the 1980s and the following decades as a result of particular patterns of co-optation and subversion between political leaders and religious groups. Issues such as abortion, marriage equality, gay rights, and even the defense of U.S. Christianity became key issues in elections and the popular corporate media. This "values" revolution involved activism on various fronts, including the Supreme Court and local contexts of states where the question of whether a zygote is a person may appear as a ballot referendum and where abortions are increasingly effectively outlawed. The Tea Party, which emerged in 2009, represents the blending of libertarianism and social conservatism.

The Culture Wars

The following quotations illustrate a growing resentment of the politics of multiculturalism. This is but one manifestation of the "Culture Wars," which began in the 1980s with the presidency of Ronald Reagan. While Christmas is still a national holiday, certain segments within the population perceive attempts to deploy more inclusive attitudes toward other holidays celebrated more or less at the same time (i.e., Hanukkah, Kwanza) as an attack on the very essence of an American identity.

Bill O'Reily (FOX News pundit)

All over the country, Christmas is taking flak. In Denver this past weekend, no religious floats were permitted in the holiday parade there. In New York City, Mayor [Michael] Bloomberg unveiled the "holiday tree," and no Christian Christmas symbols are allowed in the public schools. Federated department Stores—that's Macy's— have done away with the Christmas greeting "Merry Christmas."

. . .

Secular progressives realize that America as it is now will never approve of gay marriage, partial birth abortion, euthanasia, legalized drugs, income redistribution through taxation, and many other progressive visions because of religious opposition. But if the secularists can destroy religion in the public arena, the brave new progressive world is a possibility. That's what happened in Canada.

The O'Reilly Factor (December 7, 2004)

Source: Media Matters for America, "FOX Hypes Stories to Claim 'Christmas Under Siege.'" http://mediamatters.org/research/200412100006 (retrieved November 8, 2011).

Patrick Buchanan: 1992 Republican National Convention Speech, August 17, 1992

The following are excerpts from prime-time speeches given by Patrick Buchanan, a conservative political commentator in the United States who challenged George H.W. Bush in early primaries but endorsed his candidacy at the nominating convention of the Republican Party in 1992. He has had a wide and defining influence in the Culture Wars.

Like many of you last month, I watched that giant masquerade ball at Madison Square Garden—where 20,000 radicals and liberals came dressed up as moderates and centrists—in the greatest single exhibition of cross-dressing in American political history.

One by one, the prophets of doom appeared at the podium. The Reagan decade, they moaned, was a terrible time in America; and the only way to prevent even worse times, they said, is to entrust our nation's fate and future to the party that gave us McGovern, Mondale, Carter and Michael Dukakis.

. . .

The malcontents of Madison Square Garden notwithstanding, the 1980s were not terrible years. They were great years . . .

Most of all, Ronald Reagan made us proud to be Americans again. We never felt better about our country; and we never stood taller in the eyes of the world.

. . .

The presidency is also America's bully pulpit, what Mr. Truman called, "preeminently a place of moral leadership." George Bush is a defender of right-to-life, and lifelong champion of the Judeo-Christian values and beliefs upon which this nation was built.

Mr Clinton, however, has a different agenda.

At its top is unrestricted abortion on demand. When the Irish-Catholic governor of Pennsylvania, Robert Casey, asked to say a few words on behalf of the 25 million unborn children destroyed since *Roe v. Wade*, he was told there was no place for him at the podium of Bill Clinton's convention, no room at the inn.

Source: "1992 Republican National Convention Speech," Monday, August 17, 1992, Patrick J. Buchanan, Official Website http:// buchanan.org/blog/1992-republican-naitonal-convention-speech -148 (accessed November 11, 2012).

In the months leading up to the 2004 presidential elections, Buchanan wrote familiar words.

Who is in your face here? Who started this? Who is on the offensive? Who is pushing the envelope? The answer is obvious. A radical Left aided by a cultural elite that detests Christianity and finds Christian moral tenets reactionary and repressive is hell-bent on pushing its amoral values and imposing its ideology on our nation.

The unwisdom of what the Hollywood and the Left are about should be transparent to all. But if this assault on the sensibilities of the majority continues, the candidate of Hollywood and the Left, John Kerry, will pay a price in November.

Thus, the great battleground of the culture war, after the schools, is the courts. And here, the elected branches, especially Congress, have been derelict in permitting their powers to be seized by judicial collaborators of the moral minority.

Source: Patrick Buchanan. "The Aggressors in the Culture Wars," March 8, 2004. http://www.theamericancause/patculturewars. htm (accessed November 8, 2011).

Jerry Falwell (1933–2007)

Jerry Falwell organized the Moral Majority in 1979 to combat what he believed was an affront to the traditional Christian ideals of the United States. In the following quotations, he asserts a clear vision of who Americans are and what the content of their beliefs ought to be.

Someone must not be afraid to say, "moral perversion is wrong." If we do not act now, homosexuals will "own" America! . . . If you and I do not speak up now, this homosexual steamroller will literally crush all decent men, women, and children who get in its way . . . and our nation will pay a terrible price!

Source: Jerry Falwell. "Hostile Climate," People for the American Way, 1977. http://www.sullivan-county.com/news/mine/ quotes.htm (accessed December 22, 2011).

A quotation from a sermon given in March 1993.

Modern U.S. Supreme Courts have raped the Constitution and raped the Christian faith and raped the churches by misinterpreting what the founders had in mind in the First Amendment of the Constitution . . . [W]e must fight against those radical minorities who are trying to remove God from our textbooks, Christ from our nation. We must never allow our children to forget that this is a Christian nation. We must take back what is rightfully ours.

Source: Jerry Falwell, "Sermon," March 1993. http://www.sullivan -county.com/news/mine/quotes.htm (accessed December 22, 2011).

Jerry Falwell, "God Is Pro-War"

In a message to the American people, Jerry Falwell uses scripture to justify the war in Iraq, suggesting that the war fulfills the work that God has intended Americans to accomplish. This statement was made in response to many who claimed that the war on terror was wrong, and it calls upon American Christian ideals to justify the war.

One of the most notable biblical commands to live in peace is in Romans 12:18: "If it be possible, as much as lieth in you, live peaceably with all men."

With the Bible clear on our responsibility to live peaceably, it seems that there would be no reason to ever go to war. However, if one depends on the Bible as a guidepost for living, it is readily apparent that war is sometimes a necessary option. In fact, just as there are numerous references to peace in the Bible, there are frequent references to God-ordained war. . . .

Throughout the book of Judges, God calls the Israelites to go to war against the Midianites and Philistines. Why? Because these nations were trying to conquer Israel, and God's people were called to defend themselves.

President Bush declared war in Iraq to defend innocent people. This is a worthy pursuit. In fact, Proverbs 21:15 tells us: "It is joy to the just to do judgment: but destruction shall be to the workers of iniquity."

One of the primary purposes of the church is to stop the spread of evil, even at the cost of human lives. If we do not stop the spread of evil, many innocent lives will be lost and the kingdom of God suffers.

We continue to live in violent times. The Bible tells us war will be a reality until Christ returns. And when the time is right, Jesus will indeed come again, ending all wars.

Source: Jerry Falwell. "God Is Pro-War," World.net Daily, January 31, 2004. http://www.wnd.com/news/article.asp?ARTICLE _ID=36859 (accessed December 21, 2011).

Jerry Falwell, Comments Made during "700 Club" (September 13, 2001)

The following passage features excerpts from Jerry Falwell that claim that the attacks made on America on September 11, 2001, were a result of the abandonment of Christian values in America.

And I agree totally with you that the Lord has protected us so wonderfully these 225 years. And since 1812, this is the first time that we've been attacked on our soil and by far the worst results. And I fear, as Donald Rumsfeld, the Secretary of Defense, said yesterday, that this is only the beginning. And with biological warfare available to these monsters—the Husseins, the Bin Ladens, the Arafats—what we saw on Tuesday, as terrible as it is, could be miniscule if, in fact—if, in fact—God continues to lift the curtain and allow the enemies of America to give us probably what we deserve.

. . .

And, I know that I'll hear from them for this. But, throwing God out successfully with the help of the federal court system, throwing God out of the public square, out of the schools. The abortionists have got to bear some burden for this because God will not be mocked. And when we destroy 40 million little innocent babies, we make God mad. I really believe that the pagans, and the abortionists, and the feminists, and the gays and the lesbians who are actively trying to make that an alternative lifestyle, the ACLU, People For the American Way—all of them who have tried to secularize America—I point the finger in their face and say "you helped this happen."

. . .

In other words, when the nation is on its knees, the only normal and natural and spiritual thing to do is what we ought to be doing all the time—calling upon God.

Source: Jerry Falwell. "Jerry Falwell Transcript," September 13, 2001. http://www.thisistrue.com/falwell-transcript.html (accessed December 21, 2011).

Religious Nationalism: Examples from around the World

The followings excerpts present a sampling of exclusivist conceptions of nationalism, from Hindutva to religious Zionism, to Sinhala Buddhism in Sri Lanka. The focus here is on definitional documents or formulations of "who we are" and what religious justifications and sources are deployed to vindicate exclusionary conceptions of the "nation." Many of these examples reflect how national geography transforms into sacred topography and how the mythologies of origins of the nation are recounted. Each exclusivist articulation of a national identity is immediately followed by an inclusivist interpretation that also draws selectively on religious and cultural vocabularies, narratives, histories, and memories.

Hindu Nationalism (India)

The first selections in this section are from the writings of Veer Savarkar, who developed the concept of Hindutva in the context of British colonialism in India. He articulated an exclusivist and chauvinistic interpretation of Indian identity, one that rendered Muslims and Christians as, by definition, "unauthentic." The second selection is from the writings of Mahatma Gandhi, whose interpretation of an Indian identity was inclusivist, that is, it included all religions and minority groups. Another important distinction between the two interpretations of an Indian identity is how geography becomes intricately linked to and imbued with sacredness.

Veer Savarkar, "Essentials of Hindutva"

To this category of names which have been to mankind a subtle source of life and inspiration belongs the word Hindutva, the essential nature and significance of which we have to investigate into. The ideas and ideals, the systems and societies, the thoughts and sentiments which have centered round this name are so varied and rich, so powerful and so subtle, so elusive and yet so vivid that the term Hindutva defies all attempts at analysis... Prophets and poets, lawyers and law-givers, heroes and historians, have thought, lived, fought and died just to have it spelled thus. For indeed, is it not the resultant of countless actions—now conflicting, now commingling, now cooperating—of our whole race? Hindutva is not a word but a history. Not only the spiritual or religious history of our people as at times it is mistaken to be by being confounded with the other cognate term Hinduism, but a history in full. Hinduism is only a derivative, a fraction, a part of Hindutva. Unless it is made clear what is meant by the latter the first remains unintelligible and vague...

What Is a Hindu?

Although it would be hazardous at the present state of oriental research to state definitely the period when the foremost band of the intrepid Aryans made it their home and lighted their first sacrificial fire on the banks of the Sindhu, the Indus, yet certain it is that long before the ancient Egyptians, and Babylonians had built their magnificent civilization, the holy waters of the Indus were daily witnessing the lucid and curling columns of the scented sacrificial smokes and the valleys resounding with the chants of Vedic hymns—the spiritual fervor that animated their souls. The adventurous valour that propelled their intrepid enterprises, the sublime heights to which their thoughts rose—all these had marked them out as a people destined to lay the foundation of a great and enduring civilization. By the time they had definitely cut themselves aloof their cognate and neighbouring people especially the Persians, the Aryans, had spread out to the farthest of the seven rivers, Sapta Sindhus, and not only had they developed a sense of nationality but had already succeeded in giving it "a local habitation and a name!" out of their gratitude to the genial and perennial network of waterways that run through the land like a system of nerve-threads and wove them into a Being, they very naturally took to themselves the name of Sapta Sindhus an epithet that was applied to the whole of Vedic India in the oldest records of the world, the Rigveda itself. Aryans or the cultivators as they essentially were, we can well understand the divine love and homage they bore to these seven rivers presided over by the River, "the Sindhu", which to them were but a visible symbol of the common nationality and culture.

. . .

Hindus, a Nation

The activities of so intrepid a people as the Sindhus or Hindus could no longer be kept coopted or cabined within the narrow compass of the Panchanad or the Punjab. The vast and fertile plains farther off stood out inviting the efforts of some strong and vigorous race. Tribe after tribe of the Hindus issues forth from the land of their nursery and led by the consciousness of a great mission and their Sacrificial Fire that was the symbol thereof, they soon reclaimed the vast, waste and but very thinly populated lands . . . As time passed on, the distances of their colonies increased, and different settlements thus formed, though they could not efface the old ones, grew more and more pronounced and powerful until the ancient generalizations and names gave way to the new. Some called themselves Kurus, others Kashis or Videhas or Magadhas while the old generic name of the Sindhus or Hindus was first overshadowed and then almost forgotten. Not that the conception of a national and cultural unity vanished, but it assumed other names and other forms . . . At the last great mission which the Sindhus had undertaken of founding a nation and a country, found and reached its geographical limit when the valorous Prince of Ayodhya made a triumphant entry in Ceylon and actually brought the whole land from the Himalayas to the Seas under one sovereign sway. The day when the Horse of Victory returned to Ayodhya unchallenged and unchallengeable, the great white Umbrella of Sovereignty was unfurled over that Imperial throne of Ramchandra, the brave, Ramchandra the good, and a loving allegiance to him was sworn, not only by the Princes of Aryan blood but Hanuman, Sugriva, Bidhishana from the south—that day was the real birth-day of our Hindu people.

Source: V. D. Savarkar. *Essentials of Hindutva (1921-2)*. http://www .savarkar.org/content/pdfs/en/essentials_of_hindutva.v001.pdf (accessed November 8, 2011).

Mahatma Gandhi

I know that many have been angry with me for claiming an exclusive right for the Congress to speak for the people of India as a whole. It is not an arrogant pretension. It is explicit in the first article of the Congress. It wants and works for independence for the whole of India. It speaks neither for majority nor minority. It seeks to represent all Indians without any distinction. Therefore those who oppose it should not count, if the claim for independence is admitted. Those who support the claim simply give added strength to the Congress claim.

. . .

And who are the minorities? They are religious, political and social: thus Mussalmans (religious), Depressed Classes (social), Liberals (political), Princes (social), Brahmins (social), non-Brahmins (social), Lingayats (social), Sikh (social?), Christians— Protestants and Catholic (religious), Jains (social?), Zamindars (political?). . . . Who are the majority in this medley? . . .

I know that the fashion is to talk of the Hindus forming the majority community. But Hinduism is an elastic, indefinable term, and Hindus are not a homogeneous whole like Muslims and Christians. And when one analyses the majority in any provincial legislature it will be found to consist of a combination of the so-called minorities. . . .

Source: Mahatma Gandhi. "The Fiction of Majority," *The Collected Works of Mahatma Gandhi (electronic edition)* Vol. 77: 16 October, 1939–22 February, 1940. http://www.gandhiserve.org/cwmg/VOL077.PDF (accessed November 14, 2011).

Sinhala Buddhism (Sri Lanka)

The first selection is an analysis by comparative theorist David Little of the case of Sri Lankan ethnoreligious nationalism. An interesting aspect concerning the emergence of Sri Lankan nationalism relates to the rhetoric and activism of Anagorika Dharmapala, who explicated a connection between Buddhist revivalism and purity and the rejuvenation of a Sinhalese Buddhist identity, under the colonial context of the 19th and early 20th centuries. Dharmapala's name is also closely associated with the phenomenon known as Protestant Buddhism, which emphasizes freedom of conscience and a preoccupation with one's interior experience as well as with ideals of freedom from religious institutions and freedom of conscience. This form of Buddhism emerged in the colonial context and among middle class sectors in the urban centers. In the selection reproduced here, Little reflects on how the colonial framework enabled the emergence of particular exclusivist conceptions of identity. The discussion of the colonial context is also related to the retrieval and appropriation of the Mahavamsa. The Mahavamsa constitutes a series of documents that are dated to the sixth century. The movement of Buddhist revivalism and later of exclusivist Sinhalese political domination builds upon some key passages in the origin mythology of Sinhala Buddhism (selectively read from the Mahavamsa) and its national project and mission. Accordingly, Prince Vijaya, the leader of the Sinhala who were descendants of Aryan migrants from Bengal in the fifth century BCE, arrived in Sri Lanka upon the death of the Buddha. It was believed that the Buddha predicted that the wisdom of his teachings will be preserved for millennia in the island of Sri Lanka (or Ceylon) by the Sinhalese who came to inhabit it. The Buddha subsequently visited the island three times, thereby sacralizing it. Thus retaining and celebrating cultural, religious, and territorial hegemony and integrity has become the particular mission of the Sinhalese people. This mythology, obviously, functioned as a root cause of the prolonged civil war on the island. The second selection is by Rohan Edrishina, who is a legal scholar at the University of

Colombo, Sri Lanka. He writes on the challenges of negotiating competing narratives of nationalism in Sri Lanka.

David Little on the Colonial Legacy in Sri Lanka

The British, who occupied Sri Lanka in the late eighteenth century, introduced a number of aggressive political, educational, and religious policies that eventually provoked a counter-reaction by the Buddhist clergy, leading to what has been called Buddhist revivalism. That movement had a profound impact on the shape and dynamics of Sri Lankan politics by the time the British granted Sri Lanka independence in 1948.

. . .

In the early nineteenth century, Christian missionaries, their activities encouraged or condoned by British colonial authorities, attacked Buddhism and attempted to replace it with Christianity. That was accomplished most directly by establishing a new system of church-run schools, and by effecting the gradual withdrawal of all government support from Buddhism.

. . .

A leading exemplar and formative figure of Buddhist revivalism was Don David Hewavitarne (1864–1933), who forsook his Christian schooling and became a Buddhist monk, changing his name to Anagarika Dharmapala, "the homeless guardian of the Dharma."... his thinking profoundly influenced the ideal of "restoring the land as a whole a Sinhala Buddhist hegemony with language and culture as subsidiary themes." Dharmapala was responsible for introducing race consciousness. In his hands, Vijaya, the father of Sinhala, was taken to be the progenitor of an "Aryan" people, "a unique race ... in whose veins no savage blood is found." Such ideas are not present in the *Mahavamsa*, but are a product of the nineteenth century,

A central theme of Dharmapala—the unity of country, nation, and religion—was transformed in the 1950s by the leaders of a monastic orders into a message of enormous political potency. Sri Lanka was envisioned as a territory dominated politically and culturally by Sinhala Buddhism.

It is striking that no spokesman of this group has ever spoken clearly and specifically about the fate of the minorities in [Sri Lanka]. Alternatively, it has been vaguely suggested by some exponents ... that the minorities would be part of this socio-political entity in so far as they merge their own cultural identity with that of the Sinhala Buddhists. Stated differently, the world view expressed in the usage, country, nation, and religion envisages a hegemonic Sinhala culture empowered to place its stamp on other cultures in order to bring about [a] homogenous utopia.

Source: David Little. "Religion and Ethnicity in the Sri Lankan Civil War," in Robert Rotberg, ed., *Creating Peace in Sri Lanka: Civil War and Reconciliation* (Cambridge, MA: World Peace Foundation, 1999), pp. 41–56.

Rohan Edrishina on Competing Nationalisms in Sri Lanka

On the one hand, you find a Sinhala nationalism, deeply intertwined with Buddhism, the religion of the majority in the country (hence references to Sri Lanka being a Sinhala Buddhist nation). There is, therefore, a feeling that people who are not Sinhala Buddhists (an ethnic and religious identity) somehow have a lesser claim to the island in terms of legitimacy. You also have a mind set of majority and minority. It is often said . . . "it's all right for the minorities to have rights, so long as those rights do not infringe on the rights of the majority." Then, of course, you have a complicating factor: the Sinhala Buddhists are a majority with a minority complex. The peace process of 2002–2003 and the spread of evangelical Christian groups in recent years have contributed to the resurfacing of this complex. There is a feeling of vulnerability among Sinhala Buddhists, an apprehension that Sinhala is a minority language, used only in Sri Lanka, and that Theravada Buddhism in its pristine form is practiced only in the island of its homeland, Sri Lanka. Special measures are therefore necessary to protect and preserve both the Sinhala language and Theravada Buddhism. In contrast, the Tamil language and culture can be found in India, Malaysia, Singapore, and South Africa.

. . .

On the other hand, the competing Tamil nationalism is less intertwined with religion. It is a more secular nationalism, with emphasis on language, on a geographically based homeland. It is a nationalism that has evolved over the years. Some Tamils would describe it as a type of defensive nationalism. It began by focusing on issues of political representation and language. It has evolved over the years to issues of discrimination and equality, and then to a struggle for autonomy and self-determination.

...

The challenge for the Sri Lankan peace process is then to try to evolve or work out a compromise to reconcile these two nationalisms within a united country. What are the options in constitutional/political terms? The Sinhala Buddhist nationalist position wants a unitary, centralized, majoritarian nation-state with constitutional and legal protection of the Sinhala language and Buddhist religion, while offering protection to the rights and freedoms of minorities. The Tamil nationalist position was articulated in ... the Thimpu Principles of 1985 ... [they] are:

1. The Tamil people constitute a nation.
2. The Tamil people have a traditional homeland.
3. The Tamil nation has the right to self-determination.
4. Complete equality in terms of citizenship, language, and religion.

The problem with these concepts—nation, traditional homeland, self-determination, and equality—is that they are vague, ambiguous, and have no clear legal definition in law.

Source: Rohan Edrishina. "Religion and Nationalism in Recent Peace Initiatives in Sri Lanka," in David Little and Donald Swearer, eds., *Religion and Nationalism in Iraq: A Comparative Perspective* (Cambridge, MA: Harvard University Press, 2006), pp. 87–96.

Israel: Religious Zionism

The first selection in this section is from a reflection given by a prominent rabbi of the settlement movement in the Occupied Territories. He writes about his commitment to settling the land and how this commitment is grounded in his religious orientation. He also expresses his disillusionment and disdain of the military's collaboration in the process of unilateral disengagement from the Gaza Strip in 2005. The second selection is from the writings of Yeshayahu Leibowitz, who was a prophetic religious voice in Israel. He did not hesitate to voice his critique of both religious and secular Zionists. He always grounded his critique in his deep religiosity.

Rabbi Shlomo Aviner, Chief Rabbi of Be El, "I Sacrifice Myself for the Land"

Some sacrifice themselves for Torah, day and night. I don't make light of them—G-d forbid. Yet that isn't really part of the real world. I am ready to risk my life for the Land. I don't understand all this pilpul [debating] about what's more important, the people or the land. If I risk my life so that the Land remains in our hands, then I am also doing the People a favor. How can people not understand that?

Sure I am full of love of the Jewish People, Israel. What I do constitutes love of Israel. Yes! I am full of love of Israel! What I do sanctifies G-d's name. Abandoning parts of our land is a profanation of G-d's name. For that we waited two thousand years?! I'm no saint, but for my land, I am ready to risk my life, even if it involves a sacrifice; even though it's hard. . . . I am a soldier, a soldier of G-d, a soldier in the I.D.F., the Israel Defense Forces, the army defending our people and our land, the army defending us against three hundred million external enemies and three million internal enemies. Therefore, I must be a good soldier, the best I can. In my wallet I've got a document that says "Fighter." Yes, I am a fighter.

Source: Rabbi Shlomo Aviner. "I Sacrifice Myself for the Land," *Machon Meir: Torat Eretz Israel*. http://www.english.machonmeir .net/index.php?option=com_jmultimedia&view=media&layout =default&id=3728&Itemid=28 (accessed August 16, 2012).

Yeshayahu Leibowitz on the Religious Significance of Israel

Some of my predecessors in this debate seem to enjoy the pleasant illusion that the establishment of the state of Israel and its existence enhance the prestige of Judaism in a religious sense, both among the Jews and among the nations. I have written and said much about the status of Judaism in the Israeli state. This time I shall confine myself to recounting a conversation I had with Ben-Gurion some twenty years ago. He then said to me: "I well understand why you demand so insistently the separation of religion and state. Your object is that the Jewish religion reinstate itself as an independent factor so the political authority will be compelled to deal with it. I will never agree to the separation of religion from State. I want the state to hold religion in the palm of its hand." The status quo, which formally interweaves elements pretending to be religious with the secular executive and administrative system of the state—an integration which the representatives of "religious national" Judaism make every effort to perpetuate—reflects the cast of mind of a man who entertained a bitter hatred of Judaism. It was this conversation with Ben-Gurion that I alluded when I once wrote: "The status of Jewish religion in the state of Israel is that of a kept mistress of the secular government—therefore it is contemptible." The state of Israel does not radiate the light of Judaism to the nations, not even to the Jews.

I vehemently oppose the view that Zionist theory and practice are necessarily or essentially connected with the idea of "light to the nations." . . . I reject the attempts to adorn the state of Zionism with a religious aura. Rather than exalt Zionism and the state, these efforts devaluate religion, turning it from the service of God into the fulfillment of human needs and aspirations.

Source: Yeshayahu Leibowitz. "The Religious and Moral Significance of the Redemption of Israel," in *Judaism, Human Values, and the Jewish State* (Cambridge, MA: Harvard University Press, 1992), pp. 106–122 (selections are from pp. 115–116).

7

Directory of Organizations

The phenomenon of religious nationalism points to the enduring but varied roles religious identities, practices, traditions, and institutions play in the dynamics and cycles of various conflicts around the world. The recognition that religion is a relevant factor in the analysis of conflicts also has generated a novel preoccupation with how religion and religious people and leaders may influence peacebuilding processes. One central impetus for religious peacebuilding, on the levels of both research and practice, is an attempt to counter the presuppositions and assumptions engrained in a conception of religion as a cause of violence. This chapter features a list of organizations and groups devoted to exploring and practicing religious peacebuilding. Some groups and individual practitioners focus on the kind of resources religious traditions offer for peacebuilding and nonviolent modes of protest and exchange. Others focus on what religious individuals and leaders do in certain contexts to promote peace and the cessation of violence. Some invoke their prophetic role, such as "speaking truth to power." Others try to bridge differences through interfaith dialogues, faith diplomacy, and other activities. Others generate change and sustainable development through activation of their networks, institutions, and legitimacy within the community.

Berkley Center for Religion, Peace, and World Affairs, Georgetown University, Washington, D.C.

http://berkleycenter.georgetown.edu

The Berkeley Center was established in 2006 at Georgetown University in the United States. It focuses on the study of religion, ethics, and public life. The establishment of this center reflects the intent of Georgetown University to invest in becoming a leading voice in the interdisciplinary study of religion and in global inter-religious dialogue. The center, therefore, is one of numerous other institutional efforts of the university to fulfill these goals. Other centers and programs at Georgetown include the Prince Alwaleed Bin Talal Center for Muslim-Christian Understanding, the Program for Jewish Civilization, and the Catholic Studies Program. Further, in collaboration with the School of Foreign Service, the center offers a Religion, Ethics, and World Affairs (REWA) certificate. The center uses teaching, research, and service to examine the problems facing democracy and human rights globally, economic and social development, international relations, and inter-religious dialogue. The center operates on the belief that a critical look into faith and religious values is important when assessing international issues and for promoting peace and development. Focusing on building knowledge, dialogue, and action in areas critical to international affairs, the center hosts a number of different programs. These programs include "Religion and Ethics in World Politics" headed by Thomas Banchoff; "Globalization, Religions, and the Secular," headed by José Casanova; "Religion and U.S. Foreign Policy/Religious Freedom Project," headed by Thomas Farr; "The Church and Interreligious Dialogue," headed by Chester Gillis; "Law, Religion, and Values," headed by Michael Kessler; "Religion and Global Development," headed by Katherine Marshall; "Religion, Conflict, and Peace," headed by Eric Patterson; and the "Religious Freedom Project," headed by Timothy Shah. The "Religion, Conflict, and Peace" program scrutinizes, in a comparative fashion, the interface between religion, culture, and political frameworks and identities. It produces important case studies (all available on the center's website). Other projects include "Religion in China and the United States," "Faith and the

Global Agenda," and "American Values in Public Life," among other foci of interest and research. The center's website provides interviews with various practitioners and intellectuals, as well as broad statistical data involving issues of religion, conflict, peace, and diplomacy.

Center for World Religions, Diplomacy, and Conflict Resolution (George Mason University)

http://crdc.gmu.edu/

Through a gift from the Catalyst Fund, the Center for World Religions, Diplomacy, and Conflict Resolution (CRDC) was established in 2003. Its goal is to connect peacemakers, activists and officials who aim to broker peace agreements and accords, at indigenous and global levels, partnering with them in new ways, helping garner support for their causes, and connecting citizen diplomats, students, and policymakers. The CDRC began the Interfaith Peace and Justice Initiative of Greater Washington D.C., which is a group that includes leaders of Muslim, Jewish, and Christian communities who work to create interfaith relationships and interaction while nurturing the relationships between people of different faiths. The center's areas of pedagogical specialization include cultivating creative conflict resolution techniques and citizen diplomacy skills, international education seminars and field experience, conflict resolution analysis of current events, and organizational consultancies. Beyond developing educational resources and international seminars, the CDRC also cultivates a network of peace-builders from across the globe. The stated goal of the center is to stimulate substantive change in contexts of intractable conflicts. The emphasis is on developing innovative approaches to diplomacy and foreign policy. The sites of constructive change reside in the sphere of civil society, a sphere that can be invigorated through education in conflict resolution, peer mediation, and the introduction of innovative religious, spiritual, and cultural forms of conflict resolution (including the cultivation of effective collaborative development projects). The center has benefited from the leadership of Marc Gopin, a scholar and practitioner of religion and conflict resolution. Gopin has worked and written extensively on the negative and positive roles of religion in conflict and peacebuilding.

Fellowship of Reconciliation (FOR)

http://forusa.org/

The Fellowship of Reconciliation was founded in 1914 in Cambridge, England. FOR-USA was established the following year. FOR is an international interfaith movement with many branches across the globe. The membership of this movement is truly ecumenical—Jews, Christians, Buddhists, Muslims, and others are included. The point of departure of the FOR's mission is recognition of the essential unity of all creation. With this as a guiding framework, the FOR seeks to resolve human conflicts. The organization's goal is a peaceful world that enables full human flourishing regardless of nationality, race, religion, sexual orientation, and other divisive markers. FOR is fully committed to nonviolent modes of resistance, and it has been an adamant activist against militarism. It has been concerned with domestic and international issues of peace and justice. The belief in the unity of all creation enables members of FOR to identify with anyone who faces injustice, refuses to participate in war or war preparations and instead works to abolish war, works towards a social order in which all people can benefit, strives for fair rulings for offenders and compassion for victims of crime, shows respect for all personalities, and avoids bitterness in the face of controversy. For years, FOR has been working to educate those involved in the Israeli-Palestinian conflict, attempting to build bridges between the groups. FOR's efforts included protest against militarism, racism, and economic injustice. In 1998, it developed Interfaith Peace Builders which worked with other organizations to use nonviolent opposition against settlement expansion, home demolition, military checkpoints, and military incursions. Interfaith Peace Builders eventually became a separate entity supported by FOR. FOR has also been involved in other conflict zones. In Afghanistan, for instance, FOR expressed opposition to the war and occupation of the country. The organization's efforts in the country include raising awareness of the impact of the war on the lives of Afghans as well as exploring alternative nonviolent options.

International Center for Religion and Diplomacy

http://icrd.org/

Located in Washington, D.C., this organization's mission is to engage seemingly intractable identity-based conflicts that challenge conventional and official forms of diplomacy and thus might benefit from religious or faith-based diplomacy. The International Center for Religion and Diplomacy (ICRD) tries to incorporate the idea that religion can become integral to thinking about conflict resolution in contexts of identity-based conflicts. ICRD combines official and unofficial diplomacy efforts to try to decrease the number of young people engaged in violent militancy, promoting alternative modes of achieving peace and creating a stable global environment. The organization was established to implement the conclusions of the groundbreaking work by Douglas Johnston and Cynthia Sampson, *Religion: The Missing Dimension of Statecraft* (New York: Oxford University Press, 1994) as well as the follow-up works by Douglas Johnston, *Faith-Based Diplomacy: Trumping Realpolitik* (New York: Oxford University Press, 2003) and *Religion, Terror, and Error: U.S. Foreign Policy and the Challenge of Spiritual Engagement* (Santa Barbara, CA: Praeger, 2001). ICRD views itself as a bridge between politics and religion. The organization trains people in peacebuilding, sends teams to areas in which conflict exists or is beginning to manifest overtly, and corresponds with religious leaders and theologians whose ideologies contribute to conflict. The ICRD works in conflict zones such as Pakistan, where it works with teachers at Islamic religious schools, training them in techniques of conflict resolution. The ICRD was able to aid in the development of the peace agreement that ended the Sudanese civil war that was signed in 2005. The ICRD has also focused on cultivating institutional structures to support the endurance of peace accords over time.

Peace Brigades International

www.peacebrigades.org

Peace Brigades International (PBI) started in 1981 with the idea of creating a nonviolent international organization that could act as a third party that intervenes in conflicts through creating political spaces for various local organizations to act and affect change. The organization provides protection to local defenders of human rights. The motivation to establish PBI came from a group of practitioners of nonviolent resistance, and the inspiration derived from the work of the Shanti Sena peace army in India. The organization has a mission of making nonviolent resolutions viable and desirable. PBI tries to do this by creating an international presence and concern for local initiatives as well as creating a culture of justice and peace. They also support political and social initiatives as well as encourage active nonviolence instead of the use of violence. PBI works through educational programs to inform and train locals in different ways to use conflict transformation within their societies.

Program in Religion, Conflict, and Peacebuilding, Joan B. Kroc Institute for International Peace Studies, University of Notre Dame

http://kroc.nd.edu/

The Joan B. Kroc Institute was established in 1986 and reflected the aspiration of Father Theodore Hesburgh (at the time, the president of the University of Notre Dame) and Kroc for a world without the threat of nuclear holocaust. The Kroc Institute has expanded its scope, developing into a central voice in peace research and peace education. The institute offers an undergraduate supplementary major and minor in peace studies as well as joint practice-oriented MA and PhD programs with the departments of sociology, history, psychology, theology, and political science. The institute is fully integrated into the broader context of the University of Notre Dame. Since its establishment, the Kroc Institute has developed into a renowned organizaon for the study of the reasons for violent conflict and strategies to create sustainable peace. Professors at the Kroc Institute research war, genocide, ethnic and religious conflicts, and methodologies for peacebuilding and conflict transformation. The mission of the institute is to understand the factors that create conflict and the conditions needed for sustainable peace. The institute's Religion Conflict and Peacebuilding Program looks at the versatile roles of religion in conflict and peacebuilding. The program recognizes that religion has caused violence and peace and that religion has been at the center of many conflicts around the world. The program thus searches for ways that religious communities can work toward peace. One project looks at the fact that many religious leaders have tried to use reconciliation as a way to create peace and examines the usefulness of reconciliation as a part of justice and peace in peace building. The program has also published various books on relevant topics and cases.

Tanenbaum Center for Interreligious Understanding

https://www.tanenbaum.org/

The late rabbi Marc H. Tanenbaum's wife, Dr. Georgette Bennet, created the Tanenbaum Center in 1992. The namesake of the center was a scholar dedicated to inter-religious relations and protecting those who were victims of bigotry. After his death, his wife tried to continue his legacy by creating the center. The mission of the Tanenbaum Center is to create a reality in which people of different faiths live in harmony, not in a truce but in respect of the differences that separate them. The center tries to change the way people think and act by confronting ignorance through educational and inter-religious programs. The Tanenbaum Center created the Religion and Conflict Resolution program, which identifies and studies peacemakers in conflict zones, sharing information about them to inform others about their methods and work. The center has also profiled these peacemakers in various publications that are available for broad consumption. In 1999, the center also created the Religion and Diversity Education program for elementary students to teach multicultural and multireligious lessons as well as to address the fact that children were not being taught about diversity and religious identity. The center also provides many other programs that teach people about religious diversity around the world.

United States Institute of Peace

http://www.usip.org/religionpeace/index.html

In 1984, the United States Institute of Peace Act was passed by Congress and signed by President Ronald Reagan, creating the United States Institute of Peace (USIP). The institute was created in hopes of providing Americans with the training, education, research opportunities, and peace information necessary to create international peace and resolve conflicts between nations without the use of violence. The mission of the institute is to find new ways to prevent and stop international conflict without the use of violence. The institute features a Religion and Peacemaking program that researches and identifies the best ways for religious leaders and communities to promote peace nonviolently. The program focuses on diverse conflict zones, including Pakistan, Afghanistan, Iran, Iraq, Colombia, Sri Lanka, and Nigeria. In the case of Iraq, for instance, USIP promotes religious reconciliation and pluralism through collaboration with the Council of Representatives' Religious Affairs Committee. In Sri Lanka, USIP engages in the training of religious leadership who represent each of the country's four main religious communities. The training focuses on conflict transformation theory and technique, with the intention of enabling the implementation and sustainability of local peace initiatives. The program also works with other programs to implement strategies for working in areas of conflict. The institute's Health and Peacebuilding program looks at the connection between health, conflict resolution, and reconstruction. This program develops strategies to protect civilians caught in war, dividing work between nongovernmental organizations (NGOs) and local health agencies while also looking at health initiative work to prevent gender-based violence.

American Friends Service Committee

http://afsc.org/

The American Friends Service Committee (AFSC) was established in 1917 as a way for people who conscientiously objected to war to serve in some alternate capacity. The committee is an organization that allows people of all faiths with a commitment to social justice, peace, and humanitarian service to join. The American Friends Service Committee is dedicated to the beliefs of the Religious Friends Society, also known as Quakers. These beliefs are grounded in the appreciation of the worth of all people and the ability of love to overcome anything. It is a principally pacifist religious outlook. The mission of the group is to express Quakers' beliefs with dedication to nonviolence, faith, and love. Members of the organization maintain the belief that any conflict or situation can be transformed. The Service Committee has been present in the Central Lakes Region of Africa, where it has aided in democratic processes and elections to avoid the civil conflicts that have been present in the region during the end of the 20th and beginning of the 21st centuries. AFSC has also been present in Palestinian territories and Israel for years and has supported an end to Israel's occupation of Palestinian territories. AFSC supports self-determination for Israelis and Palestinians, and has opposed U.S. rejection of Palestinian membership in the United Nations (2011). Likewise, AFSC works in other regions of the globe, from Burma, Somalia, and Zimbabwe to Mexico, North Korea, and Brazil. The foci of activities range from campaigns to advance withdrawing U.S. troops from various fronts around the world to shaping a just federal budget, strengthening relations that prevent conflict, providing peaceful alternative for youth in conflict zones, responding to humanitarian crises, and much more.

Baptist Peace Fellowship of North America

http://www.bpfna.org/home

This nonprofit organization was formed in 1984. This organization understands its mission of peace to be grounded in Christianity. Its mission is to equip, mobilize, and gather Baptists to the goal of building just peace. Its work spreads across various fronts. In an effort to avoid conflict following elections in Liberia, Baptist Peace Fellowship of North America (BPFNA) sent its members to train local laity and clergy members in conflict transformation. BPFNA has also issued statements against Islamophobia in North America that has caused the harassment of Muslims in America and stopped the construction of mosques in some areas. The organization has called upon its members, who are part of Baptist congregations, to find other ways to face conflict and to speak out against discrimination against Muslims. BPFNA deploys the method of conflict transformation, which understands conflict as inevitable but attempts to illuminate where conflict can become productive for undergoing systemic change nonviolently.

Buddhist Peace Fellowship

http://www.bpf.org/

The Buddhist Peace Fellowship (BPF) is mainly composed of practitioners of dharma (people dedicated to seeking and fulfilling their duty as determined by their role in the divinely ordained natural order) who support social engagement and compassionate social justice. The group was founded in 1978 with the proclaimed intention to promote socially engaged Buddhism, which is grounded in a view of the profound interdependence of all life. Thus the liberation of the individual is intricately linked to the liberation of others and the communities in which one lives. This strand of Buddhism is closely associated with the Buddhist monk and leader Thich Nhat Hanh. Specifically, the group's goal is to assist people to liberate themselves from their suffering—on individual, social, and institutional levels. It focuses on global issues of gender injustice, militarism, corporatism, and environmental justice, among many other issues. The BPF has also acted to support Buddhists in Asian countries such as Thailand, Burma, and Mongolia, while also expressing concern over the aggressive actions of Buddhists in Sri Lanka. The group has also participated in marches and protests and sent letters to legislators to get support in stopping the Chinese government's ill treatment of Buddhists.

Caritas Internationalis

http://www.caritas.org/index.html

The inception of Caritas Internationalis is dated to the end of the 19th century. It is a confederation of 165 Catholic development, relief, and social service organizations that work in over 200 countries. Caritas focuses on less developed countries because of the likelihood that these contexts will be prone to the eruption of violence and other crises. In Sudan, Caritas's volunteers helped with water sanitation, nutrition, emergency preparedness, and peace and conflict training. Caritas Sri Lanka supported people there during the Sri Lankan civil war through programs that have provided shelter for people who have lost homes, schools for children, work programs for people that have been displaced, and counseling for those that face emotional trauma. In the Middle East and North Africa, Caritas work focuses on migration and human trafficking, peacebuilding, humanitarian work, and HIV/AIDS. There is also an understanding that the conflicts in Somalia, Israel/Palestine, Lebanon, and Iraq suggest the need for reinforcing interfaith dialogues.

Catholic Peacebuilding Network

http://cpn.nd.edu/

With headquarters located at the Kroc Institute for International Peace studies at the University of Notre Dame, the Catholic Peacebuilding Network (CPN) was created in order to better define the role of the Catholic Church in preserving peace and justice in the world. Although the organization is based upon religion, not all members are Catholic. All members, however, have a respect for Catholic teachings concerning justice and peace, and a respect for the interactions of Catholics with other faiths. Academics and practitioners who wished to step away from the view of religion as a divisive force and instead use the Catholic faith to study and practice peace building define the scope of this peacebuilding network. The goals of the organization are to increase the involvement of scholars and practitioners while finding the best strategies for peacebuilding, developing a theology of peace, and increasing the role of the Catholic Church in peacebuilding in conflict zones. CPN held a series of conferences annually from 2004 through 2008 to help people better understand and engage in peacebuilding and through a collaboration of 20 scholars and practitioners developed a series of essays on the topic. The CPN is currently working on aiding existing peacebuilding programs by providing training and advising in a way that combines practice and theory. In the future, CPN plans to develop teams that can address the Church's peacebuilding needs, provide peace studies training in Catholic schools, develop educational tools

on Catholic peacebuilding, and provide more research on
Catholic peacebuilding.

Catholic Relief Services

http://crs.org/

Catholic Relief Services (CRS) was founded by the Council of
Catholic Bishops in 1943 to serve survivors of World War II in
Europe and has continued its mission to serve since then. In
accordance with Catholic beliefs about the sanctity of human life,
the mission of CRS is to help those that are deprived and in poverty. The CRS claims the Gospel of Jesus Christ as its motivating
factor but asserts that their activists will help any person in need
regardless of religion, race, or ethnicity. CRS offers aid and development assistance in conflict zones. To promote peacebuilding,
CRS helps cultivate civic organizations that aim to give people
tools for self-reliance and sustainability. When entering an area
of conflict, the CRS carefully analyzes the situation in order to
determine how to help in prevention and peacebuilding processes, with a frequent focus on human rights education and
advocacy. Other foci of the organization's activities include
human trafficking, sanitation, agriculture, emergency response,
food security, public policy, and similar issues. The organization
serves populations across the globe from Africa, Asia, and
Europe, to Latin America, the Caribbean, and the Middle East.

Christian Peacemaker Teams

http://www.cpt.org/

In search of a new way to express faith while promoting the use of
organized nonviolence, the Christian Peacemakers Teams (CPT)
was created in 1986. Motivated by the group's commitment to
Christianity, its mission is to provide nonviolent alternatives to
those entangled in violent conflicts. The CPT focuses on the development of nonviolent institutions and on training for conflict
intervention. The CPT has violence reduction projects such as
the Aboriginal project, which started in 1999 and protests the
industrialization of aboriginal areas without the consent of
the aboriginal people. The CPT also has a project in Israel/

Palestine in which they stand alongside Israelis and Palestinians who protest the Israeli military occupation, settler harassment, and home demolition. In the Africa Great Lakes (Burundi, Kenya, Rwanda, Tanzania, and Uganda), the organization focuses on establishing connections with human rights organizations, peace groups, civil society leaders, and church leaders to comprehensively understand the dynamics of conflict therein.

Coalition against Genocide

http://coalitionagainstgenocide.org/

The Coalition against Genocide (CAG) is a spectrum of organizations and individuals, primarily located in North American contexts. The coalition came into being as a coordinated reaction to the Gujarat genocide. CAG emerged in response to the potential visit to the United States (in 2005) of Narenda Modi, the chief minister of Gujarat, who is widely believed to have instigated the related communal violence. The coalition successfully prevented the visit but continued to exist afterward, advancing a critique of ethnocentric policies and sentiments in India and promoting more inclusivist interpretations of Indian identity. The coalition consists of diverse organizations, including the Alliance for a Secular and Democratic South Asia, American Federation of Muslims of Indian Origin, Association of Indian Muslims of America, Association of South Asian Progressives, Building Bridges of Understanding, Coalition for a Secular and Democratic India, Coalition against Communalism, and many more organizations of similar tenor. This list of organizations and their stated objectives highlight how local, ethnocultural conflicts can be influenced by diasporic communities. The success of the CAG in preventing the visit of Modi stresses how and why expatriates (even third- and fourth-generation Indian Americans) can become important players in local conflicts.

Community of Sant'Egidio

http://www.santegidio.org/pageID/2/idLng/1064/THE_COMMUNITY.html

The Community of Sant'Egidio was founded in 1968 in Rome by Andrea Riccardi, a high-school student who attracted other students in a call to actually practice the Gospel. Identifying itself as a "church public lay association," it has grown into a movement of over 50,000 lay people devoted to spreading the message of the Christian gospel and charity work in Italy and in over 70 other locations around the world. In the spirit of the Second Vatican Council, some of the principles of the community include solidarity with the poor, ecumenism, and dialogue as a mode of co-operation across religious divides and as a method of conflict resolution. The community's peace work is intricately connected to its vocation to work with the poor and the weak. There is a broad understanding of the interconnections between war and poverty. Some members of the community were able to aid in fratricidal conflicts in Mozambique and Guatemala by offering the organization's service as a credible negotiator.

International Committee for Peace Council

http://www.peacecouncil.org/index.html

International Committee for Peace Council (ICPC) is a group of individuals from different spiritual and faith backgrounds who come to work together and understand each other for the common cause of humanity. Membership in the community is by invitation only to people who are known and respected within their communities and people who are committed to working toward peace. The first meeting of the council took place in 1995, with religious leaders articulating seven interrelated threats to peace: religious intolerance; war, violence, and the arms trade; environmental degradation; economic injustice; the population explosion; patriarchy; and oppressive globalization. The council supports local peace practitioners and also operates on the level of the United Nations, governments, and nongovernmental organizations. Projects and activities of this council included support and participation in the Dhammayietra in Cambodia (in 1996, 1997, and 1998), an annual peace walk by Buddhist monks and nuns through minefields and conflict zones. The cease-fires between the Khmer Rouge and the government are largely attributable to these marches. Other activities included intervening for peace and human rights workers in Chiapas, Mexico; organizing an international appeal for the return of Kosevar refugees; and rehabilitating child soldiers in Sudan in the aftermath of the civil war there. ICPC also supported moderate Israeli and Palestinian plans to end Israeli-Palestinian violence. Members of the group also met with local peacemaking groups and leaders in Northern Ireland.

Jewish Peace Fellowship

http://www.jewishpeacefellowship.org/index.php?p=about.who _we_are

This U.S-based organization emerged out of three antiwar Jewish organizations. Jewish Peace Fellowship (JPF) is grounded in an appeal to Jewish ideals and experiences that promote and inspire a nonviolent orientation and approach to conflict. The JPF is focused on promoting peace and freedom to all persons, regardless of religious, ethnic, or cultural affiliation. The organization was established in the midst of World War II, in 1941. At the time, images that were coming from the Nazi regime profoundly challenged the organization's pacifist foundations. The organization's primary focus is connecting individuals working toward peacebuilding and providing a forum for discussion of nonviolent resistance. While during World War II the organization was isolated, it gained momentum during the antimilitarism climate when the United States was involved in Indochina (1945–1975). However, as the United States shifted its focus to the Middle East, JPF once again found itself in a precarious position, as its antimilitaristic position had critical ramifications to Jews in Israel and around the world. The moral dilemmas faced by this organization bring to the fore the difficulty inherent in negotiating a particularistic agenda along with humanistic and universal values.

Lutheran Peace Fellowship

http://www.lutheranpeace.org/

Seattle-based Lutheran Peace Fellowship (LPF) is a group of Lutherans dedicated to peacemaking work around to the world. The LPF hosts workshops for Lutheran leaders in leadership training in peacemaking, circulates advocacy material, and cultivates intra-Lutheran dialogue on questions of war and peace. Some other specific areas of activity include hunger advocacy, exploration of why nonmilitaristic options were not considered prior to the U.S. invasion of Iraq, and echoing and reinforcing the work of various faith-based organizations (FBOs) and other nongovernmental organizations (NGOs) who are trying to stop the Israeli occupation of Palestinian territories.

Mennonite Central Committee, International Conciliation Service

http://www.mcc.org/

The Mennonite Central Committee (MCC) was formed in 1920 in Chicago, initially in response to famine experienced by Mennonites in the Ukraine. Shortly thereafter, the MCC expanded its mission to help all people in need. This faith-based organization pioneered the fair-trade movement through its program known as Ten Thousand Villages. The MCC established the Mennonite Conciliation Service (MCS) in 1979, intending to actively engage in peaceful resolution of conflicts around the world. Under the leadership of the scholar/peace practitioner John Paul Lederach (starting in 1989), the MCS engaged in various conflict zones. In the 1980s and 1990s, other Mennonite peace centers emerged at Eastern Mennonite University; the Lombard Mennonite Peace Center in Lombard, Illinois; and other locations. As a result, the MCS was discontinued in 2004, but the MCC's peacebuilding activities continued. The International Conciliation Service was one of the first groups to recognize religious leaders, transnational religious moments, and faith-based nongovernmental organizations as important players in ethnic and religious conflict.

Muslim Peace Fellowship

http://mpf21.wordpress.com/

Muslim Peace Fellowship was established in 1994 with the intention to engage theory and practice of Islamic nonviolence. It was the first organization of this type. Grounding the mission of the group is an interpretation of jihad as a spiritual struggle and striving for justice and perfection. This is called the Greater Jihad. Subsequently, the group focuses on how this notion of jihad as a spiritual struggle might inform nonviolent modes of negotiating and transforming conflicts. But the fellowship essentially constitutes a gathering of Muslims who support peace and justice. The mission of the fellowship is to combat injustice while affirming the Muslim commitment to peace, to deepen their understanding of Islam to escape religious stereotyping, to develop new ways of creating sustainable peace, and to create a working relationship with other faiths. The fellowship hosts a Multi-Faith Peace internship during the summer for young adults from Muslin, Jewish, and Christian faiths, to teach them peacebuilding techniques and how to build multifaith communities.

Rabbis for Human Rights

http://rhrna.org/ (North American Branch)

Rabbis for Human Rights (RHR) has a North American branch and a branch in Israel, both of which work together to protect human rights in both locations. The Israeli branch protects the rights of Palestinian farmers, opposes the demolition of homes in East Jerusalem and Palestinian territories, and works to protect the rights of foreign workers in Israel. The North American branch actively opposes the use of torture. The mission statement of the group is grounded in the tradition of Jewish humanism. The group has spoken out against Islamophobia in the United States, recognizing the similarity of the treatment of Muslims to the past treatment of Jews in hostile anti-Semitic contexts. In Israel/Palestine, RHR not only focuses on issues related directly to the occupation of Palestinian territories, but also engages in domestic matters. Beyond advocacy on behalf of foreign labor, RHR also calls for pluralizing interpretations of Judaism, challenging the hegemony of Jewish Orthodoxy (the rabbinate) in the Israeli state.

Sabeel Palestinian Liberation Theology Center

http://www.sabeel.org/

Sabeel (established in 1990) is a movement among Palestinian Christians that is based upon the teaching of Jesus Christ and seeks to deepen the faith of Palestinian Christians as well as unite them to work for social action. Sabeel also seeks to encourage groups around the world to work for a just, enduring peace that is based on prayer, while informing others of the situation, identity, and presence of Palestinian Christians. Sabeel has created a community-building program, which recognizes the civic and economic restraints placed on Palestinians and works to instill knowledge of the political situation, partly through providing for witness trips that expose visitors to the daily sufferings of Palestinians under Israeli occupation. Sabeel also underscores the need for ecumenism. It features a clergy program that strives to get past the denominational differences of churches by supporting local clergy, uniting denominations in thought and action, and creating a theology of liberation in response to the Israeli-Palestinian conflict. The theopolitical challenge of a Palestinian liberation theology is to combat the currency of the theology that informs Christian Zionists (especially in the United States). Christian Zionism views the establishment of the state of Israel and the ingathering of Jews in the land as chapters in a messianic saga of return. Within this theological framework, Christian Palestinians are silenced. The Christian Zionist outlook has influenced the making of U.S. foreign policy in the Middle East. It has wide popular appeal.Thus part of the focus of Sabeel is to challenge the theological premises undergirding Christian Zionism as well as expose the political, social, economic, spiritual, and cultural implications of this outlook to the actual Palestinian inhabitants of the land of Palestine (as well as those who became uprooted in the course of a protracted conflict).

Salam Institute for Peace and Justice

http://salaminstitute.org/new/

This nonprofit organization focuses on research and education. The institute is also involved with issues concerning conflict resolution, human rights advocacy, nonviolent resistance, and development. A particular preoccupation of this institute revolves around the need to build bridges between Muslim and non-Muslim communities. This necessitates research on philosophical and theological questions concerning Islam and peace as well as intercultural and inter-religious interface. The institute has

engaged extensively in overseeing projects on interfaith and intercultural dialogue, peacebuilding, conflict resolution, sustainable
development, conflict resolution, and community development in
Muslim countries. The institute has worked in areas as diverse as
the West Bank and Gaza, Turkey, Iran, Sri Lanka, Mindanao in the
Philippines, Africa, and the Balkans. For example, in collaboration
with the US Institute for Peace, the Iran program involved arrang-
ing for a delegation (in 2007) to Iran. The delegation met with
Iranian scholars and engaged in a focused discussion of peace, conflict resolution, and theoretical and practical approaches to peacemaking. The follow-up was the sending of an Iranian delegation
to the United States to continue and further cultivate the conversations that took place in Iran. In the different context of Chad, the
Salam Institute engages in work to strengthen efforts toward educational reforms. The underlying motivation here is that effective
civic education for peace and diversity may be directly related to
reduction of ethnic and religious tension and violence.

United Religions Initiative

http://www.uri.org/about_uri/

United Religions Initiative (URI) is an international interfaith network that connects—across religious, cultural, and geographic
boundaries—individuals who have established themselves as
working for constructive change toward social justice and peace
on a grassroots level. URI's global office is in San Francisco, and
the network is active in over 70 countries. Members of the group
work together to harness their collective power to confront violence that is motivated by religion and to combat social, economic, and environmental problems that destabilize political,
economic, and social structures and contribute to poverty and
other humanitarian crises. URI has developed a Traveling Peace
Academy to develop relationships and capacities to engage in
interfaith cross-cultural training that is set to address local concerns. URI contains many cooperation circles (CCs), activist-
initiated groups of interfaith cooperation and collaboration that
are independent and self-funded. The URI network involves over
500 CCs that focus on issues as diverse as AIDS, economic
empowerment, civil war orphans, climate change, and urban conflict. One of these cooperation circles is the Sudan Inter-Religious

Council, which tries to increase tolerance, create more dialogue between different religious leaders, and protect religious freedom and cooperation between different religious groups.

World Conference on Religion and Peace

http://www.wcrp.org/

The World Conference on Religion and Peace first began in 1961 intending to create a platform for leaders of the major world religions to discuss ways to promote peace. The mission of the group is to involve religious communities on a national and regional level. Religion and Peace contains a conflict transformation program that works to encourage cooperation within religious communities. For example, Religion and Peace has worked on issues of reconciliation in Southeast Europe following the Bosnian and Kosovo conflicts by encouraging cooperation, peacebuilding, and discussions between different religious groups to create a space for civil society. Religion and Peace also worked with the Inter-Religious Council to broker a peace accord that helped transform Liberia, and the organization has been involved in conflict prevention and sustaining peace in Guinea since 2001. Other achievements include the convening (in Bangkok, 2009) of approximately 120 prominent religious leaders and other representatives of Buddhist, Hindu, Muslim, Christian, and other traditions from Sri Lanka and Thailand, with the intention to cultivate a fertile ground for cooperation toward healing and reconciliation in the aftermath of a devastating civil war; in cooperation with the United Nations Children's Fund (UNICEF), Religion for Peace works toward a multiyear inter-religious initiative to protect children affected by ethnic and religious strife. These are but a few examples of the many areas of activities of this organization.

8

Print Resources

Religion and Modern Nationalism

The Emergence of the "Nation"

Robert E. Alvis. *Religion and the Rise of Nationalism: A Profile of an East-Central European City* **(Syracuse, NY: Syracuse University Press, 2005).**

This book studies the relevance of religion to the emergence of nationalism in the Eastern European city of Poznaň. The author focuses on a critical period of formation, beginning in 1793 with the Prussian annexation of the city and concluding with the revolution of 1848 to 1849. The revolution resulted in Poland regaining control over the area. This work is an example of micro social history. The author scrutinizes local primary resources in documenting changing patterns of cultural and social identifications. This form of micro social history enables the author to challenge arguments that inform secularist narratives concerning the emergence of nationalism in the 18th and 19th centuries as an entirely novel phenomenon and orientation that is in contradistinction to the antecedent religious background. An interlocutor who exemplifies this kind of a secularist orientation is Mark Juergensmeyer and his classification of religion and (secular) nationalism constituting two distinct and competing "ideologies of order." In contradistinction, Alvis exposes the influence, along with liberalism and Romanticism, of Catholic and Protestant traditions in the emergence of modern national sentiment in Poznaň, a city on the cultural and geographical border between Poland and Germany. The author demonstrates how religious identifications,

271

regardless of their elasticity, provided resources and anchors for the cultivation of national sentiments.

Benedict Anderson. *Imagined Communities: Reflections on the Origin and Spread of Nationalism* **(London: Verso, 2006), updated edition.**

This groundbreaking work in the theoretical study of nationalism first appeared in 1983. The author studies the processes and conditions involved in the emergence and spread of modern nationalism. He attributes the emergence of this phenomenon to territorialization of religious faiths, fragmentation and decline of antique kinship, development of print capitalism, and changing conceptions of time and space. He also explores how nationalist sentiments spread in the contexts of anti-imperialist resistance. Unlike other functionalist theorists (who view the rise of modern nationalism as a necessary development due to changing structural and cultural conditions), Anderson appreciates the relevance of antecedent religious worldviews in the process of selective retrieval and appropriation.

Adrian Hastings. *The Construction of Nationhood: Ethnicity, Religion, and Nationalism* **(Cambridge: Cambridge University Press, 1997).**

This work focuses on the role of religion in the construction of modern nationalisms. In particular, the author focuses on the cases of the English, the Irish, South Slavs, and Africans. The author deconstructs a prominent scholarly modernist argument (see works by Eric Hobsbawm, John Breuilly, Ernest Gellner, and Benedict Anderson, for example) that nationalisms were invented in the closing decades of the 18th century and can be explained causally only as the upshot of the Age of Revolution. This book begins with the conceptual assumption that modernist differentiation of ethnicity, religion, culture, and nationality is complex and reflective of a particular modernist orientation that needs to be problematized. Engaging with the histories of nationalism illustrates that religion cannot be marginalized and/or bracketed from a broader sociopolitical and cultural analysis. Nationalism, the author argues, is both theory and practice. As a political theory, it entails the right and aspiration of a nation to self-determination in the form of statehood. In practice, rather than a universalist commitment to a political self-determination, what would motivate people's passions and commitment to such a political project are particularistic sentiments of value and prestige of their nation. Religion and ethnicity as dynamic and fluctuating identity markers become pivotal in the analysis of the content and development of nationalist sentiments.

Anthony Marx. *Faith in Nation: Exclusionary Origins of Nationalism* **(New York: Oxford University Press, 2003).**

This work portrays the emergence of modern nationalism as the upshot of complex processes of state-building in early modern Europe. The author explores the cases of Spain, France, and England and how political elites manipulated and capitalized on religious and ethnic cleavages to centralize and legitimize their authority and control. Marx revises the modernist argument that situates the emergence of modern nationalism in modernity and with the values associated with the French Revolution. Instead of viewing modern nationalism as exemplifying the decline of exclusionary norms, Marx postulates that this social and political phenomenon was born out of intentional exclusionary practices in the service of absolutist monarchs. The civic and liberal norms that characterize modern Western democracies, therefore, conceal through a process of "collective amnesia" the illiberal origins of these democracies. This work illuminates why the labels of religious and secular nationalisms could be misleading, both historically and in contemporary cases. Instead, religion is intricately related both to the emergence and reproduction of national identities.

Anthony D. Smith. *Chosen Peoples: Sacred Sources of National Identity* **(Oxford: Oxford University Press, 2003).**

Smith argues that modern nationalisms are not at all modern and that their enduring capacity to mobilize strong attachments and sentiments resides in their deep cultural resources. There are four categories of these resources: the myth of ethnic election, a long-standing attachment to a particular topography, a yearning to recover a golden age, and a belief in the power of mass sacrifice to fulfill a glorious redemption. This work represents an articulation of an ethnosymbolist approach to nationalism. The author resists classifying nationalism as an entirely modern phenomenon. Instead, Smith underscores that the modernist approach does not take seriously the sacred roots and resources of the nation as

well as nationalism's religious dimensions: a belief in the sacredness of the community, territory, and historical narrative as well
as normative sense of "choseness." The theoretical underpinnings
of this work suggest a significant influence of the sociological-
functionalist interpretation of religion found in the work of Emile
Durkheim. Accordingly, nationalism amounts to the worship of
one's community or people. Modern nationalism is distinct in
that it represents a relocation of the redemptive dimensions of
religion to the political and social project.

Public Religion, Conflict, and Violence: A Global Perspective

Gabriel Almond, Scott Appleby, and Emmanuel Sivan. *Strong
Religion: The Rise of Fundamentalisms around the World (The
Fundamentalisms Project)* (Chicago: Chicago University Press,
2003).

This coauthored book draws on many of the conclusions articulated in the Fundamentalisms Project, edited by Martin Marty
and Scott Appleby, an interdisciplinary scrutiny of "fundamentalist movements" around the globe. *Strong Religion* focuses on the
structures, cultural contexts, and political landscapes in which a
variety of radical religious movements emerged. These movements include the Islamic Hamas and Hizbullah as well as the
Catholic and Protestant paramilitaries of Northern Ireland, the
Moral Majority and Christian Coalition in the United States, and
Sikh and Hindu radical nationalists in India. This work provides
both insightful analysis and thick descriptions of various groups
as well as a broad theoretical explanatory framework.

The Global "Resurgence" of Religion

Scott Appleby and Martin Marty. *Accounting for Fundamentalisms (The Fundamentalisms Project)* (Chicago: Chicago University
Press, 1994).

This edited volume, part of the multivolume Fundamentalisms
Project, focuses on the characteristics of fundamentalist movements and the rhetorical strategies that fundamentalist leaders
use. In their attempts to identify patterns of behavior and

engagement with social and political structures, the authors explore religious fundamentalist movement in various contexts and suggest that one of the main factors of fundamentalism is historical, while other factors substantially relate to the bodies of the religious traditions upon which fundamentalist leaders and individual actors draw as well as to their specific and local histories and grievances. The authors of this volume explore cases in Judaism, Christianity, Islam, Hinduism, Sikhism, and Buddhism and how various movements in these religious contexts change over time, their recruitment patterns, and the dynamic changes in their ideological and organizational structures.

Scott Appleby and Martin Marty. *Fundamentalisms and Society: Reclaiming the Sciences, the Family and Education (The Fundamentalisms Project)* **(Chicago: Chicago University Press, 1993).**

This volume of the Fundamentalisms Project focuses on three important spheres of interactions of fundamentalist movements, namely personal relationships such as family, science, and education. While exploring different fundamentalist groups from a range of religions, the authors are careful to avoid generalizations; they make the important assertion that not all fundamentalist groups are extremist. The book also contains essays that suggest fundamentalist groups are not all opposed to modernity; instead, they are more focused on maintaining tradition, and some are not opposed to using technology. Some essays in the book also explain that many fundamentalist groups have trouble effecting politics and are more effective in the spheres of education and relationships.

Scott Appleby and Martin Marty. *Fundamentalisms and the State: Remaking Polities, Economies and Militance (The Fundamentalisms Project)* **(Chicago: Chicago University Press, 1993).**

The contributors to this volume explore whether fundamentalist movements are inclined to engage in political activism and whether their activism and vision have been effective in terms of their desired goal of transforming political, social, and cultural structures. The interdisciplinary contributors to this volume explore the cases of the antiabortion movement in the United States, the Islamic war of resistance in Afghanistan, Shi'ite jurisprudence in Iran, among other topics of similar complexities. The volume also scrutinizes the influence antisecularist movements have exerted over national and international politics. Contributors examine five continents, with a special focus on cases that involve Judaism, Islam, Christianity, Buddhism, Hinduism, and Sikhism.

Scott Appleby and Martin Marty. *Fundamentalism Comprehended (The Fundamentalism Project)* **(Chicago: University of Chicago Press, 1995).**

The book explores common patterns and characteristics of fundamentalist movements and whether it makes sense to use the category of fundamentalism at all (being a particular American designation of a particular American movement). Some of the contributors challenge the use of the designation fundamentalism as entailing antisecular religious protest and attitude. The final essay of the volume is authored by Scott Appleby, Emmanuel Sivan, and Gabriel Almond and is designed to retain the basic premise of the Fundamentalism Project, namely that certain groups and movements around the world share certain characteristics ("family resemblances") and that identifying those characteristics, including behavioral patterns of interactions with other social, cultural, economic, and political structures could enable a comparative and insightful analysis of religion and politics around the globe. The book identifies three main characteristics of fundamentalist groups: the oppositional stance against the world outside their group, their genuinely religious nature, and their structure as an authoritarian absolutist group in a pluralistic world that compels them to make compromises.

Scott Appleby and Martin Marty. *Fundamentalism Observed (The Fundamentalism Project)* **(Chicago: University of Chicago Press, 1991).**

This edited volume provide an introduction to various reactionary religious movements around the globe. The contributors explore the social, political, cultural, and religious contexts underpinning the emergence and ideological belief systems of various movements. How and why certain religious articulations made sense as responses to secularity, modernity, colonialism, and postcolonialism, among other specifically historical conditions. The contributors cover cases from Protestant fundamentalism and Roman Catholic traditionalism in North America; Protestant fundamentalism in Latin America; Jewish fundamentalism in Israel/Palestine; activist

Shi'ism in Iran, Iraq, and Lebanon; Islamic fundamentalism in South Asia; and Sunni fundamentalism in Egypt and the Sudan.

Talal Asad. *On Suicide Bombing* **(New York: Columbia University Press, 2007).**

This work engages the Orientalist presuppositions underlying the mainstream analysis of "religious violence" or "religious terrorism" in the wake of the tragic events of September 11, 2001. The author problematizes the premises that inform the "clash of civilizations" thesis, popularized by the Harvard political scientist Samuel Huntington. The paradigm of the clash of civilizations, which states that conflict in the post–Cold War era will erupt along civilizational lines, defined by irreconcilable values, has dominated the media and also become a pretext for waging war. Asad deploys the theoretical tools of anthropology and religious studies to deconstruct this paradigm and to further ask whether there is such a thing as religious violence and whether it is categorically different than other forms of violence.

Benjamin R. Barber. *Jihad vs. McWorld* **(New York: Times Books, 1995).**

This work exemplifies the force of the secularism thesis in generating a bifurcated analysis of religion as it relates to contemporary life. The author basically posits that the central conflict of our time revolves around consumerist capitalism versus religious and tribal fundamentalism: Jihad versus McWorld. What this argument betrays is the underlying normative assumption of the secularism thesis. Accordingly, modernity not only entails the differentiation of the spheres of social interactions, nor does it only translate into the centralization of human rights conventions and values. Instead, the secularization of the world will ultimately result in the diminishing relevance of religion in public life and even its ultimate disappearance. This normative dimension of the secularism thesis is grounded in the Enlightenment critique of religion and in dominant 19th-century critiques (that became definitional of the social sciences), a tradition that led to the analysis of religion as a mere form of "false consciousness" that mature civilization will evolve out of. Barber argues that the global capitalist economy contributes to the erosion of national boundaries and to the emergence of cosmopolitan identities. At the same time, this force of capitalism breaks down large political units back into smaller and smaller tribal identification. This development explains the rise of religious and tribal counterforce to the cosmopolitanism associated with capitalism and neoliberalism.

Jose Casanova. *Public Religions in the Modern World* **(Chicago: University of Chicago Press, 1994).**

This seminal work challenges, but at the same time reaffirms, certain aspects of the secularism thesis. The author offers a groundbreaking explanation for the resurgence of religion to political and public life. In his analysis of what he terms "de-privatized" religions around the world, the author intends to offer a critique of the normative presumption of the secularism thesis that religion will eventually disappear through a process of confinement to the "private" sphere, going about the business of offering individual salvation. Casanova observes how in the 1980s and 1990s, religious institutions and individuals began to challenge and transform social and political systems, illuminating the conceptual and practical problems with the claims of the modern secular nation-state for neutrality vis-à-vis religion and culture. The de-privatization of religion in various contexts also brings to the fore important connections between religion and public morality. The book is grounded in five empirical cases that span two religious traditions: Protestantism and Catholicism in Spain, Poland, Brazil, and the United States.

William Cavanaugh. *The Myth of Religious Violence: Secular Ideology and the Roots of Modern Conflict* **(Oxford: Oxford University Press, 2009).**

This book focuses on the task of deconstructing the prevalent argument that links religion to violence. The author argues that this motif underlies much of the theoretical work and popular perception of religion. The author offers critiques of nine influential thinkers, from Mark Juergensmeyer to Scott Appleby, and how their position on religion and politics is broadly reflective of an internalization of a secularist narrative that builds on what the author renders the "myth of religious violence." This refers to the view of the European wars of religion as a moment of fanatical contestations that gave birth to tolerance, the supposedly defining attribute of modernity. Religious violence, in other words, is something of the past and antithetical to modernity. This myth is also reflective of the secularist presumption that religion is somehow a transhistorical and transcultural phenomenon. The author undertakes deconstructing this categorization of religion and historicizing the wars of religion, illustrating that even in this context, sometimes Catholics fight Catholics and Protestants fight Protestants. Thus construing these wars as purely about doctrinal disagreements is highly skewed and a historical. This book constitutes an important contribution to the critique of the secularism paradigm and its pervasive influence in the social sciences and popular perceptions.

Fawaz A. Gerges. *The Far Enemy: Why Jihad Went Global* **(Cambridge and New York: Cambridge University Press, 2009).**

This work scrutinizes the myth that rhetorically depicts a globally unified and homogeneous Islamist struggle against a supposedly Christian West. Through careful research, the author illustrates internal divergences within Muslims in various contexts of conflict. The militancy of a group like al-Qaeda with its focus on a global jihad is, the author concludes, a minority voice within diverse and internally complex Muslim voices and identities. The strategy of al-Qaeda with its global outlook and scope is contrasted with the more local focus of religious nationalists. The latter are preoccupied with transforming the Muslim world on a case-by-case basis. The author explores the rise of the jihadist movement, its structures and philosophies, and the various complexities that make it increasingly difficult to categorize it as a unified movement.

Slavica Jakelic. *Collectivistic Religions: Religion, Choice, and Identity in Late Modernity* **(Burlington, VT: Ashgate, 2010).**

This work is animated by several questions. First, how can one explain collectivist religions in European contexts? By "collectivistic religion," the author means public religions that provide the resource and very ground of people's identity and belonging. These religions are thoroughly contextual as well as socially and culturally embedded; they are often defined in relation to some "other." Often people are willing to die for such identities and understand themselves to be born into it (religions here do not constitute a choice). Prominent examples beyond Hinduism and Judaism include even "collectivistic Christianities" such as Orthodox Christianity in Serbia and Catholicism in Poland. The second question relates the observation about collectivistic religions in Europe and the presumption of secularism as entailing the individualization of religion. Third, if collectivistic religions are not some remnant from a primordial past, but rather constitutive of modernity, how might empirical and theoretical study of such religions intervene in conversations concerning the role of religion in collective and public belonging? The author brings together important conversations concerning religion, nationalism, and identity in late modernity.

Mark Juergensmeyer. *The New Cold War? Religious Nationalism Confronts the Secular State* (Berkley: University of California Press, 1993).

This work provides an early example of deploying a secularist paradigm as an explanatory framework for the resurgence of religion. This secularist paradigm interprets modern nationalism as constituting a categorically distinct orientation than the one provided by a religious worldview. The success of nationalism in the modern era, subsequently, had to entail the marginalization of religion. The "eruption" of religion to the political scene, therefore, needs to be analyzed as a form of rebellion and confrontation between what the author renders as two competing "ideologies of order." The synthetic construct of "religious nationalism" is synthetic because it represents a form of negotiating and mutual accommodation between the religious worldview and the secular fixation on modern nation-statehood. The author provides various examples of religious nationalisms, from the Middle East, South Asia, Central Asia, and Eastern Europe. In the author's analysis of various religious leaders around the globe, he identifies their common rejection of the dominant Western interpretations of secular nationhood. The rise of religious nationalism is further explicated as a mode of critiquing the decadence and ills of modernity. Still, Juergensmeyer underscores the very modernity of such religious activism.

Mark Juergensmeyer. *Terror in the Mind of God: The Global Rise of Religious Violence* (Berkley: University of California Press, 2000).

This book catalogues instances of violence associated with religion and/or religious justifications. An updated version of this book reviews the devastating events of 2001, in light of a broader analysis of the 1993 World Trade Center explosion, Hamas suicide missions, the Tokyo subway nerve gas attack, as well as violent activism of the Christian Right in the United States. This book includes interviews with individuals who engaged in terrorist activities, including the spiritual leader of the Hamas, Sheik Yassin. The intention is to uncover where and how precisely religion comes in as a motivating factor to engage in violent terroristic activities. The author illustrates why religiously justified acts of violence depend on broader "cultures of violence" rather than merely on the individual actions and beliefs of those who carry out the attacks. For instance, a broad conception of time as apocalyptic can trump ethics of engagement appropriate for ordinary time.

David Little and Donald Swearer, eds. *Religion and National-ism in Iraq: A Comparative Perspective* (Cambridge, MA: Harvard University Press, 2006).

This work represents a printed version of a conference that took place at the Harvard Center for World Religion at Harvard Divinity School in 2005. The conference's point of departure is that the internal contestation and even civil war in Iraq in the aftermath of the U.S. invasion of 2003 offered a ripe opportunity to discuss patterns of religious nationalisms in a comparative perspective. Therefore, leading scholars presented their assessments of questions of religion, ethnicity, nationalism, and conflict in the contexts of Bosnia, Sri Lanka, and Sudan. The editors' introduction offers an extensive overview of various approaches to the analysis of the role of religion in conflict, from those that dismiss religion as epiphenomenal to those that essentialize religion as a cause of conflict. The editors also illuminate the comparative role of the legacy of colonialism in many ongoing ethnoreligious national conflicts.

Pippa Norris and Ronald Inglehart. *Sacred and Secular: Religion and Politics Worldwide* (New York, NY: Cambridge University Press, 2004).

This book provides another example of an attempt to rethink the secularism thesis that predicted the disappearance of religion. Recognizing that religion is not disappearing the authors wish to recover some of the insights of 19th-century theorists such as Emile Durkheim and Max Weber, who identified a connection between industrialization and the decline of religion. However, Norris and Inglehart attempt to nuance those theoretical positions through an empirical global study. At the same time, they wish to maintain the analytic relevance of the concept of secularism. The authors argue that eulogizing the secularism thesis is grounded too much in the particularities of specific anomalous cases such as that of the United States, where religiosity flourishes despite industrialization and postindustrialization processes. The authors correlate a sense of existential insecurity with rise of religiosity. Accordingly, existential insecurity concerning political, social, and physical flourishing entices the rise of religiosity, whereas prosperity is positively correlated with a decline in religiosity (with the United States as an outlier case). The authors propose that whereas, by and large, and in the contexts of postindustrial societies, religion is declining (measured primarily through attendance in communal prayer houses), the world's population is becoming more religious (in sheer numbers) because a decline in religiosity is also positively correlated with low birth rate. The book offers regional case studies of religiosity in the United States and Western Europe, the Muslim world, and postcommunist Europe. The authors draw extensively on empirical data based on the World Values Survey conducted from 1981 to 2001. This survey was conducted in approximately 80 societies and attempted to represent the major religions. The book also draws on Gallup International polls, the International Social Survey Program, and Eurobarometer surveys.

Elizabeth Shakman Hurd. *The Politics of Secularism in International Relations* **(Princeton, NJ: Princeton University Press, 2008).**

This author argues that the subfield of international relations (IR) theory has been dominated by what she calls the discourses of secularism, subsequently delimiting its conceptual scope and ability to interpret the phenomenon of religious resurgence around the globe and especially Muslim politics. Hurd identifies two primary variations of the discourse of secularism: Judeo-Christian (which characterizes the American case) and laicism (which characterizes the French case). While laicism entails the normative presupposition concerning religion's eventual disappearance, the Judeo-Christian model imbues the political and the public sphere with a selective appeal to antecedent religious affiliations beneath the appearance of formally separating the stage from religious institutions. The Judeo-Christian paradigm tacitly presupposes that the values associated with secularity and modernity are rooted in the Judeo-Christian civilizational background. Here we see reflected a deep-seated orientalism. The laicite model is too interlaced with orientalism and with a tautological equation of modernity with secularity. The author argues that only through deconstructing the dominance of these discourses in IR theory and more broadly on the level of popular culture will analysts be able to analyze the resurgence of religion, generally, and Islamic politics, more specifically.

Jack Snyder, ed. *Religion and International Relations Theory* (New York: Columbia University Press, 2011).

This edited volume features theoretical attempts to reframe international relations (IR) theory. The three dominant paradigms in IR—realism, liberalism, and constructivism—are insufficient as frameworks for the analysis of religion as it relates to political formation and to political subjects. The events of September 11, 2001, made it all too clear that there is a disjunction between the relevance of religion to international politics and how international politics is theorized in the academy and often by policymakers. The authors featured in this volume set as their objective to rectify the analytic deficiency of IR paradigms.

Monica Toft, Daniel Philpott, and Timothy Shah. *God's Century: Resurgent Religion and Global Politics* (New York: W. W. Norton, 2011).

This work undertakes an empirical exploration of the role of religion in various conflicts around the globe. The coauthors focus both on where and why religion might contribute to belligerence and when can it function positively to bring about peace building and sociopolitical reconciliation in healing. The coauthors illustrate the limitations of the secularism paradigm in explaining the role of religion in global affairs. They argue that since the 1960s, there has been an observable reversal in the marginality of religion associated with secular ideologies. Partly, this reversal can be explained as a result of the failures of "secular ideologies" such as nationalism and socialism to deliver in various contexts. The work also highlights that the supposed forces that posited themselves as antithetical to religion (democracy, globalization, and technology) are instrumentalized by religious ideologies and forces.

Stanley J. Tambiah. *Leveling Crowds: Ethnonationalist Conflicts and Collective Violence in South Asia* **(Berkeley: University of California Press, 1997).**

This work scrutinizes the patterns of civilian riots in South Asia, connecting the discussion to a broader exploration of ethnonational conflict and patterns of collective violence. The primary cases studied in this work are those of Sri Lanka, Pakistan, and India. The author explores patterns of collective violence by situating his examination of each case in an analysis of its political, economic, and religious contexts. This work draws extensively and insightfully on a range of social theoretical analytic tools as well as on a deep anthropological knowledge of the cases under examination.

Other Selected Books on Religion, Society, and the Discourses of Secularism and Orientalism

Talal Asad. *Formations of the Secular: Christianity, Islam, Modernity* **(Stanford, CA: Stanford University Press, 2003).**

This seminal work offers a critique of the assumptions underlying the bifurcated categories of religion versus the secular, and their pivotal function in construing the concept and subject of modernity. This work generated a heated debate and a scholarly subgenre that might be classified as secularisms studies.

Peter Berger. *The Desecularization of the World: Resurgent Religion and World Politics* **(Washington, D.C.: Ethics and Public Policy Center, 1999).**

This work represents an unusual reassessment of the secularism thesis marshaled previously by the same author. Unlike his earlier work, Berger here argues that the normative and descriptive coupling and association of modernity with the decline of religiosity is not only empirically flawed, but perhaps even the opposite is the case. Modernity, in any case, does not necessarily entail a diminishing religiosity.

John Esposito. *Who Speaks for Islam? What a Billion Muslims Really Think* (New York: Gallup Press, 2007).

This book challenges essentializing conceptions and perceptions of Islam through an exploration of diverse populations in 35 predominantly Muslim nations.

Roxanne L. Euben. *Enemy in the Mirror: Islamic Fundamentalism and the Limits of Modern Rationalism* (Princeton, NJ: Princeton University Press, 1999).

This work explores Islamism (and specifically the thought of the Muslim Brotherhood activist Sayyid Qutb) by articulating how it confronts the limits of modern rationalism in a mode akin to Christian fundamentalists, postmodernists, conservatives, and communitarians. The author, therefore, challenges explanatory frameworks that render the emergence of Islamism as a reactionary force to social and political displacements associated with colonialism and postindependence Muslim contexts.

Timothy Fitzgerald. *Religion and Politics in International Relations: The Modern Myth* (London: Continuum, 2011).

This work offers a critique of the discourse of religion in international relations and especially the unreflexivity characteristic treatments of religion within the annals of IR theory.

Petito Hatzopoulos and Pavlos Hatzopoulos. *Religion in International Relations: The Return from Exile* (New York: Palgrave Macmillan, 2003).

This work problematizes the secularist foundations of, and assumptions informing, international relations. It confronts the presumption that public and politicized religion is necessarily a threat to security and an obstacle for peacebuilding. Therefore, the authors propose reframing international relations and substantially engaging religions in thinking about global issues.

John Kelsay. *Arguing the Just War in Islam* (Cambridge, MA: Harvard University Press, 2007).

Through a careful exploration of resources within the Islamic traditions, the author explores the contestation of the meanings of the concept of militant jihad (as opposed to the greater spiritual jihad) to capture the diversity of opinions and interpretations of the analogue to the just war discussion in Western and Christian contexts. This work provides an important example of the complexity of the connections between religion and violence—an antidote to simplistic renderings of these connections.

Gilles Kepel and Anthony F. Roberts (translator). *Jihad: The Trail of Political Islam* **(Cambridge, MA: Harvard University Press, 2002).**

This work attempts to develop an explanatory framework for the "resurgence" of Islamist political movements in the late 20th century. The author provides an intricate picture, looking at ideological formations, political and global contexts, and domestic coalition formation. He explores diverse areas from Egypt and Iran, to Turkey and Malaysia.

Emran Qureshi and Michael Anthony Sells. *The New Crusades: Constructing the Muslim Enemy* **(New York: Columbia University Press, 2003).**

This edited volume features important critiques from a variety of disciplinary lenses of the assumptions inherent in the clash of civilizations theory.

Jeffrey Stout. *Democracy and Tradition* **(Princeton, NJ: Princeton University Press, 2004).**

The author draws together resources of U.S. democratic history and culture (Walt Whitman, Ralph Waldo Emerson, James Baldwin, Ralph Ellison, Martin Luther King, Jr., among others) in order to portray democracy in the United States as a tradition of ethical practice. The book portrays democracy as a self-correcting enterprise in which a national community's orienting principles of justice are perpetually subjected to further criticism and enrichment in light of the best practices, exemplary practitioners, and self-critical reflective resources that constitute the tradition itself. The book articulates a "deflationist" understanding of the secularization of U.S. public life. On this account, public discourse is "secularized" when fellow citizens do not necessarily share one another's presuppositions about religion in public, political interaction. The result overturns the impasse between those who seek to marginalize explicit participation by religiously identified and motivated actors in U.S. public and political life, on one hand, and theological traditionalists who view American democracy as empty of ethical content and symptomatic of the deficiencies intrinsic to modern liberal political life, on the other.

Ivan Strenski. *Why Politics Can't Be Freed from Religion* **(Cambridge: Wiley-Blackwell, 2010).**

This work intervenes in debates about religion, politics, and power and how particular historical developments have conditioned those debates. The author offers a critique of prominent intellectuals working within the discursive secularisms scholarship (e.g., Talal Asad).

Ronald Thiemann. *Religion in Public Life: A Dilemma for Democracy* **(Washington, D.C.: Georgetown University Press, 1996).**

This work draws on legal scholarship, philosophy, and political theory to explore the role of religion in public life in the U.S. context. The author exposes the conceptual and practical limitation of the presumption of an absolute wall of separation between church and state. Instead, he suggests to reintroduce James Madison's outlook on the principles of liberty, equality, and toleration. Consequently, the author develops a revised interpretation of political liberalism that negotiates between communitarian and liberal interpretations of the debates concerning the publicity of religion.

Hent de Vries and Lawrence Sullivan. *Political Theologies: Public Religions in a Post-Secular World* **(New York: Fordham University Press, 2006).**

This groundbreaking volume addresses, from a variety of disciplinary approaches, the questions and meanings of postsecularisms. Postsecularism denotes a realization that once we accept the realization of the parochial dimensions of the normative assumptions inherent in the doctrine of secularism, we need to reassess the interrelations between the political and the religious. The book covers topics from the gods in the Greek polis, to Augustine's two cities, to classical debates about political theology by thinkers like Carl Schmitt and Walter Benjamin as well as the French controversy over the wearing of the Muslim headscarf, among other topics.

Religion and Ethnonational Conflict (Select Cases)

India

Christopher Jaffrelot, ed. *Hindu Nationalism: A Reader* **(Princeton, NJ: Princeton University Press, 2007).**

Looking back at the thoughts of Hindu nationalistic leaders and Indian history, this book attempts to understand the political goals and beliefs of the Bharatiya Janata Party (BJP), a Hindu nationalist party in India. Although the BJP lost national control in 2004, the political party remains important to Indian politics; therefore, an understanding of its views of secularism, relations with Muslims, and religion is important to developing an idea of the direction that Indian politics is taking. Through the writings of Hindu nationalists and other documents from Hindu nationalist groups, the book provides an informative view to those not familiar with the development of Hindu nationalism in politics.

Arvind Rajagopal. *Politics after Television: Religious Nationalism and the Reshaping of the Indian Public* **(Cambridge: Cambridge University Press, 2001).**

Rajagopal draws a connection between the development of Hindutva, an ideology that focuses on uniting India around an exclusive Hindu identity, and television. Rajagopal starts with a discussion of the broadcasting of a Hindu epic Ramayana on the secular government–owned television station, and explains that this was important because it set the scene for the discussion of Hindu nationalism. The fact that the showing of a Hindu epic was accepted on TV was important not only because it showed that the Indian people were accepting of modernization because the show combined a traditional Hindu tale with the modern invention of television, but also because it suggested a specific Hindu modernization for India. The books goes on to describe how the Indian People's Party was able to capitalize on the moment by advertising itself as the nation's rescuers from the Congress Party's stagnation and failure, offering economic reform and religious identification. The creation of this Hindu nationalism, which was able to reach even Indian people who were no longer residents of the country, was important to the founding of the Hindu nationalist groups that led to the Ayodyah-Babri mosque conflict.

Ratan, Sudha. "Hindutva: The Shaping of a New 'Hindu' Identity." *Southeastern Political Review* **26, no. 1 (1998), pp. 201–217.**

The author investigates the environment that contributed to the development, organizational structure, and popularization of the Hindu nationalist message in the form of Hindutva. The paper continues by looking at how the Bharatiya Janata Party (BJP) has used Hindutva themes to gain political power. Furthermore, it looks at how historical development of Hindutva as a political ideology fostered an anti-Muslim atmosphere and contributed to religious violence.

Peter van der Veer. *Religious Nationalism: Hindus and Muslims in India* **(Berkeley: University of California Press, 1994).**

In this book, van der Veer goes against the idea of the modern state necessarily being a secular nation-state and instead uses the example of a modern nation-state that contains religious identities that are seminal to its foundations. The author points out that although India attempted to become a secular nation after independence, existing religious roots could not be ignored. In observation of the fact that religion and more specifically Hinduness have been increasingly important in India, van der Veer brings up the possibility of a modern religious nationalism. Hindu traditions and identities, which cut across the barriers of socioeconomic class because of they are based in religious identities, were liberally used in the formation of an ideology to unite the Indian nation. Rather than religion being lost in the formation of a nation-state, van der Veer claims that religion can be used as the foundation of a nation, bringing people together in a way that ethnic and regional boundaries cannot.

Ashutosh Varshney. *Ethnic Conflict and Civic Life: Hindus and Muslims in India* **(New Haven, CT and London: Yale University Press, 2002).**

Varshney focuses on the question of why religiously motivated violence has erupted in some Indian towns but not others. Through the study of towns with similar ratios of Muslims and Hindus, the importance of the structure of civil society in relation to ethnic violence can be observed. The importance of this work is that while recognizing the critical role of the state in fostering ethnic tensions, it also illuminates the agency of local actors in decreasing the likelihood of interethnic violence.

Israel/Palestine

Joyce Dalsheim. *Unsettling Gaza: Secular Liberalism, Radical Religion, and the Israeli Settlement Project* **(Oxford: Oxford University Press, 2011).**

The author engages in an ethnographic study with settlers in Israel/Palestine. Her analysis exposes relations of ideological continuity rather than discontinuity between so-called mainline secular Israelis and the religious Zionists who inhabit the settlements in the Occupied Territories. In critiquing conventional modes of analyzing divides in Israel along a rigid interpretation of categories such as "religious" and "secular," the author exposes the fallacy inherent in singling out the settlers' interpretations of Israeli nationalism as inhabiting peace and as one juxtaposed with secular (liberal) Zionism. Instead, the author explains secular and religious Zionism as subsumed within a singular analytic frame. Secular and religious Zionists, in other words, are more similar than dissimilar, and it is the perception of deep antagonism that becomes a conceptual and practical obstacle to understanding the Israeli-Palestinian conflict and even broader conceptual engagements with the interface between religion and political formations.

Loren D. Lydbarger. *Identity and Religion in Palestine: The Struggle between Islamism and Secularism in the Occupied Territories* **(Princeton, NJ: Princeton University Press, 2007).**

Through his years of experience living in Palestine and over 80 interviews with Palestinians, Lydbarger offers a new view of how the identities of Palestinians have been changed by the struggle between Islamists and secular nationalists. Activists within Palestinian societies faced with peace negotiations, occupation, and fragmentation of Palestinian life have had to create a new identity despite the inherent divisions in Palestinian societies. Although some scholars have divided Palestinians into two groups, those that are pragmatists and accept territorial compromise and extremists who rely on armed conflict, a deeper internal struggle between Islamists and secular nationalists is reflected in Palestinian society.

Ehud Sprinzak. *The Ascendance of Israel's Radical Right* **(New York: Oxford University Press, 1991).**

Sprinzak gives an analysis of the political right in Israel. The ascendance of the radical right stemmed from the military victory of 1967 and its interpretation by some Israelis as amounting to the fulfillment of a divine saga and destiny. When speaking of the radical right, Sprinzak is referring to the extreme commitment of religious Zionists to settle the Occupied Territories and how this commitment is deeply entangled with anti-Arab sentiments. In this first thorough account of the radicalization of Israeli political and social orientations, Sprinzak explores the emergence of radical elements across the Israeli political spectrum. He portrays the ideologies and structures of a variety of movements.

Idith Zerthal and Akiva Eldar. *Lords of the Land: The War over Israel's Settlements in the Occupied Territories, 1967–2007,* **translated from Hebrew by Vivian Eden (New York: Nation Books, 2007).**

This work provides a well-rounded historical account of the emergence of the settlement movement in Israel and how its accomplishments expanded beyond the settlement of the territories occupied in 1967 to include a social, political, and cultural transformation of the broader Israeli society. The authors describe the history of ideological and strategic symbiosis between successive Israeli governments as well as the religious settlers and their leaders.

Sri Lanka

Ananda Abeysekara. "The Saffron Army, Violence, Terrorism: Buddhism, Identity, and Difference in Sri Lanka," *Brill* **48, no. 11 (2001), pp. 1–45.**

The author of this article proposes an alternative approach to the conceptualization of the relationship between religion and violence. Abeysekara believes that a much more nuanced approach must be taken to understand religion, violence, civilization, and terrorism. Abeysekara's approach to understanding religion and violence problematizes the traditional paradigms proposed by authors such as Tambiah in "Buddhism Betrayed?" Abeysekara proposes that we expand the traditional parameters we use to define such terms as "religion" and "terrorism," and instead, for example, recognize the multifaceted nature of religion (i.e., as doctrinal, as spiritual, as political, etc.).

Mahinda Deegalle. "Is Violence Justified in Theravada Buddhism?" *Ecumenical Review* **(April 2003), pp. 122–131.**

The author of this article reflects on three points mentioned by Hans Ucko in February 2002: (1) every religion is against violence, (2) we live in a world of violence, and (3) is there a place for justifying violence in our religious traditions? This is an especially interesting article because Deegalle takes an in-depth look at the justification used for violence within the primarily nonviolent Buddhist tradition. She uses three examples—*The Pali Canon, The Pali Chronicles*, and *Sinhala Medieval Literature*—to explore Buddhist attitudes toward violence. Her work illuminates the role of the Mahavamsa text, which tends to be the primary work cited when assessing the source of violence within Buddhism. While Deegalle concludes that the overwhelming consensus among scholars of Buddhism is that Buddhism does not justify violence under any conditions, her assessment of the Mahavamsa text and its ability to disturb the pacifist image of Theravada Buddhism is intriguing. The complexity with which this single controversial myth is interpreted, perpetuated, and received to promote national interests echoes similarities of religious narratives used in other contexts to promote violence for the sake of national unity and religious protection.

Patrick Grant. *Buddhism and Ethnic Conflict in Sri Lanka* **(Albany: State University of New York Press, 2009).**

In this book that focuses on the conflict in Sri Lanka, Grant puts forth the idea of progressive inversion, in which religion that supports inclusion is used to exclude people. The author scrutinizes how three modern Sri Lankan Buddhist scholars facilitated the transformation of Buddhism in Sri Lanka into an exclusive religion. Instead of being used to free people, religion in this context is instead used to reinforce existing prejudices and unite people in opposition to another group.

David Little. "Religion and Ethnicity in the Sri Lankan Civil War," in Robert I. Rotberg, ed., *Creating Peace in Sri Lanka: Civil War and Reconciliation* (Washington, D.C.: Brookings Institution Press, 1999), pp. 41–56.

In this chapter, Little explores the role religion plays in defining ethnicity. The author problematizes an understanding of ethnicity in purely genetic or hereditary terms, articulating the contours of identity as laden with religious significance. Little utilizes the case of Sri Lanka to demonstrate how ethnicity serves not only to differentiate and classify people, but also to evaluate them comparatively. The majority of Little's work is dedicated to outlining what he believes to be the four primary causes of the rise of modern Sinhalese Buddhist nationalism: (1) the reaction to British colonialism, (2) the existence of religious national epics that provided the material conditions for nationalism, (3) the reaction to a perceived threat and unfair advantage of the Tamil minority, and (4) the majoritarian dictatorship of the British that resulted in preferential constitutional law. In outlining the primary causes for Sinhalese Buddhist nationalism, Little demonstrates how certain political, economic, and social factors can fuel the construction of religious nationalism. Little provides analytic tools to explore how and why religion becomes involved in nationalistic campaigns, and the ways in which such opposition to religious pluralism within a community or nation can be overcome.

Chelvadurai Manogaran. *Ethnic Conflict and Reconciliation in Sri Lanka* (Honolulu: University of Hawaii Press, 1987).

The objective of Manogaran's book is to explicate the geographical determinants of the conflict in Sri Lanka and how the varying ethnogeographical regions within the country play and have played a role in colonization, agricultural development, education, employment, and national integration. The book provides a background about the ethnic and political origins of the tension between the Sinhalese Buddhist majority in the south and the Tamil Hindu minority in the north. The author not only insightfully engages the lasting effects that colonial powers (Portuguese, Dutch, and British) had on the country's social, political, and economic development, but also provides a historical context within which to understand the Buddhist revival movement, and ultimately Buddhist fundamentalism.

Stanley J. Tambiah. *Buddhism Betrayed?: Religion, Politics, and Violence in Sri Lanka* **(Chicago: University of Chicago Press, 1992).**

Tambiah's book questions the apparent irony that exists when violence is perpetrated in the name of Buddhism, a religion whose basic tenets are nonviolence and pacifism. Tambiah's work is especially helpful because it thoroughly explains the historical (both pre- and postcolonial political, economic, and social) context for such violence. Tambiah outlines institutional structures as well as national events that helped lay the foundation for ethnic hostilities between the Sinhalese and the Tamils. He demonstrates the great complexity of this ethnoreligious and political conflict, ultimately providing an explanation for the conflict within Sri-Lanka that is more nuanced than previous efforts.

Northern Ireland

James Anderson and Ian Shuttleworth. "Sectarian Demography, Territoriality and Political Development in Northern Ireland," *Political Geography* **17, no. 2 (1998), pp. 187–208.**

In this article, the authors deal primarily with the questions of territory in Northern Ireland and the role that sectarianism has played in the development of policy in Northern Ireland. They acknowledge that sectarianism is an important consideration and is deeply rooted in the society of Northern Ireland. Yet they believe that exaggerating sectarian concerns has led to poor policy decisions. In that vein, they warn that there is a fine line between simply studying sectarianism and actually promoting it. This work seeks to dispel the idea that religion is the primary dividing marker in Northern Ireland. In fact, the authors see political ideals as much stronger markers of identity.

Claire Mitchell. *Religion, Identity and Politics in Northern Ireland: Boundaries of Belonging and Belief* (Burlington, VT: Ashgate, 2006).

This book presents the complex roles of religion in Northern Ireland. The author underscores that the Troubles in Northern Ireland cannot be viewed as religious. However, religion functions as a critical marker of social difference, religious symbols and ideas might constitute and inform group identities, the practice of religion can facilitate the construction of a community, religious beliefs can also become politically salient, and religious institutions are politically influential.

Patrick Mitchel. *Evangelicalism and National Identity in Ulster: 1921–1998* (Oxford: Oxford University Press, 2003).

In Mitchel's book, he denounces the place that Christians, especially the evangelical church, have taken in respect to the conflict in Northern Ireland. Instead of offering a peaceful alternative to the conflict, the church has been shaped by the conflict. Political leaders like Ian Paisley have been able to gain a position representing evangelicalism and have adopted a closed stance in which theology is used to legitimize the actions of Unionists and support tribal nationalism instead of adopting an open stance that would accept the most peaceful route that includes compromise. Because the evangelical church has been caught in politics in Ireland, Mitchel suggests evangelicals in Ireland should develop a stance separate from the religious organizations, asserting the fact that a Protestant state is no better than a secular state and standing in favor of a state that endorses favorable communications across religions.

Religion, Democracy, and the Modern Nation-State

United States

Jose Casanova. "Immigration and the New Religious Pluralism: A European Union/United States Comparison," *Democracy and the New Religious Pluralism* (2007), pp. 59–83.

Casanova's article studies how Western secularist states deal with the challenges that have arisen from the significant amount of immigration into America and (especially) Europe in recent decades. In many instances where the "immigration issue" emerges, the predicament involves second- and third-generation immigrants. Casanova analyzes reactions to these immigration issues through his nuanced approach to the discourses of secularism. He explicates how normative components of the secularism thesis have involved a perception of secularism as being more evolved, progressive, and modern than religious societies, and that secularist nations have used Islam as the regressive, repressive "other" to help develop and define their national identities. In this article, Casanova specifically analyzes the French banning of Muslim headscarves in schools. His analysis explicates how the legislation in some ways actually contradicts what it claims to do. His discussion of how American religious pluralism has developed from first Protestantism, to Christian, to Judeo-Christian holds important implications for how the United Sates may be able to better incorporate and function effectively with Islam.

Nicholas Guyatt. *Providence and the Invention of the United States* (New York: Cambridge University Press, 2007).

Providence (God's will) has often been used to describe decisions and changes in a nation. What sets Guyatt's work apart is his specific examination of the providential thinking within American exceptionalism. Throughout history, people have looked at their situation to define the goals of God, and Guyatt finds no difference when tracing the history of the United States. There are three types of providence: judicial, in which God judges the character of the people and their leaders and decides whether to support them; historical, in which God has his chosen roles for all people to play; and apocryphal, in which the last days are being played out. While Puritans may have originally endorsed to historical providence, believing that England was the chosen land of God, the Puritan Restoration destroyed that idea and replaced it with an apocryphal providence. This vision was then replaced with a historical providence that claimed that America was now God's chosen land. This vision was then replaced with an apocryphal vision by abolitionists, until a historical vision of providence was finally taken on by Americans after the Civil War. The book provides an important look into the way that Americans have used the language of providence to justify their actions throughout history.

Robert Wuthnow. "Religious Diversity in a 'Christian Nation': American Identity and Democracy," *Democracy and the New Religious Pluralism* (2007), pp. 151–168.

This article reports on an extensive research program that examined how the majority of Christian Americans are responding to the growing presence of other religions, particularly Islam. The findings suggest enduring prejudices and stereotypes that Americans hold regarding Muslims. The study also reports that Americans will not object to treating Muslims in ways that contradict the fundamental constitutional principles of religious freedom and civil liberties.

Islamic Contexts

Abd Allah Ahmad An-Na'im. *Islam and the Secular State: Negotiating the Future of Sharia* (Cambridge, MA: Harvard University Press, 2008).

In this book, An-Na'im questions the place of Sharia in societies with a Muslim majority. By rethinking the relationship between religion and secular societies, a positive role for Sharia can be envisioned. The Quran does not support the enforcement of Sharia by the state; rather, it insists on the voluntary compliance of people through adherence to pluralistically acceptable civic reason. Indeed, throughout history, Sharia has remained separate from the state. It is only in recent history that this has changed. The state makes legislation that should fit all regardless of religious affiliation; just as the state should be free from the control of religion, Sharia should be free from the control of the state. In fact, the idea of an Islamic state in which Sharia is enforced is more consistent with European ideals, while Islamic principles are more in tune with ideas of human rights and citizenship. That there are trends in Islamic contexts toward homogenizing Islam and subordinating state infrastructures to a codified interpretation of the tradition reflects an enduring colonial thread. Rather than analyzing Islamism as representing a reactionary force, this interpretation illuminates the force of Western categories and conceptions of religion as well as the secular. The author explores in depth the three cases of Turkey, India, and Indonesia and how theoretical questions concerning religion and the political play out in each instance.

Ali Mirsepassi. *Democracy in Modern Iran: Islam, Culture, and Political Change* **(New York: New York University Press, 2010).**

In this work, Mirsepassi looks at the question of whether an Islamic society can accept democracy and answers that Islam is not inherently opposed to democracy. With a change in social institutions and day-to-day exchanges, democracy can work in an Islamic society. Taking a closer look into Iran can give insight into how Islamic countries like Iraq and Iran can work with democracy. By dropping the usual views that place Islam in opposition to democracy, or countries like Iran in opposition to the West, an understanding of how Islam can work with democracy becomes available. Viewing democracy as compatible with Islam can aid a new view of modernity in the Eastern world.

Mansoor Moaddel. *Islamic Modernism, Nationalism, and Fundamentalism: Episode and Discourse* **(Chicago: Chicago University Press, 2005).**

This work divides Islamic political formations into three distinct yet interrelated moments, thereby analyzing different ideological discourses in comparison to social structures. The three periods encompass the development, in the 19th century, of Islamic modernism, Middle Eastern nationalism, and eventually Islamic fundamentalism. It is crucial to analyze those periods and discourses in relation to one another, scrutinizing how they interface. It is also pivotal to engage in localized and contextualized analyses that not only study the interaction between ideology and social structures, but also focus on different Islamic countries' surrounding factors such as education, global economic trends, and colonialism. Each of these variables works differently in different Islamic contexts and thus assists in explaining the various modes of entry into broader discussions of Islamic modernism, nationalism, and fundamentalism.

Joan Wallach Scott. *The Politics of the Veil* **(Princeton, NJ: Princeton University Press, 2007).**

Scott argues that the 2004 ban against wearing religious symbols in French public schools was geared toward the Muslim headscarf and that it is connected to traditional French republicanism and orientalism. In other words, at the heart of the veil controversy is not the desire to protect little Muslim girls and provide them with a choice, but rather a deeper concern with the erosion of French-ness as a result of the increasing presence and visibility of Muslim French citizens. The belief that the French secularist identity embodies a universal political truth has amplified the French republican creed of secularism, universalism, and abstract individualism, and construed it in juxtaposition to Islam. The current hostility towards Islam in defense of French secularism provides a contemporary manifestation of the deep-seated orientalism informing the French colonial structures in North Africa. French nationalism, the author underscores, contradicts itself by depriving Muslims of the human rights that it strives to protect. To overcome this problem, a dialogue must be created that can overcome the assumptions that have been entangled in French political culture. Likewise, the author argues that in analyzing the veil controversy, what is overlooked is the conceptions of identity that the girls who wish to wear the hijab aim to express.

M. Yavuz. *Secularism and Muslim Democracy in Turkey* **(Cambridge: Cambridge University Press, 2009).**

Yavuz's book reveals that the rise of Islamic activists within Turkish politics proves that Islam can stand the test of democracy and economic liberalization. Although Turkey provided an example of a secular majority Muslim nation-state with Islam as the main religion, initially this status was maintained due to a state-controlled and enforced secularization. With a weakening state and the rise of explicitly Islamic national political players to the helm of the state, Turkey now presents a fascinating illustration of Islamic democracy that is not merely nominal. This Islamic state, importantly, does not stand against modernity, globalization, and integration into Europe, thereby defying the presumption that somehow an Islamic state would be antimodern. The author highlights that Islamic activism in Turkey is rooted in education and economic progress, making it more adaptable to modernity.

Religion and Peacebuilding

Scott Appleby. *The Ambivalence of the Sacred: Religion, Violence, and Reconciliation* **(Oxford: Rowman and Littlefield, 2000).**

The underlying thesis of this groundbreaking work is that religion can become a source of violent as well as nonviolent militancy. In highlighting the ambivalent responses to perception of the "sacred," the author moves away from the polemical and unproductive rendering of religion as a cause of violence or as potentially highly correlated with violent conflicts. Religion and religious leaders, consequently, become an important focus for thinking about peacebuilding and conflict transformation. The author engages a variety of cases of militants for peace and reconciliation.

Harold Coward and Gordon Smith, eds. *Religion and Peace building* (New York: State University of New York Press, 2004).

This collection of essays examines various and diverse instances in which religion and religious leaders function centrally as agents of peacebuilding. The volume contains an important theoretical introduction by Scott Appleby and David Little. Other contributors to this volume explore spiritual peacebuilding resources within religions such as Hinduism, Buddhism, Judaism, and Islam.

Marc Gopin. *Between Eden and Armageddon: The Future of World Religions, Violence, and Peacemaking* (Oxford: Oxford University Press, 2002).

This work links a careful study of the potential constructive role of religion in peacemaking with the language and insights of conflict resolution. The author argues that for religion and especially religious people and leaders to engage constructively in efforts of diplomacy, healing, and reconciliation, they need to introspectively excavate their traditions and theologies, and then articulate a paradigm for peacemaking. This particular work takes as one of its tasks to articulate such a paradigm for peacemaking from within Jewish sources.

Douglas Johnston. *Faith-Based Diplomacy: Trumping Realpolitik* (Oxford: Oxford University Press, 2003).

This book was one of the pioneering efforts to challenge the theoretical and practical underpinnings of international relations and diplomacy. The underlying thesis is that conventional modes of analyzing conflicts and confronting them on the level of diplomacy overlooked and dismissed the relevance of religion as an authentic (rather than merely epiphenomenal) motivation for engaging in conflicts. The book explores five seemingly intractable conflicts, and where religion might fit in as a peace-promoting force. Those conflicts include Kashmir, Sri Lanka, Israel/Palestine, Bosnia-Herzegovina, and the Sudan.

Douglas Johnston and Cynthia Sampson, eds. *Religion: The Missing Dimension of Statecraft* **(New York: Oxford University Press, 1994).**

This pioneering work begins with a recognition that conventional diplomacy is not equipped with the tools and resources needed to engage in seemingly intractable conflicts that rage along lines of identity: nationality, religion, and ethnicity. Religion, the authors argue, is the missing dimension of diplomacy and international relations. This book subsequently documents a series of contemporary cases where religious leaders and individuals have played constructive roles in conflict resolution. The cases range from Europe to Central America and Asia to Africa.

John Paul Lederach. *Building Peace: Sustainable Reconciliation in Divided Societies* **(Washington, D.C.: United States Institute of Peace, 1997).**

This work explicates the importance of advancing a holistic approach to peacebuilding, one that is multidimensional and attentive to horizontal relational patterns as well as vertical policymaking and formal decision making. The work provides the inductive insights of a veteran peacemaker who challenges from the ground up conventional approaches to diplomacy and peacemaking that cannot sufficiently approach and engage conflict zones defined by deep ethnic, cultural, religious, and national cleavages.

Daniel Philpott, ed. *The Politics of Past Evil: Religion Reconciliation and the Dilemmas of Transitional Justice (Kroc Institute Series on Religion, Conflict, and Peacebuilding)* **(Notre Dame, IN: University of Notre Dame Press, 2006).**

This book studies the prospect of reconciliation in the aftermath of mass atrocities. The contributors to this collection focus on how theology and politics can aid in transitional justice. The cases explored include Germany, Argentina, South Africa, and Northern Ireland.

Timothy D. Sisk, ed. *Between Terror and Tolerance: Religious Leaders, Conflict, and Peacemaking* (Washington, D.C.: Georgetown University Press, 2011).

This book explores the multifaceted roles of religious leaders—in contexts that are highly divided along religious, cultural, ethnic, and national lines—in vindicating and propelling violence and conflict as well as in mediating and reducing violent conflict and cultivating paths for peacebuilding and reconciliation. The book explores thematically the interconnections between religion, nationalism, and intolerance. It also explores transnational intra-religion contestation as represented in the Shi'a-Sunni divide within Islam. In addition, the volume features illuminating case studies of highly divided and conflictual societies, including Egypt, Israel and Palestine, Kashmir, Lebanon, Nigeria, Northern Ireland, Sri Lanka, and Tajikistan. The concluding chapter explores how a synthetic and comparative study of religious leadership could also translate into constructive policy consideration of various nongovernmental organizations as well as diplomats.

Glossary

American Exceptionalism   The view that the United States of America has a unique and/or divinely sanctioned role in the political and social history of the world.

Balfour Declaration   A statement in a letter by Arthur James Balfour in 1917 that endorsed the establishment of a Jewish national home in Palestine. The statement's meaning has been debated, and it fell short of the hopes of Zionists at the time, but it did stipulate the protection of religious and civil rights of non-Jewish residents in the area. It was approved in 1922 by the League of Nations along with the British mandate over Palestine.

Camp David Accords   An agreement between Israel and Egypt signed in 1978 that led to a peace treaty the following year. The agreement ended the fighting that had been ongoing between Israel and Egypt since the first Arab-Israeli War in 1948 and set up a framework for Arab-Israeli relations.

Canaanite Movement   Cultural and ideological movement in Israel in the middle part of the 20th century that sought to establish a Hebrew nation that would leave behind the religious dimensions of Judaism.

Civil Religion   The consecrated spaces, times, symbols, rituals, myths, texts, teachings, and practices that function to integrate and unify the diverse identities and various elements of a society into a more or less cohesive whole. The features of civil religion also function to invest the societal whole with some larger, overarching significance by, for example, (1) representing the unique or exceptional origins, destiny, and/or special role of the society within the development of world history; (2) symbolically codifying, representing, and/or holding the society accountable to the orienting and guiding values that the society understands itself to be based upon; (3) articulating the society's relation to a source of transcendent significance; (4) and/or expressing the transcendent significance of the society.

Clash of Civilizations   The broadly influential account of world politics and international relations set forth most famously by the political scientist Samuel Huntington. This thesis claims that in the post–Cold War era, after the dissolution of the Cold War power configuration, geopolitical conflicts will occur along distinctively civilizational fault lines. One such fault line is the one believed to fall between Western and non-Western worldviews and values.

Diaspora   Generally, the places outside a group's "homeland" into which members of that group have been dispersed. In Judaism, the term refers to the communities of Jews existing outside the territory of modern Israel beginning as far back as the Babylonian exile in the sixth century BCE.

Dome of the Rock   The golden-domed shrine built upon the Temple Mount in the old city of Jerusalem. Islam recognizes this as the spot at which the Prophet, Muhammad, ascended to Heaven at the side of the angel Gabriel, and is one of the holiest locations in Islam. The Dome of the Rock stands above what Jews believe to be the location of the second Jewish temple, which was destroyed by the Romans in 70 CE. The wall believed to be adjacent to the foundation stone, known as the Western Wall of the temple, is considered the holiest site in Judaism.

Establishment Clause   Clause in the First Amendment in the U.S. Constitution that prohibits Congress from establishing an official state religion.

Free Exercise Clause   Clause of the First Amendment in the U.S. Constitution that restrains Congress from prohibiting the free exercise of religion.

Good Friday Agreement   Signed in 1998, the agreement involved relationships within Northern Ireland, relationships between Northern Ireland and the Republic of Ireland, and relationships between Ireland, England, Scotland, and Wales. The agreement created a Northern Ireland Assembly with a power-sharing executive, new cross-border relations with the Republic of Ireland, and assemblies across the United Kingdom with Westminster and Dublin. The agreement ended the Irish Republic's claim to the six counties in Northern Ireland. Although the agreement's proposal that paramilitary groups give up their weapons and that paramilitary leaders be released from prison caused controversy, the agreement led to the official end to the conflict in Northern Ireland.

Gush Emunim   Literally, "the Block of the Faithful." A movement established in 1974 in the aftermath of the Yom Kippur War. Influential upon efforts to actively settle the Greater Land of Israel (encompassing the West Bank and the Gaza Strip). Adherents of this "territorial maximalism" movement refer to these territories by their biblical names, that is, as the land of Judea and Samaria. In the 1980s, the movement morphed into the Yesha Council, Yesha being the acronym in Hebrew for Judea, Samaria, and Gaza.

Halakah   Literally, "the path that one walks." Refers to Jewish law codes.

Hamas   Palestinian Sunni Islamic political party that has governed the Gaza Strip since 2007. The Hamas political party relates to the militant Islamic resistance movement of the same name. The latter is often referred to as the military wing of the Hamas political party. The first charter of the group, long before its emergence as a political party, called for the replacement of the state of Israel and Occupied Territories with a Palestinian Islamic state.

Hindutva   Hindutva is the ideology of the Rashtriya Swayamsevak Sangh, a pseudoreligious organization in India. The term was coined in 1923 and means "Hinduness." It has come to be associated with Hindu supremacy, nationalism, religious exclusivity, racial purity, and militarism.

Intifada   Literally means uprising and refers to the spontaneous eruption of Palestinian resistance against the Israeli occupation. The first intifada (1987–1993) is widely regarded as nonviolent, although some of the resistance tactics included throwing stones and petrol bombs as well as engaging in suicide attacks in Israel. The second intifada (Al-Aqsa), began late in 2000 and subsided in 2005.

Jihad   Islamic term appearing in the Quran. Literally, "striving in the way of God." In specific uses, usually by non-Muslims, the term refers to religiously motivated or inspired warfare, or "holy war."

Jus sanguinis   Latin for "right of blood." Principle for determining citizenship based upon a person's having been born into a particular people group.

Jus soli   Latin for "right of the soil." Principle for determining citizenship based upon having been born in the geographic territory of a nation-state, or territories under its jurisdiction. Principle for citizenship in the United States as stated in the Fourteenth Amendment.

Knesset   The house of representatives in the state of Israel, its rules and functions were influenced by the first Zionist congress that met in Basel in 1897.

LTTE   The Liberation Tigers of Tamil Eelam. Was created by Velupillai Prabhakaran in 1975. The LTTE is a militant pro-secessionist group that was known as a terrorist organization. The group claimed to champion the cause of Tamils in Sri Lanka by fighting against the Sri Lankan government in an effort to establish a separate Tamil state.

Mahavamsa   Mahavamsa is "The Great Chronicle" that tells the story of the people who originally settled Sri Lanka. It is divided into three volumes and is considered the longest unbroken historical record (composed in the fifth and sixth centuries CE).

Manifest Destiny A term that emerged in 19th-century United States to formally designate the belief that the United States was destined to expand fully across the continent of North America ("from sea to shining sea").

Merkaz HaRav Yeshivah A Jewish educational institution founded by Avraham Isaac HaCohen Kook in 1924. Later, under the helm of his son, the yeshiva incubated the leadership of the settlement movement and religious Zionism.

Midrash Tradition of textual interpretation of the Tanach, or Hebrew bible.

Mishnah Written collection of interpretations and reflection upon the "Oral Torah" (the teachings and interpretations believed to be given by God to Moses in oral form, and never written down, yet remembered and passed on from generation to generation).

Mizrahim Israeli Jews of Arab descent.

Naqba Naqba means "catastrophe" in Arabic and is what Palestinians call the War of 1948 (this war is known as the War of Independence within Israeli and Jewish historical consciousness). This war involved the forced exile of Palestinians.

Negation of Exile An element of Israeli civil religion according to which the historical goal or ideal purpose (the *telos*) of the Jewish state includes the eventual ingathering into the homeland of Jews living in the diaspora, and reversing the effects (often considered to be anti-Jewish) of having lived in dispersion outside the homeland.

Oslo Accords An agreement signed in 1993 between Palestinian Liberation Organization (PLO) chair Yasser Arafat and Israeli prime minister Yitzhak Rabin that set the basis for peace between Israel and Palestine.

PLO The Palestinian Liberation Organization (PLO) was established in 1964 to champion the cause of Palestinian nationalism and includes different political and armed groups with varying ideologies. Although the group originally did not recognize the state of Israel, the PLO signed the Oslo Accords in 1993 that established a way to make peaceful negotiations. The Oslo Accords involved an official recognition of Israel by the leadership of the PLO.

Political Theology The political implications of theological commitments, understandings, and doctrines. Results from reflecting upon the constitutive features of religious traditions (teachings, sacred texts, narratives, myths, conceptions of salvation, moral codes, ritual and symbolic practices, etc.) with particular attention to what these imply for social, political, and public life; law; and policy in a given time or context.

Providence or Providential Mission   In Christian theology, refers to divine guidance, divine sanction, or mandate (e.g., a providential mission is an undertaking ordained and guided by God). The term is sometimes used to refer to God's using the events of human history to fulfill God's purposes.

Sharia   Literally "the path to the watering hole." Sharia is the moral and religious tradition of Islam. This is not a fixed document, but rather a growing and interpretative tradition of Islamic learning.

Shas   Shas is an ultrareligious political party in Israel that formed in 1984 in opposition to the political party Agudat Israel, which was dominated by European Jews. Shas emerged with the intention to represent the views of Middle Eastern Jews. The group was able to attract those that are not religious because it addressed issues concerning housing and employment discrimination. Throughout the years, Shas has supported educational and social funding and opposed the secularization of Israel.

Sinhala Buddhism   The majority of the Sinhalese people in Sri Lanka practice Buddhism. The version of Buddhism is fundamentally different because it is based on Mahavamsa, unlike the Buddhism practiced in many other places. In accordance with the Mahavamsa, Sinhala Buddhists believe that they are decedents of the Buddha and that their political program is intricately linked to the survival and fulfillment of Buddhism.

Tamils   A minority group in Sri Lanka that held a disproportional amount of power during colonial rule, leading the Sinhalese majority to resent them. After Sri Lanka gained independence from Britain, the Sinhalese majority took power and enacted laws that disenfranchised Tamils, which contributed to the outbreak of the Sri Lankan civil war.

Tanach   Hebrew bible.

Uganda Proposal   Proposal to establish the national home for Jews in the form of a Jewish state in the African country of Uganda, rather than Palestine. The proposal emerged from discussions between British colonial secretary Joseph Chamberlain and Zionist movement leader Theodore Herzl. The proposal was forwarded at the Sixth Zionist Congress at Basel, Switzerland, on August 26, 1903. However, it was abandoned by the Seventh Zionist Congress (convened in 1905).

"Unionists versus Nationalists"   Political factions during the Troubles in Northern Ireland. Unionists supported the union with Britain and wished to maintain it. Most of this group is Protestant. Nationalists wanted to unify Ireland into one nation. Most of this group is Catholic. The conflict in Northern Ireland was centered on the fight between these two groups.

Yesha Council   The Yesha Council is an umbrella organization for Jewish settlement groups in the West Bank and Gaza Strip. The council was formed in the 1970s as a continuance of Gush Emunim, a group that had the goal of Jewish settlement in the West Bank and Gaza Strip.

Index

About the Authors

ATALIA OMER (PhD Harvard University, 2008, Religion and Society) is assistant professor of religion, conflict, and peace studies at the Kroc Institute for International Peace Studies at the University of Notre Dame, Indiana, where she also holds an appointment as faculty fellow in the Center for the Study of Religion and Society, Department of Sociology. Her research interests include the theoretical study of the interrelation between religion and nationalism, as well as the role of national/religious/ethnic diasporas in the dynamics of conflict transformation, with particular attention to the ways that the Palestinian-Israeli conflict is symbolically appropriated and deployed in other zones of conflict. Her published works include *When Peace Is Not Enough: How the Israeli Peace Camp Thinks about Religion, Nationalism, and Justice* (University of Chicago Press, 2013) as well as articles in the *Journal of the American Academy of Religion, Journal of Political Theology, Study of Nationalism and Ethnicity, Practical Matters,* and *International Journal of Peace Studies.*

JASON A. SPRINGS (PhD Harvard University, 2005, Religion and Society) is assistant professor of religion, ethics, and peace studies at the Kroc Institute for International Peace Studies at the University of Notre Dame, Indiana, where he also holds an appointment as faculty fellow in the Center for the Study of Religion and Society, Department of Sociology. His research and teaching focus on conceptions of religious toleration and the challenges posed by oppositional forms of moral and religious pluralism for transforming conflict in European and North American contexts. His journal articles addressing issues in modern religion and conflict in public life appear in such journals as the *Journal of Religion, Journal of Religious Ethics, Modern Theology, Journal of the American Academy of Religion, Contemporary Pragmatism,* and *Soundings: An Interdisciplinary Journal.* His broader interests include the ethical and political dimensions of American pragmatist thought and postliberal theology. He is the author of *Toward a Generous Orthodoxy: Prospects for Hans Frei's Postliberal Theology* (Oxford University Press, 2010).